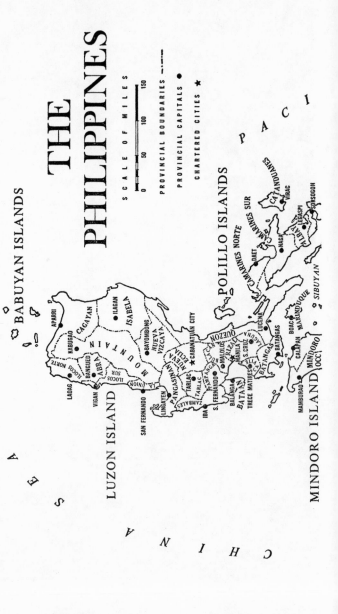

THE PHILIPPINES

SCALE OF MILES

0   50   100   150

PROVINCIAL BOUNDARIES ---·---

PROVINCIAL CAPITALS ●

CHARTERED CITIES ★

BATANES ISLANDS

BABUYAN ISLANDS

LUZON ISLAND

C H I N A   S E A

APARRI

LAOAG

ILOCOS NORTE

KABUGAO

BANGUED

ABRA

VIGAN

ILOCOS SUR

SAN FERNANDO

LINGAYEN

PANGASINAN

UNION

CAGAYAN

M O U N T A I N

ILAGAN

ISABELA

BAYOMBONG

NUEVA
VIZCAYA

NUEVA
ECIJA

CABANATUAN CITY

TARLAC

ZAMBALES

IBA

S. FERNANDO

BALANGA

BATAAN

TRECE MARTIRES

BULACAN

MALOLOS

MANILA

RIZAL

PASIG

S. CRUZ

LAGUNA

CAVITE

QUEZON

LUCENA

BATANGAS

BATANGAS

CALAPAN

MINDORO
(OCC.)

MAMBURAO

MINDORO ISLAND

POLILLO ISLANDS

MARINDUQUE

BOAC

SIBUYAN

CAMARINES NORTE

DAET

CAMARINES SUR

NAGA

CATANDUANES

VIRAC

ALBAY

LEGASPI

SORSOGON

P A C I

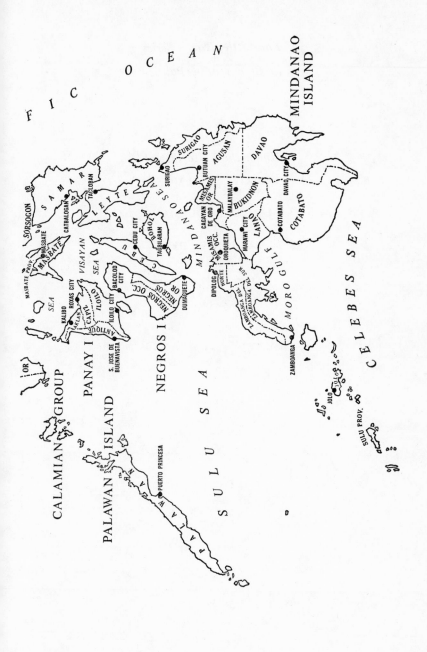

The Little, Brown Series
in Comparative Politics

Under the Editorship of
GABRIEL A. ALMOND

JAMES S. COLEMAN

LUCIAN W. PYE

A COUNTRY STUDY

Politics in the
PHILIPPINES

Jean Grossholtz
Mount Holyoke College

Boston and Toronto
LITTLE, BROWN AND COMPANY

Published simultaneously in Canada
by Little, Brown & Company (Canada) Limited

PRINTED IN THE UNITED STATES OF AMERICA

TO LUCIAN W. PYE

Foreword

THE Little, Brown Series in Comparative Politics has three
main objectives. First, it will meet the need of teachers to
deal with both western and non-western countries in their
introductory course offerings. Second, by following a common approach in the analysis of individual political systems, it will make it possible for teachers to compare these
countries systematically and cumulatively. And third, it
will contribute toward re-establishing the classic relationship between comparative politics and political theory, a
relationship which has been neglected in recent decades.
In brief, the series seeks to be global in scope, genuinely
introductory and comparative in character, and concerned
with broadening and deepening our understanding of the
nature and variety of political systems.

The series has two parts: the Country Studies and the
Analytic Studies. The Country Studies deal with a set of
problems and processes, deriving from a functional, as
against a purely structural, approach to the study of political systems. We are gratified that the participants, all
of them mature scholars with original insights of their
own, were willing to organize their discussions around a
common set of functional topics in the interest of further-
ing comparisons. At the same time, each author has been
urged to adapt the common framework to the special problems of the country he is discussing and to express his own
theoretical point of view.

An introductory book, *Comparative Politics: A De-*

velopmental Approach, written by Gabriel A. Almond and
G. Bingham Powell provides an analytic supplement to the
Country Studies. It also opens our set of Analytic Studies,
which will offer basic discussions of such topics as political
change in the emerging nations, comparative analyses of interest groups, political socialization, political communication,
political culture, and the like. We hope these books will prove
to be useful and stimulating supplements to the Country
Studies as well as points of departure in more advanced
courses.

By an imaginative use of the structural–functional approach
in analyzing a political culture Jean Grossholtz's *Politics in
the Philippines* significantly advances knowledge about both
the dynamics of public life in the Philippines and the general
problems of democratic development in the new states. She
vividly demonstrates how many traditional attitudes have contributed to the establishment of a vigorously evolving democratic polity, and with sympathetic understanding she points
to the ways in which many features of Philippine politics
previously assumed to be failings have often played a constructive role in building a more open society. She has been able
to do so because she recognizes that democracy rests upon a
social bargaining process and not just upon adherence to a
particular set of ideals developed in the West. Thus this second
volume in the Country Series represents an important contribution to general political theory and also demonstrates
how anthropological and historical insights can be systematically applied to political analysis in the developing areas.

Gabriel A. Almond
James S. Coleman
Lucian W. Pye

Acknowledgments

O NE COULD write an additional chapter in a fruitless attempt to acknowledge all the help received in producing
a volume of this sort. I would be extremely remiss, however, if I did not recognize my debts of gratitude to the
faculty and students of the Massachusetts Institute of
Technology, who set such a high standard of intellectual
vigor, the librarians, who dedicated so much effort to finding obscure books and records, the personnel of Little,
Brown, who added calm and professional advice, my
colleagues at Mount Holyoke, who sympathized with my
separate agonies, and the hundreds of Filipinos who gave
so freely of their time, their hospitality, and their own
experience. The inadequacies of the end product are all
my own.

Whatever value this volume has for academe is due to
Lucian W. Pye, whose enthusiasm and scholarship guided
me every step of the way, and to whom it is dedicated.

Jean Grossholtz

Table of Contents

xiii

Part III The Political Functions

Politics in the

PHILIPPINES

PART I

Foundations

of the Political System

CHAPTER I

Introduction

THE PLIGHT OF the emerging nations has become a topic of international concern. Their needs, their problems, their demands, their allegiance are matters of import to statesmen, international civil servants, and taxpayers. Much has been written of their prospects for economic and political development. Pessimists and optimists alike have engaged in predictions about the ability of the new nations to adapt modern governmental institutions to traditional societies and to overcome their internal disunity. There is speculation as to whether or not they can hold back the pressures of their rising populations and find the capital and competence to develop their economies. The bibliography on economic and political development defies the energies of even the most voracious reader. Still, the key to the process of development remains obscure, and the criterion for judgment illusory. Lessons learned from a study of American and British experience seem scarcely appropriate to the pressures and forces of today's environment. Yet similar elements must be present, comparable achievements must mark the path to stable political systems and viable economies.

In any survey of the prospects for democratic development of emerging nations, the Philippines stands out as a success. For here broad political participation has accompanied and motivated economic growth in conditions of sta-

3

bility and political change. Three times since independence, Filipinos have replaced the "ins" with the "outs" in free elections, and twice they have accepted an almost unknown vice-president as the legitimate national leader when strong personalities died in office. Four years of Japanese occupation and incredible destruction of economic resources were the prelude to independence, yet a decade and a half later the Filipinos had defeated a Communist rebellion and laid the foundations for sustained economic growth. Violence and corruption plague the Republic, but the fact that Filipinos have accepted democracy as a means of working out conflict and directing their development is grounds for optimism. The Philippines faces a long, hard sustained effort during which some basic social values and perhaps much of the charm of Filipino life may be sacrificed. Whether or not the leaders and the people will be able to make these decisions is a matter of broader concern. Success will build confidence in the ability of democratic government to survive, and more than that, to direct the transformation of the emergent nations.

For, like other emerging nations, the Philippines is an agrarian society in which traditional social and economic status has long dominated the political system. A small number of families controlled economic life by reason of their large landholdings, and historical experience with a hierarchical social structure encouraged their dominance of social and political life. Landlord control of the political institutions is now being challenged by entrepreneurs committed to industrialization and businesslike management of public affairs. Furthermore, public education, transportation, and communication have affected the countryside and generated widespread expectations about the use of public resources. This change has taken place within the framework of formal institutions that owe their evolution to Western experience and it has been accompanied by broadened political participation.

These impressive developments have been realized in the face of major obstacles and in spite of severe handicaps. In common with other traditional societies, Filipinos emphasize highly personal face-to-face relationships and strong family ties unsuited to the operation of legalistic, objective standards of social life. As a Catholic society, the Philippines has been subject to a strong sense of property rights and social controls, values which do not lend themselves to compromise and which do not always correlate with democratic procedures and pragmatic political action. Furthermore, the Philippines, like most of the new states, was badly shaken by its colonial experience and remains confused about its national identity. In short, the island country has experienced all the problems and forces familiar to other emerging nations, and has succeeded thus far in a transition that others are still to undertake.

Successful political development in the Philippines owes much to two related factors: historical experience and cultural patterns. Spanish colonial policy had its roots in the extension of the Catholic Church, and the emphasis on religious proselytism provided a continuing justification. Christianization proceeded rapidly in the Philippine archipelago. The political organization and economic patterns established by the Spanish administration served to enhance the influence of the religious orders. Despite important regional differences, by the end of three centuries of Spanish rule the islands had become a recognized political unit and a Christian nation. American colonial policy emphasized preparation for self-government and independence. The Americans encouraged Filipino political action and participation, extending the sense of a common political identity to larger numbers of people and incorporating a wider variety of attitudes, actions, and issues into the concept of a Filipino nation. Educational and political institutions developed, further legitimizing and extending national unity and a Filipino identity. When Filipinos gained independence in 1946, they were firmly committed to a constitutional republic and a political unity as the Philippines.

The political process developed under the American regime required behavior similar to that of traditional social and cultural frameworks. Philippine social life emphasizes the interaction of reciprocally dependent people. These relationships may be the result of direct agreement or they may be assumed, but whether explicit or implicit they represent the results of interpersonal bargaining. As in democratic politics, action in support of another is undertaken in clear expectation of eventual reward. This type of social behavior is similar to the kind of political behavior required for political bargaining, and it has been used by Filipinos to mobilize large numbers of people into the political system. It makes possible, indeed encourages, highly competitive elections that, as Robert Dahl has said, are the hallmark of democracy.

The acceptance of political unity and the existence of the political behavior required in modern democracies has eased the transition of the Filipinos to a modern political process and provides a democratic spirit that augurs well for the future. The electoral system requires political candidates to solicit support from the population and the cultural pattern ensures that voters will see clearly that this is a reciprocal relationship that can be exploited to fulfill their personal needs. The vote has become the *quid pro quo* for quite personal services, forcing the politician to trade his access to the resources of government for votes. This is the most fundamental of distribution processes and allows the inclusion of large numbers of relatively unsophisticated people in the decision-making process. Because this behavior pattern is widespread and well recognized, each new economic interest has sought its fortunes through political channels. The forces of change: literacy, industrialization, and urbanization have broadened perceptions of politics and political action and provided a basis for differentiating the electorate into specific interest groups. But, more important, the political system has become the directing, innovating system of the society, presiding over the accommodation of the host of new and conflicting interests that have developed.

In the Philippines, the political system has served three major purposes during this period of rapid change. First, it has undertaken to direct economic development and to deal in a highly pragmatic fashion with the conflicts of interest that arise among economic groups. Second, it has given the nation an identity by integrating fragmented social groups. Because every citizen has direct contact with the central government and its resources through local political leaders, the imbalances created by economic development (*e.g.,* between urban and

rural people, Filipinos and Chinese, etc.) have not been un-
stabilizing. All groups are recognized by, and thus committed
to, the political system. Third, the political system has given
legitimacy to particular methods of social interaction and
decision making. The system has been able to modernize and
commit the population to a national identity by distributing
meaningful rewards. It thus encourages people to seek the
most effective means of securing those rewards in competition
with others. As competition increases the formal structures of
the system impose limits on conflict and on rewards and losses
and thus assume a more meaningful role.

The Philippine experience has shown that political and
economic development can coincide; that mass participation
and the accommodation of peoples' interests does not inhibit development but rather contributes the energizing force
required for industrialization. The early commitment of the
population to the political system allows for a national mobilization for development. In many developing countries the
options are still open as to how to proceed in modernization.
The Philippine case reveals that the spirit of bargaining basic
to democracy can be a crucial component of that modernization. For in the Philippines, politics is bargaining and the
development of the skills required for bargaining has been
the key to democratic political development.

The concept of democracy as a bargaining process is not
new. Indeed it is reflected in the language of politics, which
includes such acceptable truisms as "politics is the art of the
possible" and "the essence of politics is compromise." These
statements imply that policy decisions are the product of assess-
ments of the relative weight of various interests in support of
or opposition to policy alternatives. Decision makers achieve
what they can of their policy choices and goals according to
the relative positions of others. Democratic government embodies the principle of bringing together political representatives of various segments of society to protect and advance
their constituents' interests in the melee of political action.
Those who would play active political roles must constantly
bargain for the continued support of a constituency and with
their peers for the wherewithal to maintain that continuous

support. This bargaining base is readily apparent in Philippine democracy. The outstanding characteristic of Philippine society is its highly politicized nature. Even the most rudimentary contact between government and citizen takes on a "political" character reminiscent of turn-of-the-century American politics when the "boss" and the "ward heeler" played key roles. Filipinos look to politics to solve their problems and public life takes on the spirited quality of an open market place where negotiations are enjoyed as much for their own sake as for their purpose.

Some of the most fundamental ideas of democratic theories make bargaining the basis of the political system. Majority rule with due respect for the rights of the minority is, as Robert Dahl has shown, a process by which representatives articulate the interests of their constituents in such a way that an aggregation of those interests can form a majority.[1] It is, of course, theoretically possible for a policy issue to be so clearly articulated as to make the formation of a majority automatic without any further explicit communication. In one sense it is presumed that an ideology serves this function. But ideology in a democratic political process has seldom achieved the required strength and formulation to create automatic majorities. Instead, the process of majority formation and decision making is one of combining more or less similar views into the best possible compromise. Policy goals are in some measure formulated with the other parties' interests in mind. The representative bases his goals on his "expectations of what others will accept."[2] Obviously this calls for skilled assessment and communication and particularly for ability in reading implicit cues and developing mutual trust. In the Philippines many of these skills are required in social relationships.

Democratic government assumes at least a limited agreement on the broad goals to be sought. Usually these are described as "freedom," "equality," and "welfare," difficult

[1] Robert Dahl, *A Preface to Democratic Theory* (Chicago: University of Chicago Press, 1956).

[2] Thomas C. Schelling, *The Strategy of Conflict* (Cambridge: Harvard University Press, 1960) p. 20.

to define when applied to any specific policy alternative.[3] The achievement of these values constitutes the "public interest" and disagreement as to what constitutes the "public interest" is as basic in democratic politics as the agreement that the purpose of the government is to achieve it. In the Philippines much of the basis for the concept of "public interest" came out of the policies of the American colonial rule. The United States recognized from the first that the islands were a potential nation and that colonial status could be only temporary. Because the aim was a Filipino government, the American administration emphasized free public education in English, road building, the establishment of communications systems, public health and sanitation, and a trained civil service. As a result, the unity of the islands, substantially achieved through Christianization, was maintained, extended, and given a framework in which a nation could develop. Even more important was the willingness to accommodate Filipino demands. The political relationship that developed between American administrators and Filipino politicians was a training ground for highly pragmatic political skills. This combination of the American concern for the people's welfare and the skills learned in the struggle to take more power from the American administration made the Filipino politician acutely sensitive to both the realities of power and the "human" character of the public interest. For the politician is a member of a society in which family, personal skill, and social status imply more important obligations than do abstract concepts of community and nation. He does not, therefore, perceive an objective "public interest" as meaningful; rather, he seeks a synthesis of the subjective demands of the people important to his status. It is these more direct considerations that condition his behavior,

[3] See the discussion of this point in Paul Ylvisaker, "Criteria for a 'Proper' Areal Division of Power," in Arthur Maas, ed., *Area and Power* (Glencoe: The Free Press, 1959) pp. 22, 28. In defining the goals to be sought in a division of power on an areal basis, Ylvisaker noted that there would be no quarrel over the basic values but there would be over establishing priorities among them. All values are compatible but only if tempered and not maximized.

and the conflicts engendered by them are played out through the electoral process.

The difficulty of defining the public interest raises the question of the distinction between legitimate bargaining and corruption. The concept of bargaining carries with it the image of a smoke-filled room where shady deals are made and public office is used for private gain. Corruption plagued the United States during its "ward-heeler" phase and it plagues the Philippines today. In a transitional system in which socialization into new roles is weak and the differentiation and integration of those new roles is only partial, the distribution and use of political influence is seriously distorted. Political influence is always unequally distributed, but a democratic system must ensure that influence is sufficiently widespread to channel the interests of all levels of society into the decision–making process. The allocation of influence by governmental structures and by organizing the electorate for political action (*e.g.,* groups and parties) provides the basis for broad participation, but it also results in conflicts of interest and necessitates negotiation and compromise. Bargaining is kept free of corruption both by the formal structures of government and legal codes and by the methods of arranging the electorate in support of particular personalities or policies. In a modern democratic system, the politician becomes a broker whose position is determined by his skill in promoting the interests of a broad coalition of interests. Thus the way in which essential political functions are performed places limits on the politician's behavior.

In modern democratic systems, functional limits are provided by periodic elections in which the politician is constrained to defend his actions against challenges from an organized opposition before an attentive and choice-making public in order to continue in office. The implication is that the politician wishes to remain in office and it has been the character of political actors since the earliest organization of social life that the advantages accruing to those who have influence over the public resources are such as to attract men who do not willingly give up that influence. Since the advantages of office holding are well known, challengers can always be found but unless there is a real possibility of their success their ability to perform the limiting function is destroyed. A significant group of non-officeholders with the power to decide between incumbent and challenger is vital. These are the limits on the politician that force him to meet certain standards of public behavior and political action. The absence or weakness of any of the limits can corrupt the bargaining process. As we shall see, weaknesses in all these limiting functions underlie the corruption of public office in the Philippines. The limiting functions described provide a natural control mechanism to force the private interests of politicians to approximate the public interest.

In our concentration on the bargaining process as the basis of the democratic political system we move away from the more traditional analysis of the component institutions and legal requirements of democracy to its dynamics. If we list all the states we designate democracies, we find an amazing variety of institutional arrangements, economic organizations, and social and cultural milieus. Studies of comparative government for many years have concentrated on describing this richness and variety. The emergence of a host of new states attempting to follow the Western model has placed democracy in an even richer variety of contexts, some of which appear inadequate to the requirements. Differences in formal structure seem less helpful for understanding democracy than the ability of the system to perform the functions required of a political system.[4] In the new states structures quite different from those in the West may process and regulate the performance of the political functions. In the Philippines the transitional character of the political system is readily apparent in the rich mixture of "modern" and "traditional" structures through which political functions are performed. By concentrating on the functions we consider necessary to an operating democracy we overcome some of the difficulties of comparison and gain insight into the patterns of change that accompany the in-

---

[4] The concept of a political system and its functions used here is adapted from that of Gabriel Almond, which served as the basis for Gabriel Almond and James Coleman, eds., *The Politics of the Developing Areas* (Princeton: Princeton University Press, 1960), Introduction.

stitutionalization and legitimation of formal governmental structures. In our analysis of the Philippine political system we concentrate on the requirements of a bargaining process and the functions it performs. We adopt as our analytic model the political functions described by Gabriel Almond in *An Introduction to Comparative Politics,* dividing them into those which generate expectations about political action and select individuals to perform political roles (political socialization, political communication, and political recruitment) and those which relate individuals to the public authority (interest articulation and interest aggregation). This type of analysis also incorporates the insights gained from recent studies on the psychological and sociological basis of politics. It is obvious that the ability and willingness to bargain is related to the individual's sense of a predictable world in which conflict is not wholly destructive and other people can be trusted. The social behavior required by the society and the identity opportunities it provides its members will condition the way in which political roles are conceived and performed and thus the bargaining process.

In conceiving of the Philippine political system as a bargaining process, we are departing from the theme that has dominated most of the literature on Philippine society, that of social and economic inequality. This tradition of study, articulated most clearly by Ralston Hayden, stressed the inequality of economic and social life that seemed to make the achievement of democracy so doubtful.[5] These fears were substantiated in some degree in the postwar period by the ease with which the Communists exploited rural unrest and, despite limited advances during the Magsaysay administration, it is still possible that the rural population will reject a government that seems unable to solve their problems.[6] The only

5 Ralston Hayden, *The Philippines: A Study of National Development* (New York: Macmillan Company, 1942).

6 See Frances Lucille Starner, *Magsaysay and the Philippine Peasantry: The Agrarian Impact on Philippine Politics, 1953-1956* (Berkeley and Los Angeles: University of California Press, 1961). This book and Jose Abueva, *Focus on the Barrio* (Quezon City: Institute of Public Administration, University of the Philippines, 1959) offer much insight into Magsaysay's weakness and strength and his personal style.

full-scale study of post-independence public policy and economic development finds substantial achievement but also
concentration of income and a basic harshness in the emergent
economic organization.[7] Social and psychological forces lie at
the root of this inequality and these forces are, for the most
part, inconsistent with the needs of democracy.[8]

It is the thesis of this study that inequality is no longer an
issue. New interests and widespread popular support are being
organized and brought to bear on political decisions by skilled
and pragmatic politicians operating in a democratic spirit. An
open bargaining process forces older interests to compete for
influence with new groups and as a result both groups are
forced to relate their needs to those of the emerging society.
Now new problems must dominate our studies of the Philippines — problems of a working democracy in a developing
country.

[7] Frank Golay, *The Philippines: Public Policy and National Economic
Development* (Ithaca: Cornell University Press, 1961) p. 415.

[8] O. D. Corpuz has written extensively on this subject. See, for example,
"The Cultural Foundations of Filipino Politics," *Philippine Motif*, I (First
Quarter, 1960) pp. 8-14.

CHAPTER II

History and Origins of the System

FOUR CULTURES and two major religions have shaped the modern Philippines. Three centuries of Spanish rule, a long history of Chinese influence, and almost fifty years of American presence have changed, but not obscured, the Malayan character of the society. The sweep of Islam to the coast of Manila Bay and the spread of Christianity from northern Luzon to the shores of Mindanao have never wholly obliterated the pre-Spanish animistic beliefs and rituals. Filipinos have listened to and accepted Western beliefs but have adapted all to their own ways and their own needs. The colonial governments interfered directly with the values of the individual citizen; the religion of the Spaniard and the technology of the American both became part of the Filipino heritage. This rich pattern of often contradictory cultural forms and values defies the Filipino's attempts at cultural description. "Just what is a Filipino?" he asks, and he questions his own identification with the rest of Asia at the same time as he condemns the lack of integrity that makes him grasp eagerly for the products and forms of the West. Such questions plague the nationalist and the scholar and they appear in the political process as doubts about the Filipino ability to operate his political institutions. For what, after all, is the Philippine political heritage? What political forms are most harmonious to his nature?

14

Spanish colonialism molded the Malay culture and society, providing the basis for a broader and more complex political unit. But at the same time Spanish rule established a social structure and an economic system inherently unequal, which seriously divided the society and impeded modernization. Although American rule continued and in some ways enhanced this basic inequality, it also set in motion pressures that were to create a competitive political process that would dominate the society and economy. Now, imbued with the spirit of democracy, Filipinos are building an industrial, businesslike, open society.

Filipinos have during several sharply defined stages in their history sought different ideals. Each period contributed to the culture and spirit of the people. Now they seek a new identity appropriate to an industrial society and their place in Asia and the world. This new identity will, however, preserve many of the gracious, human values of the Filipino past. The pragmatic quality of Philippine democracy does not obscure Filipino emphasis on a civil society in which the values of civility are highly prized.

Philippine history can be divided into six periods: the pre-Spanish, during which the Malay kinship structure and strong ruler were established as part of political and social life; the Spanish, when Christianity created a unity among the peoples of the islands and the bonds of nationhood were formed; the revolutionary, when Philippine nationalism emerged as a dynamic force and Western values of liberty and representative government were established as the touchstones of political thought; the American, when secularization, institutionalization, and political skills accompanied the transition to independence; the Japanese occupation, when Filipinos proudly lined up on the side of their Western heritage and many new and intense pressures were released into political life; and last, the period of independence, in which Filipinos are working and revealing their own distinct political style.

This chapter traces Philippine political experience in an attempt to show how both external and internal forces have contributed to the development of Philippine society and polity. We concentrate on those aspects of Philippine history which seem most relevant to the development of the political system.

ORIGINS OF THE SYSTEM

When the intrepid Magellan landed on the island of Cebu in 1521 he found a Malay population living along the coasts, organized in small colonies under chiefs known as *datus*. In the recent past, waves of people from Malaysia and Indonesia had arrived along the coasts of the islands in large outrigger canoes called *barangays*. They settled at the mouths of rivers in communities they called barangays and gradually moved inland up the river valleys and into the lowlands, pushing the older inhabitants into the hills. These original inhabitants were small negroid people with a nomadic hunting type of social organization. Remnants of this population survive today in the mountainous interior of Luzon and Negros. Known as *Aeta* but called *Negrito* by the Spanish, their small size and nomadic social structure prevented their incorporation into the political and social structure that developed among the Malays.

Security was the major problem and the society was organized with that in mind. Barangays in the more desirable and populated areas along the sea coast had to be organized as armed camps in order to protect themselves from attacks by neighbors in search of new land, chiefs in search of more power, and pirates of various types who plied the South China Sea. These coastal communities also faced the power of Islam. Brought to the Indonesian islands by Arab traders in the fifteenth century, it had spread through the area into Mindanao, whence Muslim sailing ships carried out slave raids and conquests throughout the Visayas and southern Luzon. When the Spanish arrived at Manila Bay in 1569, they found a small community of Muslims under a datu occupying a site they called Maynila. The Spanish conquest halted and pushed back Islam, confining Muslim influence to parts of Mindanao where the Spanish government never really penetrated.

The success of both Islam and the Spanish, despite the problems of supply and manpower both groups must have felt, indicates the weakness of these scattered barangays. Though there undoubtedly were cases of confederation and union of some barangays, the essential pattern remained small isolated communities holding communal lands and protecting them by a system of tactical and cultural ingenuity. Since the barangay grew from the family group, community and family were one and the same. The functions of the family could not be distinguished from those of the community. A man performing the functions of a father was at the same time performing those of a citizen. Each age group had specific community duties. A high degree of family solidarity and loyalty developed. In the barangay communities a good leader was a strong, brave man who embodied the old traditions and preferably had benevolent ancestors, and a good citizen was a loyal follower who lived up to the obligations of his community and family status. The dominant value was security and to the extent that the community was secure it was good.

THE SPANISH PERIOD

Some forty years after Magellan a group of conquistadores from the Spanish settlement in Mexico landed on the Bicol peninsula. Under the leadership of Miguel Lopez de Legazpi, they moved across Luzon, conquering as they went and meeting relatively little resistance. Many lowland and coastal natives must have escaped to the mountainous interior, but in time large numbers settled under Spanish rule.[1]

At first the Spanish adopted a system of indirect rule, maintaining the traditional authority structure and appointing the datu or *gobernadorcillo* and *cabeza de barangay* (petty governor and head of the village). Before long, however, the Spanish religious orders had established themselves in the countryside and had usurped the authority of the datus. The Spanish divided the land into large areas of jurisdiction, combining several villages whose inhabitants were commended to the Crown by one of the conquistadores, whose job it was to protect these people and help them learn the Christian faith.

[1] Felix Keesing, *The Ethno-History of Northern Luzon* (Stanford: Stanford University Press, 1962) describes the migration of peoples of northern Luzon in the face of the Spanish conquest.

In return for these blessings the *encomendero* had the right to levy tribute and require labor. This system of administration was an attempt by the colonial government to ensure Spanish rule without cost to the home government by providing incentives for Spaniards in the form of tribute collection and commerce. Along with the galleon trade that developed with Mexico it led to a hacienda, export economy and completely stultified Philippine economic development, ensured friar domination of the provincial areas, and led to the excesses that triggered Philippine nationalism and the revolts of the 19th century.

The galleon trade was established on a three-prong basis.[2] Chinese junks brought silks, tea, and spices to Manila where they traded for rice, barks, tobacco, and Mexican silver. Once a year the Manila galleon left for Acapulco in Mexico carrying in its hold the silks, tea, and spices of China and returning with 100 to 300 per cent profits in Mexican silver. The Spanish government, interested in increasing its own supply of silver rather than allowing it to seep away to the colony, restricted the trade to one galleon a year. The existence of such an attractive alternative as the galleon trade encouraged the encomendero to concentrate on acquiring and filling space on the galleon, since the high profits to be expected were sufficient to allow them to live very well for the rest of the year.

Meanwhile the religious orders were organizing the country and people around the church. By the 19th century the pattern of settlement had changed to small towns organized around the church and the central *plaza;* and an upper class of *principalia, illustrado,* or leaders of the town had come into being. These leaders were often mestizo families who were educated and imbued with Spanish culture, and who provided the native leadership of town and province, always under the direct control of the religious order and the local priest.

The governmental system of the colonial territory was, therefore, oriented around these two factors: the galleon trade as the major source of income and the major economic

2 William Lytle Schurz, *The Manila Galleon* (New York: Dutton and Company, Inc., 1959).

activity, and the provincial areas organized and, in effect, governed by the religious orders. Conflicts arose on both scores and intrigues and open battles developed between the bishops and the governors general, the holy orders and the bishops, the economic interests and the government.

THE REVOLUTIONARY PERIOD

Spanish policies had generated pressures that the colonial government could not accommodate. By the 19th century, Christianity had united Filipinos and the friar educational institutions had produced a significant number of educated Filipinos who as principalia shared certain advantages and powers with the friars in the rural areas. Children of Filipina–Spanish marriages gradually acquired land of their own and Filipino haciendas, were created. Mestizo heirs of encomenderos managed large estates, sent their children abroad for education, and developed a distinct society patterned after that of Spain.

Despite their acculturation, these Filipinos were not accepted into Spanish ruling circles, they did not share political power, and they could not expect to play meaningful roles in Spanish society. The friars continued to dominate social, political, and economic life and Filipinos were forced to follow their lead.[3]

The conditions of the peasant and tenant had degenerated as the friars demanded more in the way of tribute. In addition, the end of the galleon trade created a need for new sources of revenue, and friars and tax agents were sent to collect from the Filipinos.

By the end of the 19th century, various secret societies had developed among Filipinos. Most aimed at reform but some thought of more radical goals. Two groups with different aims and interests played out a rather stylized game. The lower classes sought complete independence as the only possible relief for their condition while the upper class, mainly mes-

[3] José Rizal's novels provide the best description of friar dominance and the life of the Filipino during this period. See particularly the new translation of *Noli Me Tangere* by Leon Ma. Guerrero, *The Lost Eden* (Bloomington: Indiana University Press, 1961).

tizo, sought admittance to the ruling group through reforms in the Spanish government. This upper-class group were not themselves interested in equality in the broader sense meant in democratic theory, but rather in equality of opportunity for those who had turned themselves into pseudo-Spaniards. Thus they seemed to say: "Here we are, we made ourselves just like you, now take us in, let us have your opportunities."

The existence of a group of educated Filipinos who could not find equal opportunity, the excesses of the friars in provincial areas, the increased demands for forced labor from Filipinos, and the attempts of encomenderos to exercise their rights after the end of the galleon trade in 1815 created demand for change, which the existing governmental channels could not handle and the friars would not recognize as important. Peasant uprisings against conditions in the provinces grew and the intellectuals took on some of this rebellious spirit, serving as propagandists for the movement. The intellectuals demanded reforms that would give Filipinos a broader role in economic, social, and political life. Under Spanish rule, leadership in the society was correlated with economic power. Informal leaders, who had no formal authority in the governmental structure, held the real power, whereas the formally designated leaders served as puppets. In the towns and provinces, despite the formal designation of village heads and governors, the friars and later (as the big haciendas developed) the landlords, were the real power. A centralized government existed but was tempered by the fact that real power lay in the hands of local chiefs (*caciques*) who controlled the local economy. The big landlords were the law on their own lands just as the friars were the law in the towns. Also during this time, the government in Spain was highly unstable, veering from extremely liberal to extremely conservative and even reactionary policies.

On January 20, 1872, a revolt broke out in Cavite among more than 200 Filipino soldiers and workers in the Spanish naval shipbuilding yards there. The revolt was put down after two days and many of the participants faced firing squads and Spanish prisons. The most noted of those who lost their lives were the three Filipino priests, Padres Gomez, Burgos, and

Zamora, who were garroted to death on the Luneta on February 1, 1872. These three became martyrs to the revolutionary movement and their death became a *cause célèbre* to the Filipino students residing in Spain, who carried on the agitation and propaganda. After the Cavite revolt and the death of many of the reform-minded leaders, many of the privileges Filipinos had won were taken away and anyone voicing dissatisfaction was imprisoned.

The resort to arms and demand for independence did not have the approval of the Filipino intellectuals in Spain or even of the middle-class Filipinos at home. When revolt broke out again in 1893, the leading intellectual, José Rizal, refused to lend his name or support to the revolutionaries and published a strongly worded repudiation of the revolt, arguing that Filipinos were not yet ready for self-government.

The actual spark plug of the revolution was the dispossessed lower urban class led by Andrés Bonifacio.[4] Their lack of education and Spanish culture eliminated any possibility of entrance into Spanish society. These were people who held no hope of being included in the ruling elite or of economic gain by any other way than to get rid of the Spaniards entirely. Under Bonifacio's leadership, they formed themselves into the *Katipunan* and organized an armed uprising.

The Katipunan started as one of several secret societies in the Philippines but it was better organized and spread rapidly outside of Manila.[5] The society promoted the idea that the Philippines had an organized civilized state at the time of the arrival of the Spanish, that they had trade with the rest of Asia, their own religion, an alphabet, and independence and liberty. They charged that the friars had not really civilized the Filipinos but had merely taught them superficial formulas of Catholicism. They aimed at uniting the Filipinos

[4] One Filipino historian argues that the revolution itself was betrayed by the upper classes and that Bonifacio's socialist orientation was obscured. See Teodoro A. Agoncillo, *The Revolt of the Masses: The Story of Bonifacio and the Katipunan* (Quezon City: University of the Philippines, College of Liberal Arts, 1956).

[5] The full Tagalog name for the Katipunan was "Kagalangalangan Kataastaasang Katipunan Ng Mga Anak Ng Bayan" or Venerable and Respectful Society of the Sons of the Country.

under a single ideology and creating an independent state by means of revolution. One conservative estimate put the membership at 100,000.[6]

Bonifacio proved a poor military leader and his popularity waned in favor of a young schoolteacher, Emilio Aguinaldo, who managed to win several major battles and thus became known as the leader of the revolution. But the Filipinos were unable to overcome Spain's military superiority and in 1897 a peace pact was signed at Biak-na-Bato. The pact provided for the payment by Spain of a sum of money (about two million Mexican dollars) for those under arms. In return for this sum, the Filipinos were to lay down their arms and Aguinaldo and other leaders were to leave the Philippines.

The Spaniards also agreed to carry out some reforms similar to those agitated for by the propagandists. The conditions were only partially fulfilled. Aguinaldo went into exile in Hong Kong, some arms and ammunition were turned in, much of the military force was disbanded and returned to peaceful pursuits. The Spaniards, on their part, paid Aguinaldo part of the funds required but did not institute any reforms or pay the remainder. Both sides, in effect, defaulted.

In 1898 war broke out between Spain and the United States and the American fleet under Commodore George Dewey, then at Hong Kong, was ordered to attack the Spanish at Manila. Dewey transported Aguinaldo and his companions back to Manila where they could raise their forces and pressure the Spanish.[7] Nothing was said, according to Dewey, about American help for Filipino aspirations. On May 1, 1898, Dewey decisively defeated the Spanish fleet in Manila Bay and laid siege to the city. Within two weeks, Aguinaldo landed at Cavite and organized his army, which proceeded to surround Manila, enclosing the Spaniards within the city. The city of Manila was surrounded by Filipino troops when the Ameri-

---

[6] James Le Roy, *The Americans in the Philippines: A History of the Conquest and the First Years of Occupation* (Boston: Riverside Press, 1914) I, p. 85.

[7] George W. Dewey, *Autobiography* (New York: Scribner's, 1916) and Charles B. Elliot, *The Philippines to the End of the Military Regime* (New York: Bobbs, Merrill Company, 1916).

cans received its surrender from the Spaniards and entered that city in June and July, but Filipinos were kept out of the city.

The fear that perhaps independence was not to come so easily and also the increased tension along the American–Filipino lines led the Aguinaldo forces to push rapidly for control over the rest of the country and to attempt to establish a legitimate government outside of Manila. The revolutionary capital was transferred to Malolos in Bulacan province, and a congress was convened in September in that city with the primary aim of writing, adopting, and, in January, 1899, promulgating a constitution.

Meanwhile relations between the Americans and the Filipinos had deteriorated drastically. The American government, unaware of the extent and intensity of the Filipino support for the revolutionary government, demanded the acceptance of American occupation of the entire Islands. The Philippine government refused to accede to this demand, and on February 4, 1899, hostilities broke out. By March 31, Malolos, the capital of the Republic, had fallen to the Americans. But it was not until April, 1902 that the last major guerilla force surrendered.

THE AMERICAN PERIOD

With the dawn of the new century, the Philippines began a new cycle of conquest and westernization. The energy and determination with which the Americans undertook their project of creating a new state on the American model elicited from the Filipinos a response which was equally energetic and intensely political and which was to give them in thirty-five years the reality of self-government and within forty-six years political independence.

The rationale of the American colonial experiment was a commitment to self-government and eventual independence. The first civilian administrators under William Howard Taft were instructed to establish municipal governments "in which the natives of the islands should be afforded the opportunity to manage their own local affairs to the fullest extent of which they were capable, and subject to the least degree of supervision and control which a careful study of their capacities and observation of the workings of native control show to be consistent with the maintenance of law, order and loyalty." [8] The early administrators also emphasized the establishment of public education and instruction in the English language, the raising of standards of public health and hygiene, the building of public roads, and water supply and irrigation facilities.

In accordance with McKinley's instructions, local governments were established and elections were held. The American Director of Education described the early elections:

> The biennial elections of municipal officers occurred in December 1905, and those for provincial governor in the following February. Unusual interest attended them. Good order was maintained everywhere, but the number of disputed elections was very great. In some provinces every municipal election was contested. In one province 19 successive ballots for governor were necessary before a candidate was chosen. Of the 32 provinces organized under the Provincial Government Act, governors were popularly elected in 29. In Cavite, Samar, and Isabela where political rights had been suspended (because of outbursts of violence and crimes) the governors were appointed by the Governor General. Of the above 29 men chosen by the representatives of the people, only one, Mr. Reynolds of Albay, was an American . . . . Several . . . had been leaders in the insurrection against American authority a few years before. Others had not previously been conspicuous in public affairs.[9]

The intent of the local government laws was clearly to give as much local autonomy as possible to the Filipinos but this plan proved impossible in practice, because of the need for central administration.

At the national level, the Philippine Commission sat as the legislative body with the Governor General as chief executive. Three Filipino members were added to the Commission on September 1, 1901. These three were distinguished, educated,

8 Letter of President William McKinley to the Honorable William Howard Taft, President of the Board of Commissioners to the Philippine Islands, April 7, 1900, cited in W. Cameron Forbes, *The Philippine Islands* (New York: Houghton Mifflin Company, 1928) 2 vols., II, Appendix VII.

9 David P. Barrows, *A Decade of American Government in the Philippines, 1903-1913* (New York: World Book Company, 1914) pp. 32-33.

and wealthy men who had at first supported the revolutionary government but had very early resigned and returned to American lines. They were members of the Federal party, which advocated statehood within the American union.

By 1907 the state of public order and the success of local government was such as to encourage the Americans to go one step further toward self-government. Elections were prepared for a National Assembly that would serve as an elective lower house of the legislature with the Philippine Commission as the appointive upper house and the Governor General with executive power.

Qualified electors were the same as those authorized for municipal and provincial elections: all male persons twenty-one years of age who had resided six months in their district and had either held local office prior to August 13, 1898, owned real property to the value of 500 pesos, or who could read, speak, or write either English or Spanish. Some 104,966 voters registered for the assembly elections and 94 per cent voted.[10]

The election for the National Assembly in June, 1907 was preceded by an active political campaign that developed into a struggle between the "ins" and the "outs"; that is, between the Filipinos serving the government and holding appointive office and those who remained outside or held elective posts. Most of the "ins" affiliated with the Federal party, which had changed its name to *Partido Progresista*. The *Nacionalistas,* who openly demanded independence, won a decisive victory, emphasizing to the administration and the world the Filipino's desire for independence. Out of the 80 seats, the Nacionalistas won 58 and the Independents 6. The Nacionalistas organized the National Assembly with Sergio Osmeña as Speaker. From 1907 until 1946 it was the only significant political party in the Philippines.

Philippine politics became one-party politics with two separate levels in the struggle for power. The first was the internal struggle among the leaders of this party, which developed

[10] United States War Department, Office of the Secretary, *Eighth Annual Report of the Philippine Commission to the Secretary of War, 1907* (Washington: Government Printing Office, 1908) Part I, pp. 202-203.

into the fight for control between Sergio Osmeña and Manuel L. Quezon. The second level was the struggle of the Filipino assembly for increased power vis à vis the Commission and the Governor General.

When the Democratic Party won the presidency in the United States, American policy was marked by rapid strides toward Filipino self-government and the extension of Filipino political power and authority. The replacement of American civil servants by Filipinos proceeded at such a rapid rate that American business interests, civil servants, and past governors general strenuously objected. In 1916, the United States Congress passed a new organic law for the Philippines.[11] The Jones Law, in effect, provided the government of the Philippine Islands with a constitution and declared the intention of the United States to withdraw sovereignty as soon as a stable government could be established.

Under the Jones Law, legislative power was vested in a legislature composed of a Senate and a House of Representatives elected by popular vote, except that two senators and seven representatives were to be appointed by the Governor General to represent the districts of the non-Christian peoples. Laws amending the tariff, immigration, currency and coinage, public domain, and timber and mining acts did not become operative until approved by the President of the United States. All measures passed by the Philippine legislature had to be reported to the United States Congress, which had power to annul them. The Governor General had supreme executive power and was appointed by the President of the United States with advice and consent of the Senate of the United States. A judiciary, composed of Supreme Court, Courts of First Instance, and Justices of the Peace, was established. The Chief Justice and eight Associate Justices of the Supreme Court were appointed by the President with the advice and consent of the United States Senate.

The increased role in government given Filipinos under the Woodrow Wilson administration created pressures for independence that made the retention of American sovereignty

[11] Public Act No. 240, 64th Congress (August 29, 1916).

tenuous.[12] Filipino politicians learned how to use the popular will for independence and their own skills to undercut the American Governor General. But the return of the Republican party to power in the United States raised questions about these policies that resulted in open conflict between Filipinos and the American Governor General.

During the period of Henry L. Stimson's governor generalship, agitation for and against independence reached a peak of activity. The Hoover administration declared itself against independence but the 72nd Congress was controlled by the Democratic party, traditionally sympathetic to Filipino aspirations. The major problem that an independence bill had to solve was the problem of adjustment of economic arrangements. The question of how to protect both domestic industries and American business interests had to be resolved and the economic base of the Philippine government had to be strengthened. An independence bill, The Hares-Hawes-Cutting bill, cleared the United States Congress and was sent to Hoover, then a lame-duck president, for approval. Hoover vetoed the bill, but the Senate and House overrode his veto and the bill became law on January 17, 1933.

A factional fight among Filipino politicians prevented the acceptance of the Hares-Hawes-Cutting Act. Quezon objected to the terms of the bill, which had been negotiated by the Philippine Independence Commission headed by Sergio Osmeña. Quezon then went to the United States to seek more favorable terms. He proposed an act that would provide for independence and free trade within two or three years, but he soon learned that chances of a more favorable act were

---

[12] A new argument for independence had gained currency among Americans by this time: the problem of ensuring Philippine security against a rising Japan and an overpopulated Japan and China. Supporters of independence often claimed that retention of the islands would involve the United States in a war for their defense. Those who supported the retention of American sovereignty claimed that, if America withdrew, Japan, China, or some foreign power would take over. The Wood-Forbes mission sent by President Harding to survey the situation in the Philippines took place concurrently with the Washington Conference and the Four- and Nine-Power Treaties had not yet been negotiated.

non-existent. The Roosevelt administration agreed to a compromise on the provision establishing permanent military bases in the islands but refused other changes asked by Quezon. A new bill, the Tydings-McDuffie Act, was introduced, passed, and signed by Roosevelt on March 24, 1934.

Within one year after the legislation was enacted, a constitutional convention was to be held in the Philippines to draft a constitution, republican in form and including a bill of rights. The constitution had to meet the approval of the President of the United States and the Philippine voters.

The Tydings-McDuffie Act provided for the continuation of trade relations as they existed for five years but after that the gradual imposition of tariff duties at 5 per cent a year for the remaining five years of the Commonwealth period.

The President of the United States was to appoint a High Commissioner who would look after American interests and whose salary would be paid by the United States. A Philippine Resident Commissioner in the United States would represent the Philippines in the American government. The United States Supreme Court continued its power of review. American sovereignty over the islands was to be completely withdrawn on July 4, ten years from the date of the inauguration of the new government.

Having achieved their one goal, independence, the Filipino politicians were faced with the question of what to do next. Although Spain had been content to rule through a religious hierarchy, the Americans had set up a government based on the popular will. The Philippines had the formal institutions of a modern state and practice in operating them. The American governors general had concentrated on the superstructure of modernization: local government, a civil service, public works, schools, roads, clean water, health services, and sound financial institutions. But American investment in the islands and a policy of laissez faire had combined to perpetuate and extend an essentially colonial economy and had led to a growing disparity between rural population and the leadership of the nation. Dependence on the American market led to doubt that ten years would be sufficient to create an economically independent Philippines. The effect of the schools and increased communications was to generate demands for social and governmental services that the government seemed scarcely able to afford. Increased tenancy, due to the attractions of large-scale production for export, had led to widespread unrest, particularly in central Luzon. Political power was subordinate to economic power and a conservative, landholding, social elite controlled access to public resources. The American period had laid the basis for a modern state but it had also engendered serious problems.

For six years, Manuel L. Quezon dominated Philippine politics, displaying a unique blend of personal charm, arrogance, and political skill. A large-scale "social justice" program was undertaken in an attempt to alleviate the tension in the countryside and ensure popular loyalty to the government. Various radical reformist movements were publicly active in the early years of the Commonwealth. Labor unions in rural and urban areas were influenced by and often led by Communists. The radical peasant movement, *Sakdalista,* uprising in 1934 in central Luzon, revealed a strength that frightened the government and gained support for the Quezon program. But Quezon's efforts and visits to the countryside were insufficient to command co-operation from local and national politicians, most of whom were themselves landlords and unwilling to cooperate. The countryside was controlled by these landlords, many of whom had their own armies and ruled with an iron hand. The Socialists under Pedro Abad Santos and the Communists under Crisanto Evangelista found supporters among peasants and intellectuals alike. In the midst of this dangerously explosive situation, the Japanese attacked and invaded the Philippines. The Japanese occupation and eventual liberation released the pressure on the countryside and brought to the fore new groups, new ideas, and new forces.

THE JAPANESE OCCUPATION

The Japanese attacked the Philippines on the morning of December 8, 1941 and destroyed, on the ground, nearly the entire American air strength. A poorly equipped joint United States–Philippine force attempted to delay the inevitable and

withdrew in accord with a prepared plan to the Bataan peninsula. President Quezon, Vice-President Osmeña, and a few
aides were evacuated and the Philippine government was
transferred to Washington. The remaining members of the
government were left in Manila and charged with doing whatever was required to protect the Filipino people.

By this time it was clear to the Filipinos that no American
troops or equipment could be expected, that all available
material was being poured into Europe, and that they were
on their own. The surrender of Corregidor on May 6, 1942
ended organized resistance to the Japanese. Remnants of
American and Filipino forces from Bataan and other combat
areas escaped to the hills, formed guerilla units, and continued to resist Japanese control. These units engaged in sabo-
tage and intelligence operations and kept alive the hope that
the Americans would return. Personal antagonisms and struggles for leadership plagued some of these units and unscrupu-
lous leaders occasionally used the resistance as a cover for
banditry. But such instances were of minor import — the
overwhelming fact was the extent and dedication of Filipino
resistance. Students, intellectuals, professional people, tenant
farmers, and masses of ordinary Filipinos joined the fight.
Numbers of urban residents and absentee landlords returned
to the countryside to escape working for the Japanese and to
assure safety for their families. They found themselves ill-
equipped for country life and depended on their tenants and
rural people for their safety and survival. For many such people this was the first awareness of the way of life of most of
their countrymen.

But many landlords and upper-class families moved to Manila, where they engaged in commercial operations, supplying
the Japanese and protecting their own wealth. In many
parts of the Philippines and particularly in the heavy tenancy
areas of central Luzon, prewar landlord–government control
was eliminated and widespread resistance prevented the Japanese from controlling the rural areas outside of capital cities
and municipal centers. Into this vacuum stepped the left-wing
peasant movements led by a united front of Socialist and
Communist parties. They organized resistance and kept the

harvest from falling into the hands of the Japanese. In many areas, local self-government was established and former tenants were given positions of power and responsibility. A guerilla movement, the *Hukbo ng Bayan Laban sa Hapon* (Peoples' Army to Fight the Japanese, referred to as Huks) was organized under the leadership of the Communist party. This was a well-disciplined organization governed by the guerilla warfare strategy of Mao Tse-tung and living off the people in the rural areas. They had a strength of 5,000 armed men, and at times they controlled whole areas of central Luzon.[13] The basis of that support was their resistance to the Japanese and the popularity of the anti-Japanese cause.

But this was only part of the story of the occupation. On the other side was the extent and intensity of collaboration, particularly among former members of the government.[14] These people worked with the Japanese to set up a civil government, end resistance to the Japanese, and restore conditions of normalcy. José Laurel, a former Senator and constitutional lawyer with a long record of friendship and sympathy with Japan, became the leader of the group. On October 14, 1943, Laurel was inaugurated President of the Philippine Republic created under Japanese auspices. The Japanese negotiated a treaty of alliance with the Republic and officially regarded it as sovereign, but in fact the Republic was a puppet regime under firm Japanese control.

After the end of the war, these men argued that they had collaborated because: (1) Quezon had ordered them to do so, (2) they were protecting the people from the Japanese, and (3) since they were neither pro-Japanese nor pro-American but pro-Filipino, the war was not their concern and they should do all possible to gain their independence from both outside powers. Throughout the occupation, President Frank-

[13] For an account of the Huk organization and its activities see Luis Taruc, *Born of the People* (New York: International Publishers, 1953).

[14] The collaboration issue is the subject of Hernando J. Abaya, *Betrayal in the Philippines* (New York: A. A. Wyn, Inc., 1946) and is covered in David Bernstein, *The Philippine Story* (New York: Farrar Straus, Company, Inc., 1947). For an able defense of the collaboration see Claro M. Recto, *Three Years of Enemy Occupation* (Manila: People's Publishers, 1946).

lin D. Roosevelt, General Douglas MacArthur, and other American spokesmen continuously declared that when the United States forces returned, collaborators would be treated as traitors. But in the confusion and chaos of the liberation period, this policy was gradually forgotten. The greatest blow to the policy was MacArthur's treatment of Manuel A. Roxas.

Roxas had been Quezon's protégé, Speaker of the Assembly and, at the outbreak of the war, a Brigadier General on Mac-Arthur's staff. He had escaped from Bataan and joined the resistance in Mindanao, but in April, 1942 he was captured by the Japanese and imprisoned. In June of the following year, he was named to the Preparatory Commission for Philippine Independence to help write the puppet constitution. Later he became food director of the puppet government. As the American army advanced on Manila, he fled to Baguio with the rest of the collaborators. A few months later, in April, 1945, he was "liberated" by the United States Army — his fellow collaborators were "captured." MacArthur immediately restored his military rank and assigned him to the intelligence branch of his own headquarters. This action along with personal commendations by MacArthur, in effect, cleared Roxas without a formal hearing. In little more than a year he was to be President of the Republic of the Philippines.

Osmeña, who had become President of the Commonwealth on Quezon's death, returned with MacArthur to the Philippines; but military authorities controlled the country and Osmeña's relations with MacArthur grew increasingly strained. MacArthur refused to accept an American political representative to help in the restoration of American authority. Osmeña's attempts to clarify policy on the collaboration issue were ineffective. He hesitated to turn to the legislature, since more than half of Congress had worked for or accepted the Japanese puppet regime. But on MacArthur's insistence, the Congress reconvened and Roxas was elected president of the Senate and became the leader of the collaboration group who now sought to clear themselves of any hint that their actions constituted treason. Roxas and his Senate colleagues opposed Osmeña's policy and refused to confirm his cabinet appointees, all of whom were identified with guerilla or non-collaboration activities. Osmeña was unable to mobilize the resources of the presidency to overcome Roxas' influence.

The culmination of the political forces and issues released by the Japanese occupation was the election campaign of 1946. Although there was some sentiment for postponing independence, the American government determined to go ahead with plans and grant independence on July 4, 1946 as scheduled in the Tydings–McDuffie Act. An election to select the first President and Congress of the Republic of the Philippines was arranged and candidates aligned themselves to do battle. Osmeña became the official candidate of the Nacionalista party. The Roxas "liberal" wing of the Nacionalista party organized themselves in support of Roxas' candidacy and eventually took the name "Liberal Party."

The Roxas campaign had three main issues: collaboration, Communism, and change. The first, and probably the most important, was an attempt by Roxas and those who had served under the Japanese to repudiate the charge of collaboration.[15] This was an extremely bitter issue, for many Filipinos had resisted to the end and at great personal sacrifice. Some of those who had served under the Japanese used their positions to protect Filipinos from the Japanese military authorities and in support of the guerillas. On the other hand, others had used the chaos of war to make fortunes in the black market and off the sufferings of their countrymen. A Peoples' Court was set up under the able young Lorenzo Tañada but the confusion of American army policy, the failure of any American political authority to provide the kind of support needed, the opposition of the legislature, and problems of finding and substantiating evidence all weakened its effectiveness. Roxas publicly stated that the men who held government jobs under the Japanese had not only remained loyal but also had resisted. Other members of the puppet

[15] On January 28, 1948, Roxas declared a general amnesty for all those found guilty of treason or of military aid to the Japanese. Abaya reports that of the sixteen official candidates for Senate on the Roxas ticket, ten had accepted high positions under the Japanese and three others had engaged in buy-and-sell operations, *Betrayal in the Philippines*, p. 241.

government, for example Laurel and Recto, presented reasoned cases for their action. They had one major argument on
their side with the Filipino people: they had remained in the
islands with the Filipinos and they knew what nearly four
years of enemy occupation had meant. Osmeña had been in
Washington, safe from danger. The Roxas campaign was an
attempt to settle forever the collaboration issue and it attracted to its banners all those who wanted collaboration repudiated.

The second issue was Roxas' cry to "save the country from
chaos, corruption and Communism." The Huks had at first
worked with other guerilla units and even had American
officers as advisors, but gradually their rigid organization and
political activities estranged American units and clashes between the Huks and other guerillas were common. During the
liberation, the Huks cooperated with American forces moving into their areas but adamantly refused to turn in their
weapons and disarm. The Americans refused to recognize the
Huks as official guerilla units attached to the United States
Army and thus eligible for back pay, educational, and other
benefits. The American army, suspicious of the Huk political goals, jailed their leaders, among them Huk *Supremo* Luis
Taruc, and held them for varied periods of time. The Huks
retaliated with a campaign charging that American military police and the Philippine constabulary (fresh from its
support of the Japanese occupation) were reimposing landlord control over central Luzon. This was all too believable to
Filipino peasants, who had watched their landlords living in
luxury in Manila while the rural people fought the Japanese.
The situation in the rural areas grew increasingly tense and,
fed by Huk propaganda, broke out in sporadic open hostilities.

As the election campaign opened, a third political force,
based on the prewar Civil Liberties Union, the old Democrata
party, and other liberal elements in the Philippines emerged.
It was led by Jesus Barrerra, a respected Supreme Court Justice, and Vicente Lava, a chemist, who later in the fifties was
convicted and imprisoned as a member of the Philippine
Communist party Politburo. This group found that the Huks
supported their aims and formed a coalition with them — the

Democratic Alliance — in support of Osmeña's presidency. Their political platform called for immediate independence as provided in the Tydings-McDuffie act, national unity against Fascism, punishment for collaborators, extension of clemency for crimes committed during the resistance, and clean honest government free of corruption. The alliance was led by intellectuals and attracted the young guerilla leaders, labor organizations, and peasants. Its aims, leadership, and support, as well as the inclusion of the Huk movement, raised suspicions in the minds of the propertied classes. The Roxas forces labeled it a Communist organization and argued that Osmeña's election would threaten the Philippines with communism.

The third issue was change. Roxas was a young man with considerable drive in comparison to Osmeña, who was old and tired. Roxas was known as a protégé of Quezon and could argue that he was Quezon's choice for president. Furthermore, he enjoyed a good reputation as an economist, and the country's most obvious problem was rehabilitation and economic recovery. Roxas argued that his election would mean an end to the era of the old leadership and the adoption of the new economic policies that would change the face of the country. In comparison with Osmeña's inability to cope with the chaos and corruption of the liberation, Roxas' campaign seemed to hold out the only hope.

The campaign took place in an environment of black markets, surplus-goods scandals, inflation, and a downward spiral in the foreign exchange reserves. Roxas campaigned all over the islands; Osmeña made one public speech three days before election. The Democratic Alliance campaigned hard in the Manila area and with the Huks in central Luzon.

Roxas won by a 200,000 vote margin over Osmeña, and his party won control of both houses of Congress. The Liberal party held eleven Senate seats to Osmeña's ten (the other three senators were under indictment for treason before the Peoples' Court) and sixty-two seats in the House. The Liberals refused to allow three Nacionalista senators, six Democratic Alliance congressmen, and one Nacionalista congressman to take their seats on grounds that their election did not reflect the popular will. One of these representatives who had won election in central Luzon was Luis Taruc, commander of the Huks. The Huks then withdrew from legal political activity and began to rebuild their guerilla organization. The collaboration issue was dead and the landed interests had returned to politics. Graft and corruption had become the dominant issue of Philippine politics.

The Independence Arrangements. With liberation came chaos and destruction. Most of the Philippine physical capital had been destroyed. Manila was in ruins, the rural areas were devastated, work animals had been butchered for food, transport facilities were nearly obliterated, and commerce had virtually halted. Food, housing, medical care, schools were vitally needed. The cost of living was estimated at 800 per cent above the prewar level.

The formal arrangements for independence took into account the need for rehabilitation of the economy. Rehabilitation began in 1945 with the transfer of $71,500,000, which had accumulated in the United States as excise taxes collected on Philippine cocoanut oil imports, and the return of $6 million in securities that had been deposited by the Philippine government before the war as surety for military equipment. These funds were supplemented by a loan of $75 million from the United States Reconstruction Finance Corporation in mid-1946.

Two major pieces of legislation established the basis for post-independence Philippine–American relations. The Philippine Trade Act provided that free trade between the countries would continue until 1954 under absolute quotas established for the principal Philippine exports.[16] After 1954 a 5 per cent tariff increase would be imposed each year until the full rate was reached in 1974.[17] The trade bill pegged the Philippine peso to the American dollar at the two for one rate

16 For a more detailed account of these measures see Garel A. Grunder and William E. Livezey, *The Philippines and the United States* (Norman: University of Oklahoma Press, 1951) Chapter XV, and Shirley Jenkins, *American Economic Policy Toward the Philippines* (Stanford: Stanford University Press, 1954).

17 The Philippine Trade Act of 1946. Public Law 371, 79th Congress, 2d session.

and declared that the rate could not be changed or convertibility suspended except by agreement with the President of the United States. The most controversial item in the bill was the so-called "parity" provision, which declared that the exploitation and development of natural resources and lands in the public domain and the operation of public utilities "shall if open to any person, be open to citizens of the United States." This would give Americans equal rights with Filipinos in the exploitation of Philippine resources, without any reciprocal rights accorded Filipinos with respect to the United States. Since the Philippine Constitution decreed that only corporations in which Filipinos owned 60 per cent of the stock could have any interest in the public domain and public utilities, a constitutional amendment was required.[18] A provision in the Rehabilitation Act required Philippine acceptance of the Trade Act before payment could be made of rehabilitation claims in excess of $500. The need for investment capital and American aid was very great and Filipinos came to understand that this restriction on their sovereignty was the *quid pro quo*. A bitter campaign ensued with President Manuel Roxas, who favored the bill, successful in gaining passage in the Congress by a one-vote margin, and acceptance by the voters in a plebiscite held March 14, 1947.

The guaranteed export market provided by the quota system encouraged the return of the prewar colonial economy and the return of the landed interests to economic and political power. The Philippine Trade Act did not overcome Philippine dependence on the United States. Perhaps this was economically impossible at the time. As a United States congressional committee pointed out in 1930, the free trade arrangements had been "established by the American Congress against the opposition of the Filipino people" but the major industries of the Philippines and foreign exchange earnings had been based on this arrangement and therefore could not be terminated abruptly without injury to both American and Philippine economic interests.[19]

[18] Article XII and Article XIII, Section 8 had to be amended.
[19] House Report 806, 72d Congress, 1st session. *Hearings on H. R. 7233 The Hare Bill of Independence.*

The other major economic measure was the Philippine Rehabilitation Act of 1946.[20] It provided for outlays of $620 million, the major part ($400 million) in war damage payments.[21] This amount was expected to cover about 50 per cent of private damage at prewar estimates, with the smaller claims paid first. A military base agreement was also negotiated that gave the United States armed forces a ninety-nine year lease on Philippine bases with the right to interfere in any situation that involved the national security.

On July 4, 1946, the Philippines became an independent Republic but was still tied economically to the United States. The character of the economy this dependence provided ensured that the landed interests would continue to have a determining voice in Philippine politics. For the Philippines depended upon the foreign exchange it earned through the export of agricultural products, products that were either grown on large haciendas utilizing tenant and unskilled labor or collected from small independent farmers by Chinese middlemen. Thus the Republic's financial status depended upon groups whose basic political interest was to secure government loans during the planting season, low-cost labor, continuation of the tenancy system, and peace and order in the countryside. Their economic power appeared to ensure their continued political hegemony, but other forces were operating to change this situation.

Young guerilla leaders with broad popular support in their home areas had entered poitics. Many, their dignity hurt by the collaboration issue and their nationalism impaired by the independence arrangements, withdrew from politics and immersed themselves in law or education. Others made their peace with the system and utilizing their popular support won places in the Congress and the civil service. They were a new brand of men with roots in the rural population and the life

20 Public Law 370, 79th Congress, 2d session.

21 It should be noted that President Roosevelt had promised during the dark days of December, 1941 and January, 1942 that *full* restitution would be made to the Filipino people. There was a good deal of controversy over American obligations in this regard. The $400 million plus $800 million negotiated as Japanese reparations later constituted a sum of $1.2 billion.

they had lived during the war and with a new sense of national pride.

A second new force was the entrepreneurs who had utilized the chaos of war and often extralegal means to grow wealthy from their commerce in surplus goods. They invested their surplus capital in commercial enterprises and, as the exchange controls were imposed, in import substitute industries. Operating on the fringes of legality, they depended on political influence with government agencies and thus played an increasingly important political role.

A third important force was the weight of the population. The war had in many ways awakened the countryside to their place in the nation; it had aroused expectations that people sought to have fulfilled, and it had poured into the rural areas, during liberation, the wealth and attitudes of the American army. Large numbers of people moved to the urban areas and even larger numbers began to expect from their government surcease from their own poverty.

Although the arrangements for independence and the election itself had returned essentially the same political and economic framework as had existed before the war, forces opposed to the *status quo* were present. A noticeable disintegration of public morality had taken place, a cynicism about the ends and means of political life was everywhere apparent, and the danger grew that disappointment with the achievements of the war would lead to anarchy and violence. The biggest problem facing the new Republic was the restoration of popular confidence in the government and in the Filipino's qualifications for governing himself. It was, simply, to establish the legitimacy of the Republic that had been born.

THE REPUBLIC OF THE PHILIPPINES

The new Republic was immediately faced with a direct threat to its survival. The Huk movement, deeply rooted in rural discontent, had successfully tapped the issues that were meaningful to the peasant. The actions of the government in the immediate postwar period had done little to gain the people's confidence. The actions of politicians and landlords substantiated the Huk arguments and enabled the movement to appear as the only organization working for the legitimate aspirations of the peasant, the liberal intellectual, and the nationalist. The government did not recognize the intensity and popularity of the Huk cause and seemed unable to deal with the situation. An almost complete lack of communication between countryside and central government and an emphasis on economic policies that appeared to be of little relevance to the masses, both undercut the government's attempt to establish its legitimate right to govern.

Throughout the Roxas administration, liberals argued for negotiation with the Huk and for an amnesty agreement that would bring them back into the framework of the political process. But Roxas refused and in March, 1948 declared the PKM and the Huk illegal and seditious organizations.

The Huk replied by changing its name to the *Hukbong Magpalayang Bayan* (Peoples' Liberation Army) and launching a military campaign against the government. In April, 1948 Roxas died of a heart attack and the presidency fell to Elpidio Quirino, who had been Quezon's private secretary and owed his position on the Liberal party ticket to his regional background, which was expected to attract votes. Quirino had no party influence and was almost unknown, which created a serious political vacuum at the center and forced Quirino to concentrate his efforts on establishing control over the party.

The Huk threat was given second place while Quirino and congressional leaders battled for control of the Liberal Party and, in effect, the 1949 nomination. Quirino tried conciliation, reversing the stern policy of his predecessor, but negotiations broke down when the Huk leaders refused to disarm their followers until reforms had been accomplished.

The 1949 elections took place amid a military campaign against the Huks and a heavy, often extralegal, use of government resources to support the Quirino campaign. Corruption in the reparations transfers, misuse of war damage payments from the United States and of United States aid had brought the government to the brink of disaster. A dangerous cynicism and disgust pervaded the electorate. Quirino campaigned as the Liberal Party candidate with half the party in opposition. José Laurel ran as the Nacionalista candidate in an attempt to clear his name and re-establish his place in Philippine politics. A bitter fight, with open warfare and violence between political groups, ensued. Quirino won by a very narrow margin in what has been called "the most corrupt election in Philippine history." [22] The greatest excesses took place in the island of Mindanao, where flying squads of voters moved from precinct to precinct and votes of dead men were recorded. A minor and abortive revolt by Laurel supporters in his home province of Batangas was quickly suppressed, but it illustrated to Filipinos the extent of government incompetence.

During 1949 and 1950 the Huks initiated a series of raids that threatened Manila itself and illustrated their contempt for the government and the armed services. They let it be known they were prepared to take over the government in 1951. The Philippine army was itself demoralized and riddled with political appointees; it seemed incapable of dealing with the Huks and through its own behavior managed to alienate the people in combat areas.

In this situation of almost complete collapse, two enterprises were initiated: first, an appeal for aid to President Truman and second, the appointment of a former guerilla leader, Ramon Magsaysay, as Secretary of National Defense with a free hand to deal with the Huks.

In answer to the Philippine appeal, President Truman sent a survey mission headed by Congressman Daniel Bell to see what had gone wrong and what could be done. The Bell mission reported that the problem was low incomes and extremely low productivity, especially in the rural areas.[23] They recommended numerous reforms aimed at raising incomes and providing for the participation of rural and laboring groups in the economy. Adequate labor legislation, minimum-wage laws, agricultural credit, tax reform, and foreign exchange controls were recommended and American aid was made

[22] Harold F. Gosnell, "An Interpretation of the Philippine Election of 1953," *American Political Science Review*, XLVIII (December 1954) pp. 1128-1138.

[23] Economic Survey Mission to the Philippines. *Report to the President* (Washington, D.C.: October 9, 1950) p. 1. (Known as the Bell Report.)

conditional on their achievement. This step sobered Philippine politicians and legislation embodying some of these reforms was passed. The report gave a sense of direction to a badly divided and confused government.

Magsaysay's appointment in September, 1950 did much to restore confidence in the government. He had been congressman from Zambales and had worked for veterans' rights in the House. Moreover, he was a big, dynamic man of Filipino, as opposed to mestizo, character. His public statements and press releases helped create the image of a poor peasant who rose to high office by his own efforts. He was a man of action and familiar with *barrio* (village) life. His middle-class origins were ignored and his rural ways and lack of the social graces required in Manila society were widely publicized. Magsaysay's personal trips to the front, where he slept in barrios, ate rice with the tenants, waded barefoot through streams, fixed his own jeep — all were faithfully reported by the news media. The first and most immediate goal of his program was to reorganize and remoralize the army so that it could fight effectively. He removed officers who did not do the job and promoted those who showed bravery and efficiency in the field. He demanded that his soldiers respect the people and their property. Under his direction the army soon began to make gains against the Huks and the people, who had previously refused to cooperate with the army, began to provide intelligence on Huk movements.

The second part of the Magsaysay program was to win the rural people back to the government's side and away from the Huks. He believed that the problem was not simply to kill Huk members, but to eliminate the conditions that made them fight the government. He began to use the army in a resettlement program organized as the Economic Development Corporation (EDCOR). This plan entailed the use of army equipment and manpower to clear large areas in Mindanao for the resettlement and rehabilitation of the Huks. The program caught on and large numbers of landless tenants who had joined the Huks in desperation were transported to Mindanao and began farming under army auspices.

On October 18, 1950 the Huk movement was dealt a blow

from which it never recovered. The government captured the Communist Politburo in Manila. From that time on government efforts showed steady results. Perhaps the turning point in confidence for the new Republic were the elections of 1951, held to elect eight senators and the provincial and municipal government officials. Magsaysay vowed they would be honest and clean and used the army, the ROTC, and a private organization, the National Association for the Maintenance of Free Elections (NAMFREL), to police the polls and report on any hint of corruption. The result was heavy gains for the Nacionalistas. The fact of free elections went a long way toward restoring public confidence and legitimacy for the political process; but that confidence and legitimacy rested on the personality of one man.

The Nacionalista party leadership, hungering for office, offered Magsaysay their nomination for the presidential campaign of 1953 and early in that year he resigned from the Liberal party and the cabinet post and began his campaign. Magsaysay carried on a grass-roots political campaign on a scale and style theretofore unknown in the Philippines. In bare feet and straw hat, he toured the barrios promising land reform, clean water, an end to graft and corruption, and a government for the masses, not for the elite. He attracted to his banner a growing group of young, intellectual, reform-minded men and women who organized as the Magsaysay for President Movement (MPM) in a citizen's good government campaign.

The result was the largest number of votes ever cast for any political candidate in the Philippines. In office his immense personal popularity made him independent of the party and the local bosses. Politicians found it expedient if not necessary to go along with Magsaysay and the party leadership and the old elite lost their hold on Philippine politics. Under the impetus of American advisers and the young intellectuals who surrounded him, Magsaysay initiated a series of rural reforms aimed at raising agricultural productivity and opening channels for continuous political communication with the masses of rural Filipinos. But Magsaysay seemed incapable of sustained interest in any one of his projects and often they deteriorated as his interest lagged.[24] He preferred to tour the barrios listening to people's particular problems and attempting to solve them then and there. The cost of his programs was very high and a series of bond issues raised government indebtedness and undercut financial stability. But they served their major purpose: to restore confidence in the government and in the Filipinos' ability to govern themselves. He brought large numbers of people into contact with the government and the presidency for the first time and established that political change was possible within the legal structure of government and that violence was neither necessary nor wise. No politician after Magsaysay could afford to ignore his goals or his image. On the other hand, the demands aroused were personal and individualistic. Rural tenants were encouraged to take their personal problems directly to the President. The emphasis of the administration on rural development seriously inhibited industrialization and the overwhelming importance of one man and his personal mode of operation prevented the institutionalization of the changes he attempted.

Magsaysay's death in an airplane crash in March, 1957 left the population stunned and the political system disoriented. Like Quirino in 1948, the vice president, Carlos P. Garcia, had little standing in the party and had achieved his place on the ticket because his Visayan Islands origin and control of Visayan votes was expected to balance Magsaysay's Luzon strength. His immediate problem was to establish control over the party in order to fight the 1957 election. A wide-open presidential race ensued. Candidates adopted the Magsaysay dress and barrio campaign style and claimed to have Magsaysay's personal support. Filipinos elected a Nacionalista president, Garcia, with only 43 per cent of the popular vote and a Liberal vice-president, Macapagal, who accumulated more votes than the winning presidential candidate.

Garcia's presidency was marked by efforts to restore fiscal sta-

---

[24] See A. V. H. Hartendorp, *A History of Industry and Trade of the Philippines,* II, "The Magsaysay Administration" (Manila: Philippine Education Company, 1961) and Jose Abueva, *Focus on the Barrio* (Manila: Institute of Public Administration, 1960) for accounts of Magsaysay's mode of operation.

bility and to find a way to regulate foreign-exchange controls and at the same time encourage industrialization. Conditions of law and order in the rural areas, achievements of the community development program, and the extended public administration allowed considerable development. But the exchange controls had by this time become a source of political influence and widespread corruption was the result. Even the various marketing and credit corporations set up for rural improvement were found guilty of misuse of funds and mismanagement. Garcia himself was an indecisive man who was slow to make decisions and lacking in the dynamic qualities Filipinos require in their leaders. His control of the party came almost entirely from his use of the resources of his office and not at all from his personal appeal to either party or voters. By 1960 corruption was widespread and confidence in the government again dangerously low.

In November, 1961 Filipino voters threw the incumbent administration out and voted into office Diosdado Macapagal and a majority of the Liberal party senatorial slate.

The Philippines had become a participant society. The population had grown from 6,623,804 in 1903 to more than 29,000,000 in 1963 and it continues to grow at a rate of 3.2 per cent per year. In the first national elections in 1907, there were only 104,966 registered voters or slightly more than 1 per cent of the population, and 93.6 per cent of them voted. In the 1957 national elections, there were 3,871,170 registered voters representing 10.7 per cent of the population, of whom 76.9 per cent voted. By 1961 the electorate had reached 7,000,000. The role that elections have come to play in the Philippines is indicative of the maturing of the Philippine political system.

The historical experience of the Philippines has gone far to create a unified, modern state. The imposition of two colonial regimes, one distinguished by its emphasis on Christianization and the unity of the Filipinos under the church bells and the other by the extablishment of secular institutions that could maintain and extend that unity, wove the bonds of nationhood. The blend of Malay, Spanish, and American cultures has resulted in a society closely tied by primary groups and preserving the warm social ties of the barangay but overlaid with a veneer of the Spanish aristocratic style and the joy in political manipulation and achievement of American politics. Filipinos accept their formal institutions but regard them as a framework for the strong personalized leadership that is their Malay heritage. Unimpressed by the equality of the American way of life, the Filipino nevertheless has a clear concept of his obligations and his rights in all social relationships. Power is for him a thing to be recognized, acquired, and used.

We shall want to examine shortly how the historical experience has been absorbed into the Filipino political culture and how the political system reflects this experience. But first, we must understand the economic and social setting of this truly emerging polity, for the capacity to bargain is rooted in the society and gives a zest to Philippine life unmatched by that of any other emerging nation.

CHAPTER III

The Economic Base

T HE CHARACTER and vitality of the emergent democratic polity is reflected also in Philippine economic life. A new spirit
of entrepreneurship is spreading through the society, increasing participation in economic life. The extent and
energy of this participation and the commitment of Filipinos to economic development stands in sharp contrast to
other developing areas. Filipinos are establishing strong
national loyalties to a new pattern of economic life, one
that better meets their individual needs. This transformation is the result not of the authoritarian and arbitrary
decisions of planning boards and bureaucrats but of the
dynamics of Philippine politics. Because politicians have
accepted popular demands as legitimate and have sought to
meet them through direct action, they have mobilized and
integrated the population, relating them directly to the
building of a Filipino nation. Rapid economic and social
change in the direction of an open, participant society is
being directed by a pragmatic political system imbued with
the spirit of democracy.

The traditional economy correlated neatly with traditional Filipino society. Large-scale agricultural production
for export provided the base for a two-class society made
up of a few wealthy landowners and masses of dependent
workers. The Philippines was, and still is, an agricultural
country. Sugar, copra, tobacco, and hemp produced on large

47

haciendas by tenant farmers constituted the basis of the economy. Low productivity and lack of capital and marketing facilities weakened the small farmers and tenants and forced them to depend upon the large landowners or Chinese merchants for capital and storage facilities. Low productivity has its roots in the land tenure pattern, the social system, and the values and attitudes of the people. Attempts to improve productivity through extension services, research, and technological improvements are hampered by the tenant's indifference and apathy. Progress in this area is slow and difficult, but key changes have taken place in the economy and polity that disrupt the traditional pattern.

Filipino leaders tended in the past to see the problem of reform as something within the province of the rich and well-born to dispense at their discretion, not as a right of those who tilled the land. Usually, as in the case of Quezon's social justice program, reforms were too late and too limited to do much good. Peasant movements and associations have existed since the 1930's but have proved ineffective as a political pressure on legislators for land reform or changes in agrarian arrangements. Pressure for reform had come from the American government and radical movements, both sources outside the legitimate political channels.

Now peasants are playing an active political role through competitive elections. Although peasant interest in or appreciation of legislation is almost non-existent, the weight of their numbers has made them a force to be reckoned with in the electoral system. Magsaysay's mobilization of the rural vote as a basis of political power created a direct linkage between peasants and the nation — a linkage that has become a major fact of political life. After 1953, no Filipino politician could forget the agrarian issue and the rural masses. For the first time peasant demands were processed through governmental channels, adding a new and more legitimate source of pressure for reform. However, the social structure, political behavior, and lack of local leadership all diminished the power of the peasantry to wrest reform through political channels.

The Philippines is industrializing and agrarian reform has

acquired new and important allies, whose interest is not improvement of rural life as such, but the release of capital and government resources from the agrarian sector. This is the pressure for industrialization led by the entrepreneurs but enjoying broad support among intellectuals, students, civil servants, and the growing middle class. Economic development is obviously tied to increased agricultural productivity. The Philippines is not self-sufficient in basic foodstuffs and must spend its limited foreign exchange on non-productive consumption goods. Furthermore, manufacturing industries must concentrate on the local market but are thwarted by the low purchasing power of the subsistence-level rural economy. Industrial-minded groups have supported land and tenancy reforms in order to increase domestic demand for manufactured goods and to release capital now tied up in land.

But even more important politically has been the support these new groups have given to a more rational tax structure and an end to heavy government loans to sugar, tobacco, and rice planters. The groundwork has been laid for conflict between the traditional political elite with its extensive landholdings, and a new competing elite whose capital requirements and need for electric power, transportation, and marketing facilities can only be met by an expanded public sector. The new entrepreneurs, raised in the Filipino tradition, have sought like their predecessors to achieve their economic requirements through political office. Such an open conflict would be an unbearable burden for the political system if it were not for the overlapping character of these competing elites. For the new entrepreneurs are for the most part sons and heirs of the landed elite. The Filipino family structure and the social consistency of the upper classes has eased the conflict and made it both academic and less painful. In this chapter, we shall attempt to define the character of this transforming trend and point out the means by which the political process has emerged triumphant over the economic conflict. Here in the Philippines one can see the broad variety of forces that must be brought to bear on politics if the commitment to economic development is to be achieved.

REGIONAL CHARACTERISTICS

The land area of the Philippines consists of over 7,000 islands, most of them small and uninhabited. Eleven islands
constitute the three major regions of the Philippines: Luzon,
the Visayas, and Mindanao. Over half the population (51.4
per cent) lives on the island of Luzon, 28.7 per cent on the
Visayan Islands, and 19.9 per cent on Mindanao.

Luzon, the largest island, can be classified into four more
or less distinct Christian Filipino regions. First in importance
is central Luzon, consisting of the lowland plains stretching
from the Lingayen Gulf to Manila. It is dominated by the
high-tenancy large-scale rice and sugar growing areas of Pampanga, Tarlac, and Nueva Ecija. These three provinces are
the core of the tenancy problem, with the heaviest population
pressure on the land. As a result, the Central Plains have
been the seat of the agrarian protest movements.

Second in importance are the Tagalog provinces around
Manila that, as could be expected, constitute the most heavily
urbanized, industrialized area of the country. The population
has shown rapid growth, largely as a result of migration. Most
of the new manufacturing establishments and commercial enterprises have concentrated in Manila and its suburbs. The
urban complex now stretches almost to Malolos, Bulacan in
the north, and Laguna province in the south.

Third is the southern part of Luzon, the home of the Bicol-
speaking peoples. This region concentrates on abaca and
copra as commercial crops, grown for the most part on small
holdings. A relatively low rate of tenancy and a relatively high
number of part or full owners characterize the area. Came-
rines Norte has significant mineral resources, notably gold and
iron ore.

The fourth region, northern Luzon, including the Ilocos
provinces and the Cagayan Valley, produces most of the tobacco and is the home of Ilocano-speaking people. The Cagayan Valley has been an important resettlement area for the
surplus population of the central plains and large tracts have
been brought under cultivation since World War II. To encourage further exploitation of the valley, work has begun on

the entension of the Manila–Damortis railroad to Cagayan.

The central islands of the Philippine archipelago are collectively designated the Visayas. The islands of Panay and Negros in the west concentrate on sugar production, with the heaviest concentration of production in the provinces of Negros Occidental and Iloilo. The sugar-growing economy has given them a distinctive culture that is reinforced by their distinctive language. The area is organized into milling districts around a sugar refinery. In the past, a very few families, controlling a large part of the land, constituted the social and economic elite.

The rest of the Visayan Islands are distinguished by mountainous terrain, poor soils, a limited amount of arable land, and large forested areas. Corn is the major food crop and copra, timber, and some tobacco are the major commercial products. Cebu City (population in 1960 251,146) is the largest city outside of metropolitan Manila. It is the commercial, political, educational center for the southern islands. Poor soils and a limited cultivable area have led many Cebuanos to migrate, and they now constitute a large part of the population of northern Mindanao.[1] As the center of the cement industry supplying all the Philippines, with a growing textile business and other consumer manufactures, Cebu has a decidedly commercial character.

The large island of Mindanao, constituting nearly one-fifth of the area of the Philippines, is regarded as the new frontier. It has been a major resettlement area but still has vast tracts of land to be brought under cultivation and major natural resources that are only now being exploited. The water-power resources of Lake Lanao and the Maria Christiana Falls are being developed and will have an estimated 400,000 kilowatt capacity. This will make possible the exploitation of the extensive iron deposits of Surigao. The Surigao ore contains quantities of nickel, chrome, and other elements that must be extracted. An integrated steel mill is planned for Iligan city. Other mineral resources include copper, gold, coal, and per-

[1] The 1960 census showed that 52.5 per cent of the population of Bukidnon named Cebuano as their major tongue and 80.7 per cent of the population of Agusan named Cebuano.

haps oil. Pineapples, grown on a single large plantation operated by Americans, and abaca have been major commercial
crops. Economic planners project that Mindanao, because of
its resources, will be a major industrial area.

The Sulu archipelago, a scattering of smaller islands, is
inhabited by small tribal groups, some of whom make their
living from the sea through piracy and smuggling. Fast native
boats (*kumpits*) carry Philippine copra to North Borneo and
return with holds full of American goods, particularly cigarettes. These items find their way around the revenue agents
and into the markets of the southern Philippines. The speed
of the boats, the extent of the area, and the numerous small islands and harbors have made the job of controlling both
smuggling and outright piracy impossible for the Philippine
Navy.

The Sulu islanders are part of the population designated
"non-Christian," which also includes the Muslims of Mindanao, the mountain tribes of northern Luzon, and the small
Negrito people (*Aeta*) who inhabit mountainous regions in
Luzon, Palawan, and other areas. Muslims constitute 5 per
cent of the population, numbering 1,317,475 in the 1960 census. Most of the Muslim population reside in Mindanao and
the Sulu Islands. The tribal people of Luzon are concentrated
in the Mountain Province, a special area created under the
American regime to handle their special problems. This province had a population of 435,839 at the 1960 census, the
majority non-Christians.

The non-Christian people theoretically enjoy special educational and other benefits but most of them continue to adhere to their traditional system, with a growing number of
educated, Filipinized non-Christians working among them as
administrators. The special Commission on National Integration handles their problems but its actions have been less than
satisfactory and its programs have been attacked for the
heavy politicizing that permeates the granting of such things
as educational benefits.[2] The non-Christian people have not,
as a group, entered the political and social process of the low-

---

[2] See, for example, the description of irregularities in the Commission in
J. L. Mercado, "Auditors Hit CNI," *Philippines Free Press*, July 13, 1963.

land Filipinos. The Muslims have been organized for political activity and have had an impact on the Philippine political process, but as yet play only a minor role. For all practical purposes, the non-Christians are excluded from the designation "Filipino." Economically the Mountain Province concentrates on rice grown on magnificently terraced mountains and on root crops, most of both crops being consumed locally. Gold, copper, and chromite mines provide important contributions to Philippine mineral resources and a growing tourist industry makes the development of hotels and semi-urbanized areas necessary. Perhaps through these economic activities, the mountain tribes will be brought into the Philippine political system.

THE AGRARIAN BASE

Although an island country surrounded by some of the tastiest fish in the world and with the majority of its population engaged in agriculture and fishing, the Philippines is a food importer, buying rice, fish, and other food products abroad. An estimated 10.5 million acres or about 14 per cent of the land area is under cultivation and probably an additional 1 per cent is under shifting slash-and-burn agriculture. One geographer pointed out in 1958 that approximately the same percentage of total land area is under cultivation in Japan, yet Japanese agriculture provided 80 per cent of the food requirements of a population of over 86,000,000 while Philippine agriculture barely supplied the requirements of a population of 21,000,000.[3] A population growth rate of 3.2 per cent annually further compounds the problem. The 1960 census reported a population of 27,087,685.

The problem is low productivity and concentration of agricultural crops for export. Forty per cent of the cultivated area is in rice but fertilizer is not widely used and only about 5 per cent of the total rice area is under controlled irrigation. Production averages eleven bushels per acre, among the lowest in Asia. Corn is grown on 26 per cent of the cultivated land and again yields are very low. Food crops in 1961 consti-

[3] Norton Ginsburg, ed., *The Pattern of Asia* (Englewood Cliffs, N.J.: Prentice-Hall, 1958) p. 325.

tuted 78.2 per cent of the total crop area.[4] The Philippines
has been close to self-sufficiency in rice but floods and other
weather conditions regularly cut production. The price of
rice in the past has been acutely sensitive to political and
economic events. Stabilization of the price of rice has therefore been a major aim of most administrations. After decontrol in 1962, the price rose sharply due to hoarding and
speculation as well as to various economic policies. The administration set up a special agency to sell rice at a "stable
price" and to relieve shortages in specific areas. During 1963,
the administration found it necessary to import rice, touching
off much political controversy.

Low productivity has its roots in the landholding pattern
and in the social system, which does not encourage innovation
or change. As reported in the 1918 census, 37 per cent of the
farms were operated by tenants, and in the main rice-growing
region of central Luzon the proportion was 60 per cent. Farm
size averages somewhere between 2.5 to 3 hectares (a hectare
is equal to 2.47 acres) with tenant farms at scarcely more than
two hectares. The Rice Share Tenancy Act provides for a fair
sharing of production between tenant and landlord based on
inputs of seeds, tools, and labor. The law also regulates landlord–tenant relations and obligations, but it has not been enforced. The law establishes a 70 to 30 sharing arrangement as
the objective but 50 to 50 is the more usual arrangement.

Income received from half the production of farms of less
than two hectares is insufficient for the food requirements of
a family of average size. Indebtedness is widespread, with the
landlord or local Chinese merchants serving as moneylenders.
The tenant borrows on his crop, since he has no other collateral, and pays back at usurious rates. Such high rates of
interest cut deeply into his income, and as a result he is
steadily impoverished.

Since the landlord's average net return is relatively high
and he receives an additional income in the form of interest

4 *Journal of Philippine Statistics* (January–March, 1962) Table 32, p. 75.
See also "Case Studies of Economic Growth: The Philippines," *Economic
Survey for Asia and the Far East, 1962* (Bangkok: ECAFE, 1962) p. 75 and
Tables 5 and 6, p. 170. (Referred to hereafter as *ECAFE Survey, 1962*.)

in loans, he has little incentive to increase production.[5] The tenants' low income, lack of land, indebtedness, and dependence on the landlord do not encourage innovation or attempts to increase production. Malnutrition is widespread, housing is inadequate, health is neglected, many children cannot attend school, and life is bare subsistence.

The Bell mission sent by President Truman in 1950 reported that "the basic economic problem" was "inefficient production and very low incomes." [6] The Bell mission recommended that agricultural production be improved by applying better methods of farming. They recommended the expansion of agricultural extension services, the rehabilitation of the College of Agriculture at Los Baños and the establishment of an experiment station there, the provision of rural banks to provide credit for productive purposes to small farmers, the opening of new lands, the purchase and resale to tenants of large estates, and measures to provide tenants with reasonable security on their land and an equitable share of the crop.

The Quirino administration began to follow some of these recommendations but the real push for improvement of the rural areas came under the Magsaysay administration. Reforms made during that time included an expanded resettlement program in Mindanao, resurgence of the College of Agriculture at Los Baños, establishment of rural banks, creation of the Agricultural Credit and Cooperative Farming Association (ACCFA) and the Farmers' Cooperative Marketing Associations (FACOMA), an expanded program of agricultural extension work, and creation of a national community development program aimed at helping the farmers to help themselves.

[5] Generosa F. Rivera and Robert T. McMillan, *An Economic and Social Survey of Rural Households in Central Luzon* (Manila: Philippine Council for United States Aid and the United States Operations Mission, 1954). This study reports that the landlords received on an average 93 pesos per hectare in profit. The landlord's average net return was equivalent to 30 per cent of the total value of the palay (unhusked rice) produced. In addition he received 12 to 15 pesos per hectare in interest paid by the tenants on loans.

[6] *The Bell Report*, p. 1.

These programs have shown some success. The countryside is not transformed but it has not the apathetic, hopeless appearance of prewar years, either. The ACCFA and FACOMA have engaged in inefficient and even corrupt operations and many of them have failed. The rural banks have difficulty collecting the money they have loaned and are thus constrained from further lending operations. Filipinos have continued to patronize the traditional loan sources who do not demand either collateral or evidence that the loan will be used for productive purposes. Many resettlement communities in Mindanao have failed and returnees have discouraged others. The College of Agriculture and its experiment station have developed into an important research and teaching institute but its findings with respect to fertilizers, disease, soils, and planting techniques have seldom been adopted by tenant farmers, because of either financial or social reasons. The community development program has had difficulty in sustaining the energy and enthusiasm of barrio people in self-help projects. Nonetheless, improvement is noticeable. One of the biggest problems of the rural areas is underemployment. The development of cottage industries is essential to the economic improvement of the rural people.

On the whole, agricultural production has lagged well behind manufacturing, as Table III.1 shows. There is a growing

TABLE III.1   *Indexes of Agricultural and Manufacturing Production*

Year	Agricultural production 1952–56 = 100	Manufacturing production 1955 = 100
1952	93	69.9
1954	89	88.8
1956	109	115.7
1958	115	134.6
1960	121	150.1

Compiled from Table 3-7, *ECAFE Survey*, 1962, p. 74.

danger that the failure to expand agriculture to meet the food requirements of a rapidly increasing population will slow down the growth of the industrial sectors as more capital is channeled into purchases of food abroad. The coordination of economic planning to take into account the requirements of all sectors of the economy has become a major problem.

Although the Philippines is still an agrarian country, the trend is toward an increased role for manufacturing. Agriculture contributed 33 per cent of national income in 1958-60 compared with 41 per cent in 1950-52, whereas manufacturing increased its contribution from 11 per cent in 1950-52 to 16 per cent in 1958-60.[7] Fifty-six per cent of the labor force was engaged in agriculture in May, 1958, as compared to 73 per cent in 1939 and 60 per cent in 1948. Loans from the Development Bank of the Philippines in 1961 were distributed 29 per cent in agriculture and 41 per cent in industry whereas loans from all banks other than the Central Bank in 1961 were distributed 39 per cent to commerce, 32 per cent to manufacturing, and 18 per cent to agriculture.[8]

Despite these changes, the fact remains that for some time to come the Philippines must depend upon its agrarian sector not only to earn foreign exchange but also to feed a growing population and cut down imports. Increased productivity is an inescapable requirement.

RESOURCE BASE

One of the most important Philippine resources is the rich variety of hardwoods, particularly mahogany, which are world-famous. Over half the land area is in forests, and lumber and other products have been a major export. In the past these products were exported as raw lumber, but in recent years finishing industries have developed, making the forests a major resource in economic development. The government has been unable to control lumbering. Indiscriminate cutting, the lack of a reseeding program, and slash-and-burn agriculture have depleted many areas and created problems of flood control and soil erosion. The Bureau of Forests has attempted to remedy this situation by regulating cutting and by reforesta-

[7] *Ibid.*, p. 75.

[8] Central Bank of the Philippines, *Statistical Bulletin*, XIII (December 1961) Tables 22 and 35.

tion and has met with some success, but the difficulty of enforcement and political considerations have hampered its effect. The waste and loss of forest resources have been widely publicized and the role these resources will play in development has engendered concern for their protection.

Power resources have been limited but extensive development of hydroelectric power facilities in the mountainous areas of central Luzon and Mindanao have brought significant increases. An estimated 40,000,000 tons of lignite coal are scattered throughout the islands, mainly in Cebu, Polillo Islands, Batan Islands, and southeast Mindanao. Geographical distribution of other minerals and poor transportation have limited the effective use of this resource. Oil has been found in Cebu and its presence is suspected in Mindanao but exploitation has been held up and reserves seem to be limited.

Other than iron ore that exists in Samar, the Bicol area, Marinduque, and Mindanao, the Philippines has extensive deposits of chrome. Although of low grade, the chrome deposits in western Luzon are among the world's largest and are being mined largely by foreign capital. Manganese, copper, and gold are important, the largest deposits being in the Mountain Province and western Luzon.

Although resources are relatively limited, they provide a basis for the industrial growth that has become the aim of economic development planners. The Philippines is moving from the export of base metals and minerals to local refining and use and the export of finished or semi-finished goods.

THE CHINESE ENTREPRENEUR

Much has been written about the Chinese in southeast Asia, their clannish character, and the means by which they perpetuate their own culture and remain loyal to China.[9] They are regarded as a potential fifth column, growing more dangerous as China becomes an aggressive power. Estimates of the number of Chinese in the Philippines range as high as 400,000

[9] See particularly Victor Purcell, *The Chinese in Southeast Asia* (Cambridge: Oxford University Press, 1951) and G. William Skinner, *Report on the Chinese in Southeast Asia* (Ithaca: Southeast Asia Program, Cornell University, December 1950).

but most observers agree that the number is probably between 200,000 and 250,000. There is some difficulty in distinguishing between Chinese who have become citizens and intermarried and those who are aliens. In addition, no one knows how many Chinese have entered the country illegally. The Department of Justice listed 152,739 registered aliens in 1961, 137,519 of whom were Chinese.[10] Half of the total number resided in cities.

Chinese–Philippine trade contacts occurred as early as the Tang dynasty (618-907 A.D.). The first references to the islands appeared in Chinese annals in 982 A.D. and late Tang pottery has been found in recent archeological digs.[11] However, trade did not develop fully until the thirteenth century. The Spanish exploited this trade as part of the galleon system and allowed Chinese to reside in parts of the islands, particularly outside the walls of the city of Manila and along the banks of the Pasig. They became indispensable both in inter-island trade and in trade with the mainland. But they remained aliens and were subjected to extreme persecution. Periodic massacres drove them from the islands. In one major uprising in 1603, some 23,000 Chinese were killed.[12] But Chinese traders returned and became a permanent group in the islands. Some intermarried with Filipinos and the Chinese–Filipino mestizo has played a major role in politics and business. The tenuous position of Chinese business in the face of a growing economic nationalism has led Chinese to seek security through the political system. Chinese businessmen and financial interests are heavy contributors to political parties and political campaigns.

Traditionally, the Chinese have been the entrepreneurs, the business- and commerce-minded minority; but the post-

[10] Bureau of Census and Statistics, *Journal of Philippine Statistics*, XV (January–March 1962) Table 22, p. 59. The 1960 census reported 181,626 alien Chinese.

[11] *The Philippines in Pre-Historic Times* (A Handbook for the First National Exhibition of Filipino Pre-History and Culture) (Manila: October 1959) pp. 3 and 26. (The exhibition was sponsored by the UNESCO National Commission of the Philippines with the cooperation of the National Museum.)

[12] Hayden, *The Philippines*, p. 694. Horacio de la Costa, *The Jesuits in the Philippines, 1581-1768* (Cambridge: Harvard University Press, 1961).

war impetus toward industrialization has given a new status to manufacturing and commercial activity and Filipinos now seek to replace the Chinese, bringing renewed anti-Chinese feeling. Filipino economic nationalism pressures the government to adopt policies curtailing and restricting Chinese investment. The major areas of Chinese economic activity have been the retail trade, the cereals industry, and the assembly of copra for export. Important banking and financial institutions are controlled by Chinese. In the rural areas and municipalities, the ubiquitous Chinese *sari-sari* store (general store) has dominated the retail trade in textiles, canned goods, hardware, etc. Long hours, relatively large and varied inventories, and easy credit have given the sari-sari store an important place in Philippine life. The government has encouraged Filipinizing of this trade through the National Marketing Corporation (NAMARCO), which, during the period of controls, imported large amounts of goods and sold them to Filipinos at reasonable prices for resale in local markets. Since government regulation of imports and foreign exchange limited Chinese participation in the retail trade, the nationalization measures have borne some fruit. But NAMARCO suffered from some of the evils of other government agencies. Mismanagement, overexuberance, and plain graft destroyed its prestige. Furthermore, Filipinos, who at first flocked to open their own sari-sari stores, proved less adept at the business and many were unwilling to follow the practices that made the Chinese such an important and integral part of the rural economy. However, the program encouraged Filipinos to engage in commerce and the hold of the Chinese is correspondingly reduced.

The cereal industry was closed to aliens by legislation enacted in 1960. A short transition period was stipulated, in which aliens would be forced to sell their warehouses and inventories to Filipinos. The Chinese gained control of the rice and corn business by many of the same methods that made them dominant in the retail trade: easy credit, hard work, and attention to the business. In the rice areas, the Chinese provided rice on credit during the growing season when tenants and small owners could not meet their domestic needs since the price was high when rice was scarce.[13] At harvest time, the Chinese would collect two sacks for each one loaned. Indebtedness to the Chinese crippled the rural economy. Being in debt to a Chinese, the grower was constrained to sell rice to him, and in time the Chinese owned the business. Filipino politicians appeared shocked when they discovered that the food industry of the country was in the hands of aliens but the broad political influence of the Chinese prevented a rapid response.

Very much the same process occurred in the assembly of agricultural products for export. Chinese mobilization of the production of the small grower of copra, abaca, or tobacco enabled them to build warehouses and copra-drying plants, tobacco-curing sheds, and abaca-stripping mills. Since the small grower with a handful of cocoanut trees could not afford to store his copra or to dry it, except in the inefficient and wasteful home-drying process, he sold his production to the Chinese.

As a result of such activities, the Chinese financial institutions grew and constitute a major capital source in the Philippines today, further strengthening their political role. Now the problem is to find a reasonable arrangement that will allow the Chinese and Filipinos to live together in peace. The problem of finding Filipino replacements for the functions previously performed by the Chinese is inhibited by Filipino social values and behavior as much as by Chinese business acumen. The Chinese have contributed extensively to the economic development of the Philippines, but in so doing they have created serious problems for the future. Filipino economic nationalism and traditional anti-Chinese feeling often seem bent on solutions destructive not only to the Chinese but to the Philippines as well. But the political weight of the Chinese prevents such measures from being much more than "palabras" and allows cooler heads to prevail and sort out compromises on the basis of legitimate self-interest.

[13] Purcell, *op. cit.* (p. 635) reported that 75 per cent of rice mills were owned by Chinese before World War II. He noted that the mill was frequently the only buyer of rice in the area and that it acted as "banker and money lender."

PUBLIC POLICY AND ECONOMIC DEVELOPMENT

In the past, the hacienda economy and its attendant social structure shaped Filipino politics. One of the most striking features of the present, however, is the extent to which the political system and political decisions are shaping the economy. We are here attempting to describe how this change took place, how government influenced the economy in the past, the basic economic philosophy, and the political groups that have been important.

The American Period. Before World War II, the Philippines was essentially a colonial economy tied to the American market by free-trade policies and concentrated on the production of a few agricultural products for export to the United States. In the prewar period, Philippine exports to the United States amounted to 80 per cent of the total value of exports whereas Philippine imports from the United States amounted to about 60 per cent of the value of its total imports. But the resultant economic arrangement excluded the masses of people from a share in the prosperity. The last prewar administrator, describing the achievements of the American administration, added: ". . . and yet in spite of these salutary and outstanding accomplishments, neither a sizable independent middle class nor an influential public opinion has developed. The bulk of the newly created income has gone to the government, to the landlords, and to urban areas, and has served but little to ameliorate living conditions among the almost feudal peasantry and tenancy. . . ." [14]

Per capita income was estimated to be $40 per year in 1939.[15] And 73 per cent of the population depended on agriculture for their livelihood.[16] Despite American attempts to

[14] *Fifth Annual Report of the United States High Commissioner to the Philippine Islands* (Washington, D.C.: Government Printing Office, 1941) p. 34.

[15] Estimate of the Secretary of Finance cited in Kenneth K. Kurihara, *Labor in the Philippine Economy* (Stanford: Stanford University Press, 1945) p. 37.

[16] *Census of the Philippines, 1939.*

distribute governmental resources through social and welfare services, conditions worsened. The number of tenant farmers increased. A postwar survey found that the percentage of farms operated by tenants had doubled since 1903 and in some parts of central Luzon had trebled since 1918.[17]

These conditions were the result of American policies. In particular, they were due to the increase in population. Health and sanitation measures, the elimination of smallpox, and the control of cholera, as well as advances in the control of tuberculosis had lowered the death rate and created increased pressure on the land. But economic policies must bear part of the blame for the situation. The small landowner–farmer, who barely met the subsistence needs of his growing family, did not have the surplus capital required to store and hold his production until he had enough to sell directly to the user or foreign buyer. As we have noted, he sold his harvest to middlemen, usually Chinese, who processed and stored the copra, tobacco, or abaca, accumulating sufficient quantities to sell to users. High interest rates and capital needs combined to force the small owner into tenancy.

The Tydings-McDuffie Act provided for a gradually increasing economic independence by setting stages for the lowering of import quotas and raising of high tariff walls. But the change in policy came too late. A combination of population pressure, increasing indebtedness, and the effects of the world depression had created tensions near the breaking point in central Luzon.

Despite the problems it faced, the Philippine government appeared unwilling to play an active directing role in solving them. The Filipinos' own orientation and American "free-enterprise" pressures combined to limit the role government played in the economy. Government corporations had been set up to fulfill functions that conservative, land-based capital would not. But they were run by boards of directors made up of members of the traditional economic elite and were therefore not inclined to seek changes that would meet these problems.

[17] Starner, *Magsaysay and the Philippine Peasantry*, p. 13. Miss Starner's chart (p. 14) is a dramatic illustration of this point.

In short, a form of "state capitalism" had developed in the Philippines.[18] A very strong bias in favor of private property and its protection, a high propensity to consume, and a tendency to demand high short-term profits had combined to slow savings and misdirect investment. The relatively effortless and guaranteed steady profit to be gained in production for the American market did not encourage entrepreneurship or risk-taking.

The destruction of the war provided an opportunity for rebuilding a different type of economy so that independence would separate the Philippine economy from the American system. But the need for rehabilitation and traditional economic ideas together prevented those opportunities from being exploited.

Most of the physical capital had been destroyed in the war. Physical production had dropped to less than 40 per cent of the 1937 volume of production. Some means had to be found to rehabilitate the economy rapidly. The major industries of the Philippines and their foreign exchange earnings had been based on free access to the American market. There was no basis for a drastic change of emphasis on the part of the government and there was no possibility that Philippine agricultural products could meet the world market price, since production was inefficient. The guaranteed export market was re-established under the quota system and the prewar colonial economy returned. Provisions with respect to the peso prevented the Philippine government from regulating the flow of capital from the country and, since the exchange rate overvalued the peso, Philippine exports went to the United States. The import pattern reflected this situation.

The conservative, land-based economic ideas of the Philippines did not change. A large part of available investment went into commerce and real estate. A large portion of foreign exchange went into imports of luxury and nonessential consumer goods.

Post-Independence. Coupled with the government's unwillingness or inability to collect taxes, the misuse of available

[18] Golay, *The Philippines,* uses this descriptive phrase.

capital led to an excessive drain on foreign exchange reserves. Reserves steadily dwindled away despite the large sums provided. Exchange and import controls were imposed in December, 1949 and the Bell mission in 1950 recommended that further American aid be conditioned on the imposition of such controls and regulations and an improvement in the tax collection system. Import controls and special inducements in the form of tax remission and foreign-exchange allocations to "new and necessary" industries led to a rapid expansion in consumer goods manufacturing and a basic change in the political economy. High profits and a protected market encouraged the creation of manufacturing establishments to produce import substitutes, but many of these manufacturing concerns were little more than packaging or assembly plants.

During the period 1952–59, the annual rate of increase in industry was 11.5 per cent and national income showed a steady rise to 10,492,000 pesos in 1960.[19] During the period 1950–59, national income rose at 5.8 per cent per year and per capita income at the rate of 2.6 per cent.[20] Perhaps the most obvious example of growth is the average annual growth rate of gross national product at constant 1955 prices: 5.7 per cent per year between 1950 and 1960. The average annual growth rate in per capita income during the same period was 2.4 per cent at constant 1955 prices. Increases in industrial production were greatest in the period 1951-56 but growth slowed down after that and by 1958 there were signs of a slowdown and misgivings about the policy of development of industries concerned with import substitution and finishing.

Foreign trade retained its colonial pattern. In 1960, exports constituted 10 per cent of the gross national product and imports amounted to 11 per cent. Coconut products, sugar, hemp, base metals, and forest products accounted for 85 to 90

[19] For the same period, India's rate of increase was 2.8 per cent in agriculture and 5.6 per cent in industry, while Japan had a 3.7 per cent rate increase in agriculture and 14.2 per cent in industry. *Economic Bulletin for Asia and the Far East*, III (December 1961) p. 20. (Hereafter referred to as *ECAFE Bulletin.*) National income was 4,202,000 pesos in 1946 and 8,288,000 pesos in 1956. *ECAFE Survey, 1961,* Table 5, p. 170.

[20] "Development Planning and Implementation in the ECAFE Region," *ECAFE Bulletin*, XII (December 1961) Table 8, p. 19.

per cent of total exports. But the composition of imports has shown a change from consumer to capital goods.

TABLE III.2 *Distribution of Total Imports*

Year	Consumer goods	Materials for consumer goods	Materials for capital goods	Capital goods
1952–53	49%	19%	10%	22%
1957–59	35%	21%	9%	35%
1961	26.7%	22.6%	5.8%	44.9%

Data compiled from Tables 1-15, *ECAFE Survey,* 1961 and *ECAFE Bulletin* XIII (September 1962) Table 8, p. 61

The direction of foreign trade has also changed; reliance on the United States has decreased.

TABLE III.3 *Direction of Trade*

	Exports		Imports	
	1949	1960	1949	1960
United States	71%	51%	80%	42%
Europe	15%	19%	3%	13%
Japan	5%	23%	3%	26%

"Case Studies in Economic Growth: The Philippines," p. 75.

The government's role in the economy has been limited, expenditures have remained constant at 11 to 12 per cent of gross national product. Government-owned corporations that had engaged in many economic activities, from textiles to shipbuilding, are gradually being turned over to private interests. Government cocoanut, abaca, and tobacco administrations supervise their respective industries.

The major economic role of the government has been performed by financial institutions. The Central Bank, the Philippine National Bank, the Development Bank of the Philippines, Government Service Life Insurance, and the Social Security system provide investment capital, the last four accounting for nearly half of the assets of all financial institutions, excluding the Central Bank.[21] The postwar period has been marked by an increase in financial institutions and

[21] "Case Studies in Economic Growth: The Philippines," p. 76.

credit facilities. Rural Banks began operation in 1952 and expanded to 170 by 1961; commercial banks grew from twelve in 1957 to twenty-one in 1960 and their deposits grew more rapidly. Life insurance and mutual funds have developed as investment agencies. Despite the increase in facilities, total investment remains fairly low. Gross capital formation has been 12 to 15 per cent of the gross national product and net domestic saving has grown at a rate of 11.5 per cent per year (compounded).[22]

One of the most striking developments has been the extent and composition of household savings in the economy. The household sector has been the largest single contributor to domestic saving. "At the beginning of the decade, household saving took place predominantly in the form of tangible assets. By the end of the decade, however, saving in financial assets was substantially larger than saving in tangible assets."[23] This change reflected a basic change in attitude and the corollary of the development of a wide variety of non-banking financial institutions.

In the corporate sector, the United Nations report predicted that the expansion of manufacturing industries in recent years would probably slacken as a result of the adoption of the free exchange rate in 1962. But the report suggested that much of this decline could be offset by "constructive developments in fiscal policy especially in the field of direct taxation."[24] The most urgent problem "is to develop existing markets for financial instruments in . . . breadth and sensitivity. Until this is accomplished, a large portion of the nation's saving will in all probability continue to be devoted to low priority investments."[25] And if that investment pattern continues, acceleration of the rate of growth will "probably depend on the inflow of foreign capital."

The Filipino entrepreneur's tendency to invest in unproductive enterprises and packaging industries reduces the capi-

[22] "Saving in the Philippine Economy, 1951-60," *ECAFE Bulletin,* **XIII** (September 1962) p. 20.
[23] *Ibid.,* p. 21.
[24] *Ibid.*
[25] *Ibid.,* p. 22.

tal necessary for building a strong industrial base and prolongs Philippine dependence on imports for producer goods. The problem is not so much the rate of saving as the inefficient allocation of that saving. The wide variety of non-banking financial institutions that have developed in the Philippines are beginning to steer investment from low priority enterprises. The end of controls has intensified this trend by removing the greatest incentive to such investments.

The Garcia administration began measures toward decontrol and in 1960 the Central Bank adopted a policy of gradual decontrol. But the uncertainty and indecision this policy engendered among the commercial and industrial groups only intensified demands for complete decontrol. In January, 1962 the newly elected Macapagal administration adopted measures leading to full decontrol. Concomitant with this policy was a general tariff revision designed to protect Philippine industries vulnerable to competition from foreign goods.

Before the new policy went into effect, the official rate of exchange was two pesos to the United States dollar, the Central Bank free market rate was 3.45, and the black-market rate hovered between 4 and 4.30. Since decontrol, the peso has stabilized at around 3.88–3.90 per United States dollar.

In order to stabilize and meet the new demand for dollars, the government obtained from the United States government and private banking institutions a stabilization fund of $300 million. In the next few months, prices rose but price stabilization measures, such as government imports and sales of rice, curbed the excesses.

Under controls, the allocation of foreign exchange had "deliberately favored" manufacturing in order to speed industrialization and, in effect, had subsidized manufacturing. But the allocation system had ignored productivity or efficiency so that firms were established that, after the lifting of controls, were "unable to compete with foreign products either in . . . price or quality." [26] Major expansion in manufacturing is unlikely until the existing firms are consolidated and more efficient production so reduces costs that domestic goods can compete in the home market with foreign goods.

[26] *Ibid.*, pp. 7-8.

The end of controls allowed the modernizing industrial sector to come to the fore, and as the economy stabilized the Philippines began to look for markets for its goods and a broader arena to work out its industrial development. The United Nations Economic Commission for Asia and the Far East has provided the machinery for regional cooperation and the Philippines has shown an increased interest in the possibilities of an "Asian Common Market." The Association of Asian States created by Thailand, Malaya, and the Philippines in 1961 was a first step in this direction. Interregional trade has shown some increase but the biggest problem is a lack of coordination in economic planning.[27] Some Philippine industries are approaching the limits of the present domestic market and there is little probability that such industrial goods can be sold in the West. Regional cooperation has become the Philippine goal.

Land Reform. Agricultural policy in the Philippines, as elsewhere, is a complex economic and political problem. In the Philippines, a man's ties to his land are almost sacred, so that any attempt at change is a threat to the social fabric of the nation. Proposals for land reform have often failed to take into account all the social ramifications. In the Philippines, all such attempts must face the basic economic problems of too many people, a low level of technology and thus of production, and a lack of capital. At least four possible solutions have been discussed, along with any number of combinations of one or more of them.

The first proposal, which has been tried in the Philippines with only limited success, is that the land be redistributed. A part of Quezon's "Social Justice" program was to buy up large estates and divide them among the tenants who worked them. This redistribution was continued in the postwar period, and the program expanded under the Magsaysay administration. But there are problems in assessing the price of an estate and even greater problems in financing the purchase, since landlords want immediate cash and tenants can pay only small

[27] For a discussion see "The Scope of Regional Economic Cooperation in Asia and the Far East," *ECAFE Bulletin,* XII (December 1961).

sums over a very long period. Another problem is the redistribution; small lots are uneconomic and insufficient, yet larger lots would force some tenants off the estate. An even more important problem on a national scale is the efficiency of production of small versus large areas under cultivation.

The second proposal is resettlement. Unlike other Asian countries, the Philippines has large areas of fertile but unused land that could be brought into production. Much of this land in Mindanao and the Cagayan Valley particularly has been opened up by the Bureau of Lands and sold. Resettlement in government-operated colonies in Mindanao began in Quezon's time and gained impetus under Magsaysay's administration. But to be effective, such a program requires not only transporting people to a measured-off piece of land but also providing them with capital, seed, better technology, health and education services, and tools. Such a resettlement program is very expensive.

Another possibility, less drastic in nature but just as difficult, is to raise productivity. Community development and agricultural extension programs and numerous other government and private projects are attempting to do precisely that. But there are important social and technical obstacles to be overcome. There is a limit to how efficient production can be on the small plots of land now available. Furthermore, marketing, credit, irrigation, and other problems must be met through cooperative, rather than individual efforts, and such cooperation has thus far proved difficult to arrange.

Another possibility, most often articulated by the entrepreneurs and economic management groups, is to let the present system continue while concentrating on opening up urban employment opportunities. When jobs are available in the cities, the people will leave the land.

All these possibilities, however, are insufficient for the pressure of population. The population increase of 3.2 per cent annually would soon make a mockery of whatever resettlement plan the government could afford, just as no conceivable increase in productivity would meet the population's requirements, since the population expands geometrically. To continue the present system while providing for urban employment assumes that capital for development will be found and demand for Philippine products will be created, and both capital and potential demand lay in the rural areas.

In fact, a full-scale effort on all fronts is required if the Philippines is to industrialize. Congressional resistance to changes in the land tenure pattern has weakened as new industrial groups have come to share power with the landed interests. Since tenants and those who would most directly benefit from land reform do not have legislative power, or indeed any interest in legislation, it has been difficult to mobilize support for such an effort. But now the new industrial and middle-class groups, which showed their strength in the 1961 elections, have joined forces with the "agrarian reformers" to push for land reform as a part of a general economic transformation. This new alignment of interests was illustrated in the 1963 debate brought on by the Macapagal administration's bill to eliminate tenancy.

President Macapagal in his State of the Nation message in January, 1963 asked that tenants be freed from "economic peonage" to share in the work of nation-building. He reasoned that by "setting up the tenant farmers as independent landowners, we shall release tremendous productive energies that will boost economic and social development. We shall release large capital resources tied up in absentee landlordism to business and industry." [28] The President's arguments centered on the need to raise productivity and purchasing power so that industrialization and economic development could take place. Macapagal himself considered land reform the key to his whole socio-economic program, which was intended to achieve industrialization, a private enterprise economy, and a reorganization of the social structure and attendant redistribution of political power.

The proposal to eliminate tenancy and convert the agricultural system to a lease-hold relationship was not new. The important difference between this case and those of the past was the emphasis on industrialization and the relationship be-

[28] Diosdado Macapagal, "State of the Nation Message," delivered January 28, 1963. Excerpts in "A Democratic Revolution," *Philippines Free Press*, February 9, 1963.

tween land reform and the need for capital and a domestic market. The land reform bill became the object of nationwide attention, with the press almost completely behind the measure and keeping it constantly before the public. The House of Representatives passed the bill in four days, not because they favored it "but because the President wanted it passed and he was in virtual control of the House." [29] But the Senate, divided between the parties and beset with a continual leadership crisis, adjourned without acting on the bill. The President then called a special session and the Senate took up the debate, eventually passing the measure with its main provisions relatively intact. According to one reporter: "In the history of the Senate no bill had undergone more searching scrutiny than the land reform measure. No piece of legislation had been the subject of longer debate, thanks to some Nacionalista senators. Many insiders were surprised that the bill somehow managed to survive the opposition. The reason, of course, was that strong public opinion kept it alive." [30] As finally passed, the bill provided for the establishment of a lease arrangement to replace the landlord–tenant system, which would be based on a contract with specific regulations to protect both parties. A Land Authority was created with the power of expropriating agricultural lands in order to bring about full utilization of all agricultural lands and reduce large landholdings. Landowners would be compensated for expropriated land with 10 per cent in cash, at least 60 per cent in tax-free bonds, and the balance in shares in the Land Bank that would be set up for that purpose. In addition to these key provisions, the bill raised the minimum wage for agricultural laborers to 3.50 pesos per day and reorganized the Bureau of Agricultural Extension into the Agricultural Production Commission, to be staffed by agricultural college graduates who would personally teach farmers.[31]

[29] Napoleon Rama, "The Sad Fate of the Land Reform Bill," *Philippines Free Press*, June 1, 1963.

[30] Napoleon Rama, "Land Reform: Senate Version," *Philippines Free Press*, July 13, 1963.

[31] "The Land Reform Bill" in *The Manila Times*, July 31–August 7, 1963.

The measure provides the framework for a basic reform of the economy, the redistribution of investment, and a change in the basic social structure of the rural areas. But the question of implementation is crucial and will depend upon the political system itself. It is obviously a long-term reform that will take great effort and governmental resources to accomplish.

The significance of the land reform bill, like that of the other economic changes we have discussed, lies in the role that the political system has come to play. In this case, it was the political system that dominated economic interests and forced them to play out their conflict within the confines of the public business. It was the political system that provided the incentives and led the innovation.

POLITICS AND ECONOMICS

The subordination of economics to politics has revolutionary implications not only for the Philippines but for other emerging systems as well. It demonstrates that an energetic commitment to economic modernization is possible through the very methods that economic planners and administrators often condemn. In our analysis of the political system, we shall show how the dynamics of Philippine politics contributes to as well as responds to this transfiguration. We need to make clear the forces and pressures for change that have been operating.

One of the most important factors was the system of exchange and import controls levied in 1949. We have already noted the tendency to invest in import substitute and packaging industries and the "inefficient" use of capital resources they gave rise to. But the story of economic development would not be complete without an understanding of how those controls affected the political system. The limits placed on imports and the use of foreign exchange gave rise to a shortage of consumer goods and because the peso was overvalued (the official rate was two pesos to one dollar and the black market rate reached four pesos to one dollar) made it possible for the government to use judicious taxation and for licensing policies to regulate and channel investment.[32] All exchange transactions were handled through the Central Bank, which, in alliance with the economic planners, could have directed investment through its policies. But the government did not take advantage of this opportunity; the planners played little part in development. Instead, the opportunity was turned over to entrepreneurs in the form of huge profits. Filipinos saw that if they could obtain import licenses and foreign exchange, they could create manufacturing concerns to produce the goods that people wanted. The controls contributed to a change in investment patterns, attracting savings out of real estate and commerce and into industry.

The competition for import licenses became acute, and it was played out through the political system, with political influence a major component of commercial success. The great rewards guaranteed by the controls and the political character of their administration allowed aspiring entrepreneurs to make the most of their opportunity. The controls led to a vast amount of graft and corruption. Dollar allocations to pay for imports were made on the basis of political influence, tying the new entrepreneurs directly to the political system. A proliferation of consumer industries ate up capital that could have been more "efficiently" invested under different conditions. According to the economic criteria of productive allocation of investment, the government's policy failed. But in the development of an entrepreneurial spirit and a political system sensitive to economic needs, the policy was a success. Political influence determined the allocation of capital and foreign exchange, which established linkages between the new entrepreneurs and the politicians and made the political system the organizing framework for economic development. The politicians now found that they could gain support for their careers not only from the landed elite but also from the new industrial and commercial entrepreneurs as well as the increasingly politically active masses. The participant character of political life will have ramifications for the economy

---

[32] Frank Golay, *The Philippines: Public Policy and National Economic Development,* has pointed out that a study of the economy is essentially a study of the foreign exchange reserves.

diminishing the drastic inequality that had been traditional. The inefficiency and waste of economic performance under these circumstances is the price the Philippines has paid for the development of a broadly based policy and for the integration of new groups with new demands into the political consensus. The government's failure to take full economic advantage of the opportunities offered by the controls not only encouraged the development of an entrepreneurial spirit and profit-making motives but also opened opportunities to sectors of the society outside the traditional economic elite. In addition, the expansion of manufacturing and commerce provided jobs for many Filipinos and created the context for the development of an urban working class and an active trade-union movement. The controls and the government's failure to use them in planning gave impetus to the dominance of the political system and the growing participant society. The attitudes and behaviors encouraged by this period have been a major contribution to democratic development. But as we shall see they have created new problems that threaten to distort and hamper further development.

The goals of the new industrial-minded entrepreneurs are different from the goals of those who grew agricultural products for export. The industrial elite challenged the agricultural export industries' control of the political process and lent financial support to reform movements that would enhance their own interests. The disintegration of the old social–economic–political elite, whose position had already been weakened by the wartime experience, was speeded. The political process also had to find new mechanisms and channels for conflict adjustment. So long as the elite dominated politics, a common interest and background allowed them to solve conflicts through personal relationships and traditional behavior. The new group did not partake of that same background and the conflicts that arose were too deep to be solved quietly. Those in political roles now find it necessary to supervise the struggle of the economic interests through formal structures of government.

The one group that remains outside of the conflict and change are the agricultural workers and tenants. They had no general interest to promote but concentrated on their personal relationships with the landlord. The landlord, who could meet their individual needs, was the one contact with a broader authority that was or could be meaningful. Peasant movements turned easily to sporadic violence and left-wing ideas because they had to build demands where none existed. They promised the millennium precisely because nothing less could penetrate the peasant's view of the world. None were successful until the well-organized Huks took advantage of the vacuum created when the landlords left during the Japanese occupation. The activities of the Huks, Magsaysay, and ambitious politicians campaigning for the rural vote has awakened a sense of participation in the rural people. But as we shall see, the demands they bring to the political process do not lend themselves to aggregation into broad general policies. The potential and actual strength of the rural vote has been recognized and the latent demand for reform has been translated into specific policy by those at the center who depend on rural votes. Without this pressure, latent though it is, changes in the land tenure system would probably be impossible. But in combination with the interests of the new entrepreneurs, it has become a potent force for change.

As we have seen, changes in the economic structure demand more, not less, government direction; more, not less, of a role for the political system. Changes in the economic pattern have raised conflicts that only the political system can handle. The imposition of exchange and import controls, and the resultant demand for domestic substitutes for previously imported items, put pressure on the government capital and credit facilities from a new group, which challenged the dominant pattern of government support for agricultural export producers. A corollary to that change was the broadening of political participation and the pressure on the politician to distribute his resources on a broader basis. The politician could not hope to stay in office solely on the basis of his personal, family, and social ties and his attention to the older economic interests. All these changes sent conflict to the electoral process for resolution. Elections have become highly competitive and bargaining among diverse interests for influence with particular politicians has come to be the mode of operation. But the very responsiveness of the politician to immediate, individual demands has prevented the development of broad-based universalistic policies that would meet the public interest and incorporate the goals of all groups. Contemporary Filipino politics, as we shall see, is a reflection of the attempts of political actors to deal with the particular demands of those who support and pay for their political campaigns and at the same time to develop policies that will meet the general needs of a developing country. The Philippine economy now faces a new set of problems that can be divided into two main groups: first, to bring the agricultural sectors into the modern economy, and second, to create conditions of efficient allocation and use of resources and more adequate standards of economic performance. The commitment of the newly emergent industrial sectors to modernization within a democratic context is a striking achievement but it is by no means sufficient to ensure continued development. An energetic and innovating political system is necessary to cope with these problems. Much will depend upon the ability of the political bargaining process to focus and order aspirations in support of broad general policies and that ability in turn demands the transformation of some of the most characteristic Filipino social behavior.

The traditional economic system underlay the social structure and the social attitudes that were the system's means of control and legitimacy. If the economic system is changing, what of these older structures of control? As long as economics dominated politics, the social structure imposed conformity. Now that economic dominance has been displaced, what will happen to this structure? How will it handle the change? These are the questions we must turn to now.

CHAPTER IV

Philippine Social Life

THE FILIPINO lives in a society shaped by a rich variety of cultures and organizational ideas. His orientation to politics and power includes attitudes and values derived from such diverse institutions as the close-knit, hierarchical barangay with its emphasis on security and survival; the Catholic Church with its universalist civilization and its support for the privileges of the Spanish aristocratic society; and the energetic, pragmatic administrative and political structures of the American civil servant. Out of this variety, the Filipinos have achieved a degree of national unity and a commitment to democracy that stands in sharp contrast to those of other developing areas. Yet it is a society in which primary groups and personal relationships are given greater weight than the contractual and abstract values of nationhood.

Contradictions between the demands and behaviors required by this structure of direct and warm human relationships and those required by the distant and impersonal structure of the nation have been overcome by the penetration of the political system and the politician in search of electoral success. Throughout this study, we shall be pointing out how this has happened and how the contradiction gives Philippine political life its unique zest and its major problems.

In this chapter will be laid the foundations for much of

our later discussion. Knowledge of the pattern of relationships that incorporate the Filipino into his society is crucial to an understanding of how political functions are performed. The social patterns and behaviors described here form the basis of our later examination of Philippine political culture, where the focus will be on the orientation to political action that the society promotes. In our analysis of the political socialization function (Chapter VIII) the focus will be on the process of imbuing members of the society with a sense of citizenship and participation and the problem posed by the conflicts arising out of the different behaviors required by primary groups and political organizations.

Before moving on to the more specifically political aspects of social behavior, however, we need to understand the society that has grown out of Filipino historical experience. The two most striking features of this society are the degree of national unity and the overwhelming reliance on politics to solve problems. In this and later chapters, we shall point out how the society allows for, even encourages, the kind of bargaining behavior that makes political solutions possible.

A note of caution is in order. We must stress that the Philippines is an extremely complex society that defies easy generalization. Our discussion will be limited to those key parts of the structure which appear to have the greatest relevance for the political system. A more detailed study of the family system, child-rearing practices, village organization, and many other factors that bear directly on the individual's relationship to the political process would be of great value. Any such limited discussion of Philippine society is in danger of gross oversimplification since the island country is made up of many subcultures, among them the non-Christian people of the mountains of central and northern Luzon, Mindanao, and Sulu. These cultural minorities reveal some characteristics common to the Christian Filipino, but they are distinct groups that are only slowly being integrated into the total society. Since political life is presently dominated by Christian Filipinos, our description excludes these minority groups. Another major subcultural distinction is the regional linguistic group. Christian Filipinos identify themselves by linguistic region and this designation has meaning in social, economic, and political life.[1] Table IV.1 shows the language distribution by mother tongue. But it should be noted that 44% of the population speaks Tagalog and the number is increasing.

TABLE IV.1   *Percentages of Population Giving Specified Language as Mother Tongue, 1960*

Cebuano	24.1
Tagalog	21.0
Iloko	11.7
Panay-Hiligaynon	10.4
Bikol	7.8
Samar-Leyte	5.5
Pampango	3.2
Pangasinan	2.5
38 other tongues with 1% or less	

In our discussion of Philippine society, we shall ignore these subcultures and note general characteristics that appear more or less in all six regions. But it should be remembered that the regional group constitutes an identity midway between the kinship ties and the Philippine nation.

An almost reverent attitude toward land and family obligations marks the Filipino and underlies his orientation to political action and organization. Family ties and traditional social obligations have been the basis of political coalitions and electoral appeals. Now these are being transformed, but the emergent pattern will be largely determined by the nature of the social controls that have evolved out of traditional society. The forces pressing for change in the economic system have had a major impact on the society also. The monopoly of urban society held by the traditional landed elite has been broken. Their influence on urban patterns has been reduced by the new commercial and industrial groups. Now, this growing urban population, committed to a more businesslike life, mediates between the central government and the rural areas. A changing criterion of wealth has accompanied eco-

[1] The most important attempt to describe the differences among regions is Marcelo Tangco, "The Christian Peoples of the Philippines," *Natural and Applied Science Bulletin*, XI (January–March 1951) pp. 9-114.

nomic development and the shift from agricultural to industrial patterns. Before we examine the family and social control mechanisms, we must make clear the general structure of the society and particularly the urban–rural differences. Then we can move to the traditions that play such an important role in conditioning the individual's life. Our discussion will set the scene for a look at the changes in social controls and social relationships that have taken place.

URBAN–RURAL DIFFERENCES

The Philippines is still predominantly rural. The *poblaciones* (municipal centers) and provincial capitals provide rural Filipinos a contact with urban life and mediate the attitudes and values of Manila through contact with rural people in the markets, schools, and government offices. The poblacion provides the only contact with urban life for the majority of Filipinos and very few escape a heavy orientation to rural attitudes and values. The degree of difference between poblacion residents and rural people is small, but it is significant. Contact with the mass media, government, and new products is greater, as is the opportunity for education and economic mobility.

The difference between urban and rural areas in the Philippines is the basic economic pattern and values connected with land on the one hand, and commerce and industry on the other. Urban residents are employed in manufacturing and service industries and are, on the whole, much better off than their rural cousins. Both geographic and social mobility are strictly limited in rural areas, whereas in urban areas both are becoming increasingly possible. A new class of service, transport, and skilled labor groups has developed in the urban areas. These workers have a higher standard of living, considerable contact with the mass media, and, more often than not, a high school education. The influence of the urban life has in many ways undercut traditional values and ways of thinking.

Urbanization. Philippine urbanization is dominated by Manila. As the center of government, Manila has become also the center of the economy, the arts, education, and social life. The city has shown a spectacular population growth, nearly doubling in size during a twenty-year period.

TABLE IV.2　*Population of Manila*

1903	219,925
1939	623,492
1948	983,906
1960	1,138,611

Other cities have shown a remarkable growth also. Quezon City, the official capital of the Philippines, increased in population by 289,392 between 1948 and 1960, almost tripling its population. Cebu, the urban center for the southern Philippines, grew from 167,503 in 1948 to 251,146 in 1960. According to the 1960 census, 9.9 per cent of the population of the Philippines lived in cities of over 100,000 and 13.5 per cent in cities over 50,000. But nearly 30 per cent of the total urban population lived in Manila. It is difficult to distinguish between urban and rural areas, and the criteria applied to Philippine population statistics have been rather loose.

From the point of view of social change, access to mass media and education, and contact with governmental structures, these cities and even the poblaciones fulfill the urban function. The poblacion is the center of population of the municipality, like the county seat in the United States, and usually contains the municipal offices, the market, and the recreation center for the barrios of the municipality. Barrios are the smallest unit of political organization into which the Philippines (including cities such as Manila) are divided. They range in population from a few hundred to more than a thousand people.

The attitudes, information, and values of urban life that reach the mass of people originate in Manila. The urban complex of Manila and the adjacent cities and suburbs reaches as far north as Malolos, Bulacan, and southward well into the province of Laguna. The city's growth is due largely to migration. Numbers of rural young people and entire families move to the city each year. The growth of the province of Rizal, which surrounds Manila to the east, indicates this trend. The population of that province increased by 790,470 in the twelve-year period 1948-60; most of the increase concentrated in towns bordering on Manila.

The rapid growth of Manila has created serious problems of law enforcement and unemployment. Migrants from rural areas constitute most of Manila's unemployed. Unemployed persons for the entire Philippines have numbered over a million since 1950 and, in the 1960's, the number borders on two million. Even in the best growth year (1955) unemployment rose to 1.5 million. Unemployment will continue to be a serious problem for the large numbers of untrained rural young people who flock to Manila. In such a situation, the aspirations generated by the political system, the media, and education are denied in reality and young people find themselves without even the subsistence security of the rural tenant.

Socio-Economic Difference. The majority of families in the Philippines are concentrated in the lower income levels. The median family income of 905 pesos means that more than one-half of the families have incomes below 1,000 pesos.[2] This is 400 pesos less than the government-established minimum wage of four pesos per day. Of the families in the lower income brackets, 80 per cent are in the rural areas. Families

---

[2] Candido Ordinario, "Income Distribution and Expenditure Patterns Among Families in the Philippines," *The Statistical Reporter,* III (October 1959) pp. 1-10. Another, earlier study (1956) found farm income to be 223 pesos per year, which was considered hardly sufficient for the simple necessities of life. See Horst and Judith von Oppenfeld, J. C. Sta. Iglesia and P. R. Sandoval, *Farm Management, Land Use and Tenancy in the Philippines,* Central Experiment Station Bulletin 1 (Laguna: College of Agriculture and Central Experiment Station, University of the Philippines, 1957). But a note of caution has been raised against these figures by a PSSH study, which pointed out that the most important factor classifying many families in the lower-income brackets was undervaluation of income in kind. In their survey, products raised at home or made at home were valued according to the prevailing prices in the locality. Since the local price of such goods was usually lower than the price of the goods in urban areas, the figures were distorted, particularly since 47 to 64 per cent of total income of the low-income families in the rural areas was non-cash income. See "Family Income and Expenditures," *PSSH Bulletin,* Series No. 4 (March 1957).

with incomes of at least 3,000 pesos constitute the upper 10 per cent and almost one-fourth of the Manila families fall into this category. Families with incomes over 5,000 pesos constitute the upper 4 per cent of the population and are heavily concentrated in Manila. The average income of urban families was 2,427 pesos, whereas the average income of rural families was 989 pesos.

The striking fact about these income distribution figures is the evidence they give of an urban middle class able to afford education and committed to an urban, contractual way of life. The social significance of these income distributions can be seen in the low level of expenditure for education. Slightly more than 1 per cent of income is spent on education by families with incomes of 1,000 pesos or less. Since tuition is charged from the intermediate grades onward, except in the city of Manila, and students must rent textbooks, education beyond the elementary level is all but impossible for most of the rural population. The effect of the schools as a mechanism for developing national loyalties is thus reduced and the effect of the socialization process is limited.

Contact between Urban and Rural Areas. Despite quite different economic status and aspirations, the gap between city and barrio is not as great as one would expect. Certainly it is nowhere near as serious as in other non-Western developing societies, because important channels exist weaving the two groups together.

The most important channels are the upper- and middle-class mediators in the person of landlords, teachers, doctors, and government agents. These people visit Manila, read the English-language press, partake of many of the modern attitudes and aspirations as well as the economic status of the urbanites, but live in the provinces in daily contact with the rural people.

Another important channel is the barrio fiesta and other religious holidays such as All Souls Day. These are closely tied to the family structure and attendance is an important social obligation. Relatives from the city return to the home barrio for these occasions. Just as the masses of urban residents are only recently removed from their rural background, the rural resident is not so far removed from a relative who has become partially urbanized.

The mass media constitute an important channel, not because of direct contact with rural people, but because the content flows into the local communication channels. In our analysis of the way in which the function of political communication is performed in the political system, we shall look more closely at the role of the mass media. As we shall see, the political system has shown a remarkable capacity to integrate all segments of the population, and the gap between urban and rural population has been largely breached by the politician.

CHANGES IN THE CRITERION OF WEALTH

Landholding is still the respected criterion of wealth and the big landowning families, even though their wealth may have diminished or may have been channeled into industrial activity, are still the upper class.[3] Despite the tenacity of this pattern, other economic criteria are being accepted. Aspirations for a money income or a steady salary have become widespread in the rural areas, in part because of the search for security to replace the old tenant–landlord pattern, which has been seriously undermined. The landlord, more often than not, has refused to behave in the traditional, paternalist way and in many cases has moved to town or even to Manila. In another sense, the desire for a cash income is a response to the demands engendered by contacts with urban areas and their economic status and aspirations.

Education has produced higher aspirations and the attraction of government service further motivates the drive for education, in part because of the obvious dead end of tenancy and rural life. Much larger pieces of land than the rural farmer could possibly dream of owning would be necessary to change his status. But even the most lowly clerk in Manila can own a pair of shoes, a watch, sun glasses. Furthermore, he goes

[3] Demonstrated in Frank Lynch, S.J., *Social Class in a Bikol Town*, Research Series No. 1 (Philippine Studies Program, Department of Anthropology, University of Chicago, 1959).

to the movies, looks in the store windows, moves about the big and mysterious city, and in short, has fun. By contrast, life is hard in the rural barrios.

The experience of the war years also showed Filipinos some new methods of gaining wealth. Buying goods and reselling them could provide a good profit. Investing a little cash now could pay off in long-run dividends. Investment patterns began to change, slowly, to be sure, but in the direction of commercial and industrial enterprise rather than agricultural lands. Household savings, as we noted previously, grew and found its way into the modern commercial structure. Filipinos observed how the Chinese had gained a position of dominance in the cereal trade, in commerce, and in the local retail business, and they began to emulate this behavior.

In general, Philippine society can be described as essentially a two-class society with a small, developing middle class. The majority of the population are rural people with either very small plots of land of their own or (more often) tenants farming a piece of land probably less than two hectares in area. Incomes are insufficient to cover the essentials of life and certainly are not large enough to provide opportunities for participation in the larger society. The family system and the economic conditions make upward mobility very difficult and the self-made man is still a rarity in the Philippines. Changes wrought by the war and the economic changes of the postwar period have attracted large numbers of young people to the Manila area. Changing expectations of the young and the lack of opportunity to achieve their goals is certainly an important factor in prospects for stability in the Philippines. It is in this changing scene with the heavy weight of rural poverty and mass urban unemployment that the Philippine politician works.

THE FAMILY SYSTEM

The basic unit of social organization and the main instrument for transmitting cultural values is the family. In the Philippines, the family is the strongest unit of society, demanding the deepest loyalties of the individual and coloring all social activity with its own set of demands. It is important to understand the kind of behavior it encourages and the kind of alternatives it provides, for the communal values of the family are often in conflict with the impersonal values of the institutions of the larger society.

The family system is characterized by bilateral kinship, which gives equal importance to the families of both parents, generational respect, which means that the respect owed to parents, grandparents, elder brother, etc. is extended to all persons of that generation in the society, and intense solidarity among family members.[4] The family is extended to include blood relatives, often as far as the third or fourth cousin, and is limited largely by physical distance and economic difference. Kinship is extended to include non-family persons by a system of ritual co-parenthood or *compadrazgo*.

The basis of family ties is the children born to a couple, for the children bind the families of the mother and the father together. When a child is baptized it is usual for one male and one female godparent to be chosen as sponsors to look after the child's spiritual development. These individuals then are regarded as *compadres* of the father and mother and become members of their family, and the godchild becomes a member of the godparent's family. The same is true of marriage sponsors, although in marriages quite often there are four or more sponsors, who become compadres not only of the married couple and their families but also of each other. It should be noted that godparents as well as marriage sponsors have an obligation beyond that expected of such ritual roles in the United States. As compadres they are expected to take on some of the obligations of family members and to help out when needed.

The compadrazgo practice is a means of removing the danger a stranger might present by tying him to the family system. It is also used for social climbing, economic gain, or

[4] For detailed descriptions of the kinship structure, generational respect pattern, and the compadrazgo system see HRAF, *The Philippines*, I; Agaton Pal, *A Philippine Barrio: A Study of Social Organization in Relation to Planned Cultural Changes* (Ph.D. Dissertation, Cornell University, 1956); Carl Lande, *Politics in the Philippines* (Ph.D. Dissertation, Harvard University, 1958). These authors place greater emphasis on the family as an explanation for Philippine political behavior.

political rewards. Politicians, members of the landlord's family, and socially prominent persons are often chosen as godparents or wedding sponsors.

The family is the economic unit in the rural areas and it remains so, in most cases, in the urban areas. There is a well-defined set of economic expectations that call for complete response to the economic demands made by the family. The obligation to help one's relatives is very strong, with the expectations of the family and the society acting to enforce them. Children are regarded as an "economic asset" because they can be expected to care for their parents in their old age. A large family is desired as the best means of achieving social security.

Special terms of address for each family member denote each special relationship. Younger siblings are taught to treat their older brothers and sisters with respect. Lapses or rebellions in meeting respect rituals are dealt with by shaming the offender or threatening him with tales of evil spirits. This requirement of generational respect is carried over into the society and results in a pattern of behavior that often conflicts with modernizing influences.

The pattern of respect and obligation is reinforced by the belief that elders are the source of both the positive *panalangnin* and the negative *gaba*.

> . . . *Panalangnin,* which literally means grace or blessing is both given and earned. It has to be given and yet no amount of giving will enable a person to receive it if he has not earned it but if no one will give it to him he cannot possess it . . . . God, parents, old persons of skills and authority can give *panalangnin.* The possession of it is an added power and chance to succeed in any undertaking.[5]

Those who give panalangnin can also give *gaba* or curse. One incurs gaba by being disrespectful to older persons, living or dead, and once it is earned by a person it remains a hindrance to any undertaking.

[5] Pal, *A Philippine Barrio,* p. 115. Pal studied a barrio in Leyte in the Visayas and used the Visayan terms, but similar concepts exist in other parts of the Philippines.

Child-rearing practices are notable for the great affection shown children. Such practices differ somewhat from urban to rural areas, but in both cases, permissiveness and continuous display of affection are characteristic. From birth until weaning, which may be anywhere between ten months and two years, the child is constantly with his mother or another adult and his demands are met with affection and humor. One seldom hears small children crying, because some older person is there to indulge their every whim. Among upper-class children, the mother's role is quite early taken over by the nursemaid, who treats the child very much as the rural mother would. Whether rural or urban, upper- or lower-class, the child receives a great deal of attention and affection. The father also is an indulgent and affectionate authority figure. During the period of weaning, the child is expected to be irritable and to misbehave. This behavior is tolerated but the child is made to feel ashamed of himself. The parents allow the child to vent his rage but their attitude becomes a means of shaming him into his role within the family. The extended family allows the child to develop in a warm environment with the constant daily affection of a large number of adults.

The twin mechanisms of shame and fear are used to enforce the deference for age and the formal respect patterns. Lapses into uncontrolled behavior are met with ridicule and with stories of ghosts, child-eating spirits, or foreigners who will punish the children if they misbehave. At a very early age, the child moves into the activities of his age group, takes on certain household chores, and becomes an integrated member of the family. By this time, the respect rituals are unconscious. He greets older relatives by kissing their hands, shows deference for all those older than himself, and knows the fears and dangers posed by the spirits.

In the upper-class home emphasis on the formal patterns of respect is probably less. Instead, the goal is to teach the child his class role. The presence of maids and servants make this role very easy for the child to understand so that one hears a four-year-old ordering the maid to do this or that or something else and the maid obeys, though often with amusement. The child still learns the ghost stories and traditional fears, for these are the way of life of his nursemaid and it is she who has charge of him.

In these ways the child comes to understand that his personal self is tied up with the family and community and that his self-respect is in danger any time he slips from the pattern. This is the beginning of the concept of *hiya,* which will remain a threat, because of possible loss of face, throughout the individual's life. The fear of the evil spirits and the dead ancestors develops in him an unwillingness to act in strange situations when he might not understand just what is expected of him and thus might suffer a loss of face or worse. The child has a deep personal commitment to the generational respect pattern and to conformity.

The child is not taught to accept frustration and to deal with it as such. He does not learn that a certain amount of frustration will be his all through his life. Instead, his frustration is given no weight; conflict between himself and society is not recognized. Any feeling of frustration on the part of the individual, any conflict he senses, is accompanied by a sense of guilt and a fear that God or the spirits will react. The trust and mistrust in the world that a child learns about correlate with the fear of loss of self-esteem, which underlies his later attitudes and behavior. All behavior is calculated to avoid open commitments that might lead to conflict. The achievement of personal goals is in the hands of God, luck, or higher authority, and the individual can only maintain good relations with these sources of help by showing respect and living up to his debts of gratitude.

Regardless of the other roles a person may play in life, the most habitual and comprehensible are those within the family. The formal behavior that gives order to the world is learned and accepted. In any situation the respect pattern and the limiting factor that hiya produces determine response. The sense of security within the family is heightened by the lack of clear and differentiated patterns of behavior and types of responses in the non-family sphere. As a consequence, whenever possible the role outside the family is given the character of the family role. The individual finds that in school, church, and the market the same pattern prevails as the one that guides his conduct within the family. All relationships are power relationships, involving assumptions of authority. There is always a superior and an inferior. A ritualized form of language and behavior has been developed, which masks the bargaining and manipulation that takes place and allows superior and inferior to deal with one another without danger. Well-understood cues and responses serve to obscure the actual situation. Skill at this sort of manipulation and at the ritualization and use of cues is highly prized in the Philippines. These responses, the ritual, the cues, and the skills become a matter of habit. Filipinos reveal a zest for social intercourse and a spirit of manipulation and bargaining. It is a matter of pride to be good at human relations and, since all activities are seen as power relationships, it is a matter of necessity to develop these skills. People have deep personality commitments to activities in the social arena and ritual behavior protects the individual.

This type of stylized social behavior is common to rural and urban areas and among upper- and lower-class people.

In addition to the overwhelming influence of the family, other institutions of social control affect both the development of the personality and the behavior pattern common to Filipinos. For example, religion and the values it perpetuates affect personality, role, attitudes toward conflict, and development of the bargaining spirit within the society. The Filipinos' beliefs, combined with the values of the family unit, comprise a strong control system that encourages behavioral responses and has a major influence on the prospects for democratic political development in that country.

THE NATURE AND ROLE OF RELIGION

In a political sense, religion serves as a modifier of values. As the structure through which man's spiritual ideals are articulated and regulated, it conditions behavior in all spheres of life. Because Christianization was a major element of Philippine colonial experience, religion is part of the national consensus. Religion is one of the most important agencies for revitalizing commitment to the Western model of modernity.

But Filipinos have made their own religion from a blending of old and new elements and this blend plays a unique role in conditioning political behavior.

Filipinos take pride in being the only Catholic country in the Far East. With 83.8 per cent of the population Catholic, the Church serves as a unifying force. It is the main tie between the rural and urban populations, between the leaders and the led. It colors all aspects of life and serves as the social glue that binds the regionalisms together.

Filipino Catholicism is a rich blend of folk tales, *anitos,* witches, saints, and the Virgin. The tradition of making an offering (*lihi,* or in Tagalog, *alay*) to the gods to assure a good catch of fish or a good harvest is reinforced by lighting candles to the saint or the Virgin Mary.[6] The Catholic obligations of baptism, attendance at Mass, and confession are enforced as strongly as the traditional obligations and through the same channels: discussion of the results of infraction of the rules at the sari-sari store.

TABLE IV.3   *Religions of the Philippines by Percentages of Population, 1960*

Roman Catholic...........83.8
Protestant 2.9
Aglipayan 5.2
Iglesia ni Kristo........... 1.0
Moslem 4.9
Buddhist 0.1
Other 2.1

Gaba and panalangnin, which are used as control mechanisms within the family, have their roots in the pre-Spanish belief, which was a form of animism. One of the Filipino scholars of the revolutionary period explained that the anitos were a form of ancestor worship:

[6] For a description of these beliefs and rituals see the writings of Richard Arens, SVD, San Carlos University, Cebu City. Particularly, "Social Scientists Point the Way to Religious Acculturation and Accommodation," *Philippine Sociological Review,* VI (January 1958) pp. 14-18 and "Religious Rituals and their Implications for Economic Development," *Philippine Sociological Review,* VII (January–April 1959) pp. 34-45.

. . . They were not Gods, they were the souls of the ancestors and each family worshipped its own dead who were supposed to have died in order to be able to use their influence for the benefit of the living.[7]

Elements of the animistic belief remain in the form of rituals of planting and the use of charms called *anting-anting*.

Witches (*asuang*), black dwarfs (*agta*), and numerous other evil spirits populate the Filipino's world.[8] Stories of ghosts and spirits and of curses that result in terrible disasters are common. The latest sighting of the agta, the suspicion of a witch, the latest hard-luck story and its cause are discussed with serious interest at the community gathering place. Spirits are related to the souls of the dead ancestors and are powerful factors in ensuring continuation of the generational respect pattern.

Catholicism is highly personal in the Philippines; the saints are more in evidence than the Lord. The role of the saints cannot be overemphasized; they are compadres through which requests are channeled to higher authority. Nearly every household has an altar with pictures of the Virgin and of the patron saint of the town or barrio. The saints serve as liaison between the individual and Jesus Christ, who can intervene in one's behalf with God. The Filipino venerates the saint with the clear expectation that he will intercede with the Lord for the petitioner. The saints are really spiritual brokers of the society. Laws and ethical systems will never replace them in the Filipino's view.

Religious rituals are important social occasions and quite frequently serve as entertainment as well as religious obligation. The most important religious festival in the community

[7] Trinidad H. Pardo de Tavera, "Discovery and Progress," *Census of the Philippine Islands, 1903* (Washington, D.C.: United States Bureau of the Census, 1905) I, pp. 309-410.

[8] In the Bicol region, the asuang today serves the social purpose of controlling deviant antisocial tendencies. The accusation of being an asuang is greatly feared; even the merest suspicion may prove disastrous. See Francis X. Lynch, S.J., "Ang Mga Asuang: A Bicol Belief," *The Philippine Social Science and Humanities Review*, XIV, No. 4, pp. 401-427. For older beliefs see Roy F. Barton, *The Halfway Sun* (New York: Brewer and Warren, Inc., 1930) pp. 141-149 and 153.

is the annual fiesta in honor of the patron saint of the town or the barrio. Significantly, the fiesta is also the most important social occasion of the year, though it is ostensibly a religious rite to honor the patron saint and thus secure his favor for the rest of the year. It is usually scheduled for a time when people are relatively well off; that is, after a harvest. It fulfills the function of assigning status and social behavior for the community society. The lavishness of a household's celebration, the number of outside and status guests, all contribute to the household's social position. No one is turned away and a visitor must partake of food and drink in every house he enters. People borrow money by mortgaging their crops, spend their harvest money, and assure themselves of a lean diet for the rest of the year just to celebrate the fiesta. As in baptisms, weddings, and funerals, it is the time when the household can gain or lose social status in accordance with their conspicuous consumption. At no other time is the obligation of hospitality so intense. It inspires a sense of community and it strengthens the family ties by bringing members together under one roof.

The importance of the Church in daily life is still very great. The observance of the Angelus bell each day and the praying of the Rosary over the loudspeaker system of the town church each evening are daily reminders. The basic character of the religion is fatalistically expressed in the familiar terms *Bahala na* or *Talaga ng Diyos*, which translates "God will take care," or "It is God's Will," respectively.

A great part of the resistance to change is undoubtedly due to the attitude that it is the will of those with higher authority and not man's action on his environment, which determines how men will live. There is no well-developed concept of men using their skills and ingenuity to bend nature to their will. Rather, men use their skills and ingenuity to make *pakiusap* (literally, "to talk for") through the saints to the higher authority, God. In this process, the kinsmen–spokesmen, in the form of the dead relatives, are an important influence.

Thus the old and new religions combine into a belief system that encourages bargaining between inferior and superior power relations to meet the needs of the present. This combination strengthens the bonds of the family, the respect pattern, and social conformity. At the same time it inhibits individualism and innovation. These religious institutions underlie the operation of other social controls in the society and encourage the development of specific kinds of behavior.

SOCIAL CONTROLS IN THE SOCIETY

The mechanisms of fear and shame that are basic to child training continue their importance in the life of the Filipino as the fundamental social controls. Fear of gaba and of being shamed force the individual to live up to his family obligations, respect his elders, and abide by religious teachings. Shame is peculiarly potent in Philippine culture because of the great importance to Filipinos of hiya or self-esteem. The mark of the full man and the maturing individual is his capacity to protect his self-esteem and to react effectively against any threat to it.

The Filipino's strong sense of hiya means that great care has to be taken in all social relations to avoid remarks and actions that might be regarded as criticism of the person. Teachers, for example, find it extremely difficult to criticize, in a direct and pointed fashion, the work of students. The application of standards is easily compromised, and students are allowed to continue their studies even when complete failures because none of their teachers feel up to giving them a frank accounting.

Fear of giving offense leads to a cautious and ambiguous use of language, slowing down the communication process and influencing the capacity to bargain. It allows time for offers to be made, positions to be clarified and threats defined, and for the individual to analyze his position *vis à vis* the other and to make the necessary calculations.

But the vagueness of communication and the tendency to look for the well-turned phrase, the flowery compliment, the long and redundant detailing of facts in order to mask the raw conflict that may exist, lead to ambivalence and uncertainty. One can never be sure that the bargain has been made or of its exact content. Because everything is carried out without explicit definition, one can always get out of a bargain by merely denying that a bargain exists. Filipinos seem to make and break promises with impunity, but in fact they do not perceive mere words as binding. Other considerations enforced by social controls come into play.

The difficulties of direct communication lead the Filipino to use a middleman when dealing with strangers or persons whose power positions are too dangerous for direct contact. The Filipino would no more think of dealing directly with a potential employer than he would of dealing directly with God. In both cases, he uses a go-between, a middleman, to talk for him.

The pakiusap practice overcomes many of the obstacles to direct communication. The middleman who initiates the action with the other party has no direct stake in the proceedings and thus can speak more clearly. If the negotiations fail, they can be ignored as never having existed since the parties involved never met directly.

The pakiusap method, however, involves another element of social control, that of *utang na loob,* or a debt of gratitude, which is owed to those who have sacrificed for you or helped you in some way that you cannot repay. A debt of gratitude is owed to your parents, to the elder sister who cared for you when young, to the man who gives you a job, the teacher who helped you through school. They remain as permanent obligations throughout one's life. Recognition of debts of gratitude is a strong social obligation enforced by threats of gaba and a possible loss of hiya. It is considered extremely shameful not to honor such debts by obeying any request from the persons to whom one owes them.

The initiator of a request for a job, for example, searches for a middleman to whom the employer owes a debt of gratitude. If the request is honored, then the job seeker incurs a debt of gratitude both to the middleman and to the employer. For this reason, Filipino employees feel an obligation to perform quite extensive services for their employer, well beyond the duties for which they are hired.

In theory, the obligation to honor utang na loob is automatic, but in practice the individual often has to be reminded.

This is a very shameful procedure for it implies that the individual has not fulfilled his obligations and is a threat to his
hiya. In negotiations in which utang na loob is owed, the obligation of the debtor may be recognized implicitly, but if the
debtor appears to be ignoring his debt to the detriment of the
other party then explicit reference will be made to the debt.

Three factors must be emphasized in this brief examination
of social controls: the tendency to make personal all relationships; seeing human relations as the superior and inferior
status of participants; and the fact that for every service performed, whether requested or not, a *quid pro quo* is expected.

These three considerations in Filipino behavior, growing
out of family structure and religious beliefs, social control
mechanisms, and the socialization process, underlie the political bargaining process in the Philippines.

THE BASIS OF SOCIAL RELATIONSHIPS

The traditional pattern of landlord and tenant as the main
roles in the society influences the behavior of the Filipino
whether he remains as a tenant or goes to the city to work in
industrial establishments.

In the traditional argicultural framework, the tenant was
expected to till the soil and divide the production with the
landlord. Beyond this arrangement, the tenant showed deference and respect for the landlord and his family, fetched and
carried, rowed boats, and did whatever the landlord required.
On the other hand, the landlord was expected to care for his
tenants, to provide advice and, when needed, medical aid, educational opportunities, and jobs for the children. The landlord and the tenant met always in the servant–master roles
and this relationship and its expectation of complete deference from the one and enlightened paternalism from the other
conditions most of modern Philippine society.

The urban worker's relationship to his boss is based on the
same considerations. The worker is expected to do his job but
beyond that to show complete deference for the boss, run er-
rands for him, carry things for him, and perform other services, whereas the boss is expected to advise and give guidance,

lend money, and help out when the other is sick. This relationship is often a warm and personal one, but it is strictly limited to proscribed behaviors.

Leadership in the Philippines is highly personal and paternalistic, in line with the respect pattern of the family and with the deference pattern of the tenant–landlord relationship. The instinct of the Filipino is to turn to his *jefe* (chief), his landlord, or his boss for help, for guidance, for justice, for all the problems of his life. He does not seek general or communal improvements or goals. He expects the leader to be better off, to be better educated, to live more comfortably, to profit by his leadership, and to do justice to him as an individual.

The alienation of landlords in the prewar and postwar periods broke the old personal ties of loyalty demanded of both participants and the landlord–tenant relationship became more of a strictly economic and formal arrangement. The tenant, imbued with the communal orientation of barrio life, sought a substitute in the political system by transforming his expectations of particular and personal considerations to the politician. In the postwar period, as the weight of numbers began to transform political calculations and elections were energetically contested, political candidates found it necessary to perform the traditional functions of the landlord. They used the old personal and private commitments to gain support for their public roles and gradually the basis of the commitment has changed to meet the new circumstances. Personal relations and traditional social obligations still play a crucial role in Filipino voting behavior but experience with the new system is transforming attitudes toward authority. Unlike the landlord who exercised authority by personal right, the politician must seek authority from his constituents.

In the cities, a new middle-class group is growing. It is made up of educated professional people, businessmen, and small entrepreneurs. The upper income levels tend to take on the characteristics of the older upper class; the lower income levels tend to be similar to the older lower class. But the growing group of urban workers; small entrepreneurs, such as seamstresses, tailors, beauty shop operators, market stall owners;

and government employees has become commercially oriented and takes on a more entrepreneurial character.

These Philippine behavior patterns: utang na loob, pakiusap, the superior–subordinate relationships, the manipulative use of language to cover conflict and raw self-interest, the shames and fears of hiya and gaba, respect for elders, and the strong family system, all contribute to the character of the political process that has developed. In some ways, as we shall see in our analysis of the political functions, they hinder the development of "legitimate" bargaining and encourage corruption. In other ways, they provide the basis for the development of bargaining on a broad scale but limit the development of the specific components in such a way as to change the bargaining process.

*   *   *

Although on the surface a rigid, ritualized economic status pattern governs social relationships in the Philippines, in fact many channels of communication and common interest allow for change. The bargaining character of social interaction allows the transfer of interests from one personal set of relationships (landlord–tenant) to another, broader in scope (politician–voter). The expectations of the old relationship have been transferred to the new and in turn some of the expectations aroused by politicians have been transferred to the landlord. In this way the social relationships that underlay the tenancy system have been affected by the more contractual arrangements of the political process. The interaction of rural and urban areas made necessary by rapid migration and made possible by increased transport and communication facilities has introduced a new concept of the role of government as well as a new attitude toward traditional social and economic values.

The political system has been shaped by the social attitudes growing out of the old land-based economy. Now the traditional economy is breaking down and the social attitudes that supported it are undergoing change. In this situation, social controls become increasingly important for the maintenance of the system. New behaviors not based on or controlled by the old social structure must be regulated. The bargaining character of the traditional social control mechanisms allows for their penetration by political control mechanisms. Increasingly, political experience will guide social development and social attitudes.

Political participation in the form of elections lends itself easily to the older pattern. As the politician realizes that he has to win over every voter by individual favors, he finds insufficient the personal, subjective ties that formerly guided his behavior. How will the political actors and groups deal with this changed situation? What sort of limits will institutions enforce? What sort of party system will develop? These are the questions we must turn to now.

The Framework of
Political Life

PART II

The Framework of

Political Life

O UR DESCRIPTION of the historic, economic, and social base that underlies the Philippine political system reveals that the Filipinos had achieved a good measure of unity and modernization before they became independent. An educated elite dedicated to the secularization of their political institutions and the education of their people for self-government had developed in the Philippines before the end of the Spanish period. By that time also, a common religion and a centralized government had united the islands and given the people a sense of nationhood, of belonging together. The following half century of American control and influence extended the commitment to Western values largely through the public school system to the masses of people. The physical base for transforming the society — roads, communications, water supply, power sources — had been created and set into a framework of formal institutions of representative government. But the economic system, buttressed by the social structure, had come to dominate the society. Social, political, and economic power were concentrated in the same hands, and the various subsystems of the society were subordinated to this pattern.

Changes in the organization of Filipino life during the period of colonial rule had created pressures on the elite that had already become apparent in the Commonwealth

103

period. The results of American policies began to show in lower death rates and an increasing population, in the number of high school graduates who turned up at congressional offices looking for jobs, and in the expansion of the money economy to the provincial areas. The steady alienation of the traditional rural society from the urban westernized center had, by the 1930's, created a dangerous gap that was most obvious in the economic sphere but extended to social and political life also. To some extent old roles and attitudes were adapted to new situations and some accommodation was possible, but the Japanese occupation and its immediate aftermath brought all these forces to the fore as more articulate and open demands for change.

These demands triggered an expansion of the "political" sphere in the form of innovations in the use of public authority. The adaptation of the economic and social structure had effected changes, entrepreneurial in spirit, in attitudes and values. Among the most notable were the growing acceptance of acquisitiveness and profit-seeking as goals, a changing attitude toward the commercial activity of the Chinese, which had previously been held in contempt by Filipinos, and a growing distrust of the "God's Will" explanation for success or disaster. Such attitudes did not permeate the rural areas in any great measure, but they spread through the urban areas and to the provincial capitals and market centers and created a significant group of middle- and lower-middle class people who were in direct daily contact with the rural population.

Because economics had dominated politics, this entrepreneurial attitude became basic in politics also. The new entrepreneur saw the rewards to be gained by the control and use of public authority and followed his landlord predecessor into politics. Politics was opportunity; it opened the way for great rewards, and, since basic common interest and social behavior governed, it entailed few risks. This bargaining spirit permeated the Philippine political system.

Changes in the economic structure and the demands of industrialization have raised conflicts that cannot be solved by highly personal negotiations among social and economic equals. A broader set of interests must be incorporated into the compromise. Some accommodation of groups previously left out of negotiations is necessary to prevent violence and to secure their commitment to the existing system. An expanded electorate and widespread participation has established the need, if not the reality, for taking into account the effect of elite compromises on elections. The conflict between agrarian and industrial interests is too deep and involves too broad a policy to be settled by a few men with family and personal ties of long duration. The political system has had to play an expanded role in order to provide channels through which this conflict can be resolved. In a sense, the political system has come into its own. It has become the dominant system regulating and motivating economic change and policy, awakening new and more meaningful attitudes toward political action, shaping, in short, a new Filipino society.

We are here interested in the dynamics of politics, how these changes have been incorporated into the political system, and in the functioning of the Philippine bargaining process. We have already suggested some of the forces that make the political subsystem crucial in the developing countries. It should be clear from the Philippine experience that this development is not the result of simply adopting adequate institutions; it is a far more complex process in which social attitudes and cultural values play a major role. It involves commitment to a set of rules, willingness to rely on social controls, and readiness to seek relief or reward by bargaining with other interests seeking different goals.

It is precisely these considerations which give meaning and legitimacy to the formal institutions of government. In the Philippines, these institutions have assigned functions, set limits to action, and allocated authority. But their operation and use has been conditioned by the social and cultural forces and no listing of constitutional provisions is sufficient to describe the role they play. The personal, intra-elite character of political negotiations often left the legislature, for example, an empty and meaningless forum. A commitment to traditional forms of personal loyalty inhibited the development of a broad-based, disciplined party structure. But the elite system is breaking down and the constitutionally established institutions are beginning to play an increasingly important role.

This part of our study of the Philippine political system will be concerned with the character and operation of the formal institutions and the political parties. It will culminate in an attempt to draw from our study a sense of the Philippine political culture. We shall then be prepared for an analysis of the bargaining process itself and of the functions the system performs.

CHAPTER V

The Constitutional Allocation of Power and Function

THE CHANNELS through which Filipinos are related to the political actors, their knowledge of and affection for political structures and groups, their understanding of what constitutes effective political action, the formal structures through which public authority is brought to bear, all contribute to a highly pragmatic political system. At first glance, the system seems arbitrary and the formal structures almost meaningless, but closer analysis reveals that popular demands do reach the inner circles of decision making and do influence public policy. The requirements of traditional society, even though transformed by the pressures for change, are still inadequately correlated with the formal structures. The heavy commitment to personal relations rather than contractual obligations is everywhere evident. But it is also apparent that the structures and the behavior combine to force those who would successfully influence public authority to bargain constantly for the support of the electorate and of those who hold public office.

In this chapter, we shall concentrate on the constitutional framework of the bargaining process and on the way in which the formal institutions have developed. The political system, like the society as a whole, is in a transitional

107

stage, adapting its parts to something approximating a "modern" framework. The role that the formal institutions play will be determined by the Filipino context, but it is clear that the democratic system developing here will, as in other countries, utilize a combination of formal and informal patterns of organization to process popular demands and transform them into public policy. The formal structures orient and set limits to the bargaining process. A constitution defines the broad lines of bargaining power by assigning specific authority to particular governmental structures. Use of the public authority in making, applying, and adjudicating rules will be conditioned and given a special flavor by the structures established for those purposes.

The relationship between the informal organization of the electorate and the formal constitutionally established structures is interactive and interdependent. If in the Philippines the formal structures operated solely in the manner described by the constitution, without benefit of the informal political structures that have developed, there would be as many demands on the structure as there are voters, leaving it to those at the center to decide among them. This is, of course, unrealistic. Some form of collection pattern must channel demands into government in manageable (*i.e.,* negotiable) form. In the final analysis, however, policy initiatives come from the center from the formal authority structures of government. The direction the policy takes will be dependent upon the way the electorate is organized to influence those playing roles in that formal structure. But it is also clear that the political functions are themselves products of the formal allocation of authority and are shaped, in part, by those structural requirements.

THE PHILIPPINE CONSTITUTION

For the American, the first impression of Philippine government is that it is patterned after his own to a remarkable extent. This similarity is the result of the American emphasis on establishing the formal base for self-government and independence. But these formal resemblances should not be given undue weight, for, as we have already indicated, the Filipinos have proved remarkably adept at adapting foreign institutions to their own needs.

The Philippine constitution was drafted under the provisions of the Tydings-McDuffie Act signed by President Franklin D. Roosevelt in March, 1934. Beyond the specified requirements, a republican form of government, absolute religious tolerance, and a Bill of Rights, the Constitutional Convention was free to express its own political ideas in a fundamental law of its own devising. An ordinance was attached providing for a minimum of American supervision and the protection of American interests for a ten-year period. In 1946 the ordinance was dropped and the document became the Constitution of the Republic of the Philippines.

The declaration of principles in Article II defines the Philippines as a republican state with sovereignty residing in the people. The state may require citizens to serve in its defense but it renounces war as an instrument of national policy and accepts international law as part of the law of the nation. In addition, the state undertakes to aid and support the natural right and duty of parents in rearing youth for "civic efficiency," and to take as its direct concern the promotion of social justice as a means of ensuring the well-being and economic security of all the people. The rigid land laws established by the Philippine Commission were incorporated into the constitution and the sale and use of natural resources were carefully defined to ensure Filipino control. Extremely broad power is given the government to limit property rights, to engage in business, and to protect labor. These provisions give the constitution a significant social-welfare orientation.

Although heavily influenced by American experience, the Commonwealth developed along Filipino lines and came to bear the unmistakable stamp of Manuel L. Quezon. The period 1935–41 can rightly be called the period of Quezon government. Quezon dominated the political life of the Philippines, exercising control over all phases of government as well as his party. The amendments to the constitution in 1940, which included the change in the President's term from six to four years and limiting any man from holding the office more than eight years, were passed to keep Quezon in office. All the amendments were ratified in the election by a vote of nearly four to one, although only about one-half of the registered voters went to the polls.[1]

The actual powers of the President, constitutionally very great, were considerably expanded by Quezon. Presidential recommendations to the legislature were, in effect, orders. Although legislators often rebelled, Quezon maintained effective control of the government. His political philosophy is indicated, in part, by a speech he made to public school teachers in 1936. At that time, he explained that there was a difference between the political philosophy of the United States and that of the Philippines. He referred to the compulsory-service provision of the Philippine constitution as only one manifestation of the subordination of the individual to the state. The American constitution, he said, places the individual above all other considerations and imposes on the government the duty of protecting his basic rights. But "the Constitution of the Philippines entirely reverses this political philosophy. Under our Constitution what is paramount is not individuals; it is the good of the State, not the good of the individual which must prevail." [2]

The establishment of a Senate elected at large is an example of the centralization of the Philippine government and of the importance given to national rather than local government. This emphasis had its roots in the Spanish system and, despite the announced intention of the American government to develop local autonomy and grass-roots democracy, became a major feature of Philippine government. The party system, as we shall see in the next chapter, developed a vested interest in centralization. The strong executive envisioned by Quezon led him to support an upper house that, because of its election at large and the difficulties of transportation and communication in the island country, would be dependent upon presidential largess and popularity for electoral success. Also, the

[1] Ralston Hayden, *The Philippines* (New York: The Macmillan Co., 1942).

[2] "Changes in Government and Political Philosophy," speech given by the President of the Philippines at Teachers Camp, Baguio, May 22, 1936 in *Messages of the President: Manuel L. Quezon*, II, Part I.

electorate had been gradually expanded during the American occupation, and free public education gradually reduced the barrier posed by the literacy qualification, posing a threat to the oligarchy of landed interests that dominated Philippine politics. A legislature made up of members elected in small districts based on population allowed radical reform movements based on mass appeals, such as the Sakdalistas or the Socialists, to gain public office. The institution of a second house, election to which would necessarily remain in the hands of the wealthy and powerful, checked this trend. In recent years proposals have been made to elect senators by district. This suggestion, pursued most seriously by President Garcia, has been called an attempt to increase executive power by preventing the development of national personalities with support broad enough to challenge the President.

The strength of the presidency, both constitutionally and politically, has slowed the development of a responsible and independent legislature. The legislature has had little effective voice in shaping public policy. Instead, they have concentrated on negating the President's policies. The experience of the first National Assembly of the Commonwealth of the Philippines is similar to that of later legislatures. The opening weeks of the assembly were taken up with a fight between the President and Congressman Quintin Paredes over the speakership. Quezon established his supremacy, placing his man in the office, but it was a hollow victory. An extraordinary number of vetoes revealed the deep disagreement between executive and legislature; forty-four bills, constituting 42 per cent of the measures passed during the 1938 session, were vetoed.[3] The assembly, like succeeding legislatures, spent its first months on privileged speeches, forcing all legislation into the final days of the session when it had to be debated and passed without thorough consideration. Of the 148 bills enacted during the first regular session of the assembly, 93, mostly administrative measures, passed their final stages on the last day of the session.

The integration and institutionalization of policy-making procedures is one of the crucial problems of political develop-

[3] Hayden, *The Philippines*, p. 220.

ment. In the Philippines the willingness of politicians to work through constitutionally established channels has provided an important measure of stability and predictability. This acceptance of regularized procedures has been more apparent than real and only very recently has the Congress assumed a more active legislative function. The formal structures are only now becoming real channels of conflict resolution.

THE EXECUTIVE

The Filipino idea of leadership residing in one man with broad powers exercised in a highly personal manner became the dominant idea of the constitution. The constitutional grant of power has been extended in practice through an emphasis on "political" considerations. Congressmen and senators regard presidential powers as almost unlimited. The powers of the presidency have been determined largely by the political skills of the men who held the office and, as we shall see, the legislature has developed as an effective check largely because of the legislator's control of local politics.

The Constitutional Convention accepted the separation of powers in principle but, in line with the tradition of strong leadership, wrote a fundamental law that strongly overbalanced the executive *vis à vis* the legislature. For example, the executive has the right to certify measures he deems important for immediate congressional action, bypassing normal procedures; he alone can call a special session and designate the agenda for it; he has considerable independence in budgetary matters and what appears to be policy-making power in certain fields.

One aspect of his extremely broad powers arises from the unitary form of the Philippine government. Local government is subordinate to the national government and owes its limited authority to a delegation of power from the center. The President has general supervisory power over local government and as a corollary has the authority to define boundaries, divide up municipalities and barrios, and generally create or destroy local government without the consent of the legislature.

Perhaps the most useful political influence derives from the executive power of appointment. The President appoints an astounding number of officials, clerks, and laborers. Until 1955, he appointed the mayors and police chiefs of chartered cities and still appoints half of such officials. He appoints the director of the Central Bank, the municipal treasurer, health officers, and law clerks. Since he has control of the services provided by local government, he has a means for ensuring political loyalty from local government officials despite their party designations. The municipal mayor, for example, cannot control local health officials and agricultural workers, since these people work directly for national administrative offices. He is dependent on the executive in this regard. Patronage is the oil of politics: the unitary character of the Philippine government and the fact that government offers the best and, in some cases the only employment opportunities, makes that oil even more important than usual.

Presidential appointment power is subject to the consent of the Commission on Appointments, elected on the basis of proportional representation of the parties, twelve members each from the House and the Senate, with the Senate President as chairman. Nearly all appointments must be confirmed by the Commission, and in the past most have been approved with little objection because of the executive's skillful distribution of patronage and because the administration has usually had a majority in Congress.[4]

The President is the chief administrator.[5] The legislature has some limiting power since it can create executive departments, define their powers, appropriate the money necessary to their operation, and require reports or testimony as to their activities. But the political influence of the President and his control of patronage and the allocation of public funds allows him extensive independence. As chief administrator, the President must issue executive orders to provide for the execution of legislative measures, since Congress usually defines only general policy. In prescribing the rules and regulations pro-

[4] John Romani, *The Philippine Presidency* (Manila: Institute of Public Administration, 1956) p. 90.

[5] *Ibid.*, chapter IV.

mulgating legislative enactments, the President can and does stamp them with his own ideas and character. The personal, as opposed to institutional, character of leadership in the Philippines is reflected in the extent to which the President is involved in the details of administration. Often the most rudimentary administrative matter is sent directly to him for decision; personal quarrels among bureaus and officials come to the President for mediation, and he is likely to interfere in administration at all levels.

Another important part of executive power is the authority given him as commander-in-chief of all armed forces to suspend the writ of habeas corpus and place the Philippines or any part of it under martial law. The writ was suspended during the Huk rebellion but, as soon as the threat subsided, agitation for its restoration began and, in 1953, it was restored. Presidents have not used the martial law provision but from time to time have placed areas under the control of the Philippine Constabulary. The constabulary has a unit in each province that serves somewhat the same function as the state police forces of the United States. When there is a threat to law and order that the local police cannot handle, the Philippine Constabulary takes over temporarily. Violence at election time and political murders have been common enough to warrant some form of policing of the polls where local police forces either are not available or are themselves involved. But often Philippine Constabulary control has been undertaken for political ends and the constabulary's reputation, though improved by Magsaysay's efforts, suffers from a reputation for political partisanship.

In the Philippines, as elsewhere, the budget is the fundamental base of executive policies and political pressures. In line with the leadership tradition, the President is given broader authority and independence than is the American executive. The President is required to submit a budget to the legislature within fifteen days of the opening of each regular session. This budget becomes the basis of the general appropriation bill and sets off a continuous round of bargaining between executive and legislature, among legislators, and between parties. The Congress cannot increase the appropriations recommended by the President for the operation of the government except those for the Congress and judiciary. Furthermore, the President has an item veto on revenue and tariff bills that allows him to strike out of the appropriations act items he does not want without endangering the financial ability of his administration. To make his position even more secure, his veto of certain kinds of appropriations bills and measures that increase the public debt can only be overridden by a three-fourths vote of all members of each house.

The most intriguing aspect of the Philippine budgetary process is the public works budget. It is not included in the executive budget but is worked out by Congress and includes recommendations from the Department of Public Works and "pork barrel" sums for each member to be used in his own constituency. Its legislative aspects will be discussed later. Here it is important to understand that the executive maintains control of the appropriations. The budget commission, under the direct control of the President, certifies the availability of funds and releases the money, which gives the President a powerful club over the heads of congressmen and senators who must depend on pork barrel for election purposes. It also accounts for the large number of defections from the losing party to the winning party after elections.

In addition to the public works and pork barrel funds, the executive has large "contingent funds" at his disposal, to be used for emergencies at his own discretion. Presidential use of budgetary powers for political purposes is summed up in this statement by a Philippine congressman: "The President can, by pouring money into a province and through his pork barrel funds, defeat a candidate he doesn't like. So you really have to stay in good with the President." [6]

The President, both constitutionally and by political influence, has a real advantage in getting his program through the legislature. Administration measures are given top priority in Congress and broad support can be generated by the judicious use of funds and appointive power. But this situation is changing, in part because of increased sophistication of the electorate and the demands of organized interest groups. In part,

[6] Author's interview.

also, it is due to the changed relationship of legislature to executive growing out of the above factors and out of the inefficiency and indeed impossibility of the pork barrel and patronage system. Another largely unassessable factor is dissatisfaction with personal leadership and particularly with the personalities who have occupied the presidency in recent years. Much of this change and its force will be made clear in the next section; here we can only describe what has happened to indicate the change.

Philippine Presidents have usually enjoyed legislative majorities largely because of their political influence. As a result, they have hand-picked the leadership of the Congress and in consultation with that leadership and members of the majority party have worked out a legislative program. Legislation by caucus was the result, with most of the negotiation, like the proverbial iceberg, hidden from public view. Despite this system, presidential vetoes have been common, and legislative refusal to pass administration bills has also been notable.

The President can veto any legislation and a two-thirds vote of all members of each house is required to override the veto. Therefore, nine senators or thirty-five congressmen can prevent the legislature from acting against the President's will. Since most legislation is passed by Congress during the last few days of the session, the President often vetoes measures after adjournment, postponing the legislature's attempts to override the veto until the next session. Meanwhile, the President can work through the party caucus and leadership to draft a bill that will meet with his approval.

The pressure of legislation is very heavy during the month after adjournment, since a measure can become law without the President's signature if not vetoed within thirty days of adjournment. Measures automatically become law during the session if the President does not return them to Congress with his veto twenty days after he receives them. An example of the legislative jam was the end of the 1960 session, when presidential action on 400 measures passed by Congress was not made public until nearly a week after the thirty-day deadline on executive action. In this case, the President signed the budget and public works appropriations but vetoed some items, reducing the budget passed by Congress by over one million pesos. He vetoed four major bills, a measure nationalizing the rice and corn industry, an anti-graft measure, a bill to transfer the Sugar Quota Administration to the Philippine Sugar Institute, and an amendment to the Japanese Reparations Agreement.

Philippine Presidents have often returned vetoed legislation along with an executive message detailing the objections and sometimes including a revised bill.[7] There had been few, if any, explicit attempts to override presidential vetoes until 1960, when two measures vetoed by President Carlos Garcia were passed again by Congress with the required majorities. These were the anti-graft bill, designed to limit influence-peddling, the use of public office for private gain, and setting up the mechanisms for enforcement, and the bill nationalizing the rice and corn industries, which had for some years been dominated by Chinese interests.

Legislatures have often refused to pass administration bills or have so weakened them with amendments as to destroy their aim. That has been the common fate of land reform measures. The fact that most sessions are followed by one and sometimes more special sessions is evidence of the legislature's negating power. Special sessions have been called to deal with administration measures that have been ignored or defeated in the regular session. At the end of the 1963 regular session, for example, the Senate adjourned without acting on the budget, the public works appropriation bill, or the land reform bill, and a special session had to be called to deal with these measures. Extensive negotiations between congressional and party leaders are usually necessary to work out the agenda for special sessions. Important legislation, for example the 1955 and 1963 land reform bills, become the subject of wide debate and amendment and is more widely publicized and educative in nature when taken up in special sessions. In 1963, President Macapagal called a six-day special session to consider his land reform bill, which had not passed

[7] Romani, *The Philippine Presidency,* reports that Quirino, in particular, used this device. It is not clear, however, how many of such revised substitutes were accepted by the legislature. No study of Philippine legislative history is yet available.

in the regular session. Seven extensions were required and twenty-eight days passed before the Senate approved a heavily amended version.[8] During the extensive debate between supporters of the measure and their opponents, many aspects of the bill and its ramifications were clarified, and the press, which was almost unanimously in favor, gave the debate wide coverage. The special session has come to be almost a regular institution, utilized by the executive in securing passage of important but controversial measures.

The provisions for the election and tenure of the President are worth noting, for political interest has centered on them on two occasions. He is elected by direct popular vote for a four-year term and is restricted to eight years in office. The constitutional language is important because it establishes eight years, not two terms, as the criterion: "No person shall serve as President for more than eight consecutive years. The period of such service shall be counted from the date he shall have commenced to act as President."[9]

The arguments inherent in this language involve an attempt to remove the presidency from political considerations and elevate the President to statesmanship. But obvious problems in this provision came to view in 1953 and again in 1961 and led to proposals that it be changed. When an incumbent President dies (as Roxas in 1948 and Magsaysay in 1957), and the Vice-President assumes the office, should that person be elected to a second full term of his own, he would have to step down after completing his eight years in office. This provision has never been tested in practice since both Quirino, who assumed office in 1948 and ran for a second full term in 1953, and Garcia, who assumed office in 1957 and ran for a second full term in 1961, lost their re-election bids. The constitutional provision led to a wild free-for-all campaign for the vice-presidency in 1961. Since President and Vice-President

[8] In both cases, President Magsaysay in 1955 and President Macapagal in 1963 had certified the land reform bill as "urgent" and in both cases the bills were ignored in regular session and there was much opposition to the special sessions called to consider them. For an account of the debate over the 1963 measure see Edward Kiunisala, "Fighter for Land Reform," *Philippines Free Press,* July 6, 1963.

[9] Article VII, Section 5.

are elected separately, with the winner being the candidate with the larger number of votes, they could belong to different parties. Since an incumbent President has significant political resources, he is difficult to beat. Massive political and financial resources are required to win nomination, and the use of public resources in the form of budgetary allocations and public works projects is almost inevitable. If Garcia had won in 1961, the Vice-President, whoever he might have been, would have become President well before the 1965 elections, which would have helped him win a party nomination and would have provided the resources needed for the campaign. The constitutional provision for some time has been a matter of concern to constitutional lawyers, and attempts to change the presidential term by constitutional amendment have been proposed several times. Whatever the outcome of these attempts, Philippine lawyers and theorists will wrestle with the dilemma of providing for a strong President but at the same time trying to keep him above "politics."

THE LEGISLATURE

In the postwar years, the legislature has played an increasingly important role and has established a degree of independence from the executive. During the Commonwealth period, Quezon had proved able to control the legislature, although not without some serious battles. The establishment of a two-house legislature in 1940 created new problems by providing a group of men with national reputations and constituencies. The Senate is composed of twenty-four members who serve six-year terms. One-third of the membership is elected every two years. A senator's security of tenure is much weaker than that of his American counterpart. To be successful, a senator must place in the top eight of at least sixteen and, because third parties are common, usually more candidates. He must first win renomination from his party and that in itself is a major task and a major expense. Then he must campaign over eleven major islands and a host of smaller ones and contribute to the campaigns of local candidates in a wide variety of areas in order to ensure enough votes to place in the top eight. It demands much money and tremendous physical energy, as well as a national reputation that will make his name known throughout the islands.

The House of Representatives is composed of 104 members chosen by districts apportioned among the provinces by population.[10] Congressmen are chosen for four-year terms, which forces them to concentrate on maintaining their grass-roots support. A large number of "unofficial" candidates enter congressional races, drawing off many votes. Since the candidate with the largest number of votes is named the winner, many congressmen are sure to be elected with less than a majority.

The Congress convenes on the fourth Monday of January for a regular session limited to 100 days. Each house elects its own officers and determines its own rules of procedure. The Senate elects a President and a minority and majority floor leader, as well as a President *pro tempore*. The House elects a speaker and a majority and minority floor leader. In both instances, the chief officer of each house exercises great influence as a result of his control of the agenda and committee assignments. In the past, the administration's party could count on a majority in each house, and the President could influence the choice of congressional leaders and could work closely with them. However, legislative leaders have been able to weaken and even reject executive programs. We have already seen how Roxas blocked Osmeña's programs in 1945–46. The same sort of dispute broke out between Quirino and the speaker and, in 1960, between Garcia and Rodriguez. In all

[10] As in the United States, the apportionment of congressional seats leaves something to be desired. Congressional districts in the 1960 census ranged from a population of 10,309 for the lone district of Batanes to 1,179,819 for the first district of Rizal, 95,993 for the second district of Capiz to 620,430 for the first district of Negros Oriental. The population of Rizal is greater than that of Cebu, yet Rizal has only two seats, whereas Cebu has seven. An attempt to redistrict in 1961 met with failure when the Supreme Court declared unconstitutional a bill increasing the House to 120 seats (the constitutionally assigned maximum). This measure sought to distribute the sixteen additional seats by means not consistent with the distribution of population. The attempt to redistrict was reflected in the congressional elections of that year when 532 candidates vied for 104 seats. See Raul P. de Guzman and Ma. Elena Gamboa, "The Redistricting Bill of 1961," *Philippine Journal of Public Administration,* VII (January 1963).

these cases, President and legislative leader were of the same party.

The lower House initiates all appropriation, revenue, tariff, local, and private bills. All bills of local application and those authorizing an increase in the public debt originate in the House. The Senate may propose amendments to such legislation.

Legislation may be initiated by members of Congress or the executive branch but in all cases is sponsored by legislators. When the administration controls the two Houses and has strong congressional leadership, bills are passed more or less as recommended. But executive control of the legislature has deteriorated as new interests compete with the old and the government undertakes a broader role in socio-economic development. The more important business of the legislative branch is the executive program and, since these programs have been aimed at accommodation of new interests and reform, conflict has increased. However, by far the majority of bills introduced are local in nature, changing the name of barrios or municipalities or creating new barrios. Many of them die in committee but many are passed. For example, the *Official Gazette* for September 21, 1959 lists thirty Republic acts enacted by the Fourth Congress of the Philippines, second session: twelve created new barrios, seventeen changed the names of schools, municipalities, barrios, and streets, and one divided a barrio in two. During the 1962 session, the House debated a proposal to divide the province of Cebu into two. The proposal was submitted by several congressmen from Cebu who were attempting by this means to undermine the political strength of Sergio Osmeña, Jr. who controlled the province. Redrawing political boundaries has become a means of changing the distribution of political power. But often such private bills force postponement of debate of administration measures of a broader nature.

A bill is introduced and put on the calendar by title (first reading). The measure is then referred to a congressional committee for further study. Committees are of three types: standing committees like those of the United States Congress, organized in the first days of the session; select committees created by each house for special purposes, usually investigatory; and committees of the whole house that include the entire membership, meeting in closed session and not bound by house rules. The latter generally consider revenue and appropriations measures and other matters that legislators wish to deliberate in private.

Standing committees in the Philippine Congress do not play the crucial legislative role they do in the Congress of the United States, a reflection of the effects of the strong executive. Legislation by party caucus has lessened the function of the committees. Committee chairmen seldom acquire the continuity and legislative prestige of their American counterparts, since seniority is seldom considered in their selection. The committees tend to concentrate on "fiscalizing" activities, uncovering instances of executive failure or misbehavior and investigating charges made by other congressmen.[11] Some committees, for example the Senate Blue Ribbon Committee, are set up for the primary purpose of investigating charges of corruption, and provide excellent publicity for senators seeking a national reputation. Others, such as the appropriations committees, give their members great influence over public works projects and allocations.

In the course of considering a piece of legislation, committees may hold hearings and call in witnesses to testify on the bill. A large part of the legislation referred to committees is pigeonholed and very little emerges for floor consideration. Administration measures are usually reported out without amendment but sometimes several bills will be consolidated or an entirely new bill be reported out, combining elements of several others. Bills processed through committees are then placed on the house calendar (second reading). The place on the calendar determines whether it will be considered by the whole house or will die with the session. Since this decision is

11 This term is derived from the Spanish official, the *fiscal*, who was a combination of public defender, district attorney, and inquisitor. To "fiscalize" in the Philippines means to keep watch on and uncover as well as to investigate charges of graft and corruption.

made by the leadership, it gives the majority party broad influence over the legislative process. When a bill comes up for debate, the house rules how it will be handled and how many speeches pro and con will be heard. General debate and consideration of amendments then takes place. The bill in its final form must be printed and distributed to members at least three calendar days prior to passage. On the day set, the title is read and a vote is taken.

If the bill is approved in one house, it is then sent to the other, where it may be amended further and the amended versions may be circulated until differences are accommodated. The joint conference committee system is often employed to ease this process. When both houses have acted favorably on a bill, it is sent to the President, who may sign or veto it. If signed by the President, it is given a Republic act number, printed in the *Official Gazette,* and fifteen days later is put into effect. This cut and dried explanation of the legislative process obscures more than it reveals. The legislature is the scene of eloquent speeches, charges and countercharges, and even physical violence, but it is almost never possible to find out anything about the state of legislation by attending the sessions. Most work is accomplished in the last sessions of the year and particularly in the *sine die* session during which, with the clock stopped, legislators hastily consider and pass hundreds of bills. Most of the real work of the session and the negotiations that result in enacted legislation takes place in quiet caucuses in the Senate President's office or at Malacanan with the President. The factors that are most often crucial in gaining support for a measure are patronage and public works considerations.

In this discussion, we have tried to point out how the formal organization of power conditions the role that the legislature may play. Precisely because the executive not only has formal authority but also derives political influence from that allocation of power, the legislator must constantly seek to tap the resources of the President in order to extend his own political influence. Within the context of legislative authority, perhaps the most important feature is the appropriations and budgetary power, which allows legislators to influence administrative programs and policies. But the heaviest emphasis has not been on policy as such or on the department programs. Congressmen concentrate on acquiring the necessities of electoral success — public works projects and patronage as a result of the organization of the electorate and the content and expression of its demands. The informal process encroaches at all points on the formal structure.

On policy questions, the legislature in the past has been a conservative force. Legislatures have successfully opposed land reform and labor legislation, or by amendment have reduced the effectiveness of executive proposals. It is significant that the major labor legislation was passed as a result of American pressure and at a time when the Huk movement was still a threat to stability. When the military threat disappeared, the legislature returned to an obstinate stand against social welfare, labor, and land reform measures. The development of strong pressures for change from new industrial groups is changing this attitude, but the change has been very slow and an effective tax law that would bring land and real estate taxes more into line with the needs of development has yet to succeed. Unfortunately, much of the crucial negotiation on these matters has taken place in the majority party caucus. Apparently there have been real debates in which many points of view were expressed, but these are not made public. The replacement of the legislature with the majority caucus as a forum for discussion is a direct result of the organization of the electorate, which pays little heed to legislation as such. In turn, the fact that the legislature does not debate these matters publicly impairs its educative function. Congressmen are seldom held responsible for legislative actions and some have successfully maintained an image as land reform advocates among their constituents while consistently voting against such measures in the halls of Congress. This contradiction results from demands that are highly personal and narrow in character and are not aimed at broad solutions to particular problems. One scholar found in a study of agrarian reform legislation of the Magsaysay period that rural people, although strong supporters of Magsaysay, knew nothing of his legislative program and cared less.[12]

THE JUDICIARY

In such a highly political society, it is inevitable that justice will have a political cast. Certainly in the Philippines, as in other countries, there have been numerous examples of judicial corruption and bias. But more important has been the status of the higher courts and the respect given the judiciary, resulting from interest in and respect for the law. But that respect does not obscure the Filipino attitude that laws will never replace men. It is the individual leader who ensures justice, not the law. Philippine jurisprudence has a long and rich history, but it is always in danger of seeming meaningless to the majority of citizens.

Courts were established during the Spanish occupation at the national, provincial, and municipal levels. The Philippine Commission under McKinley's instructions set up courts after the American model. Before the constitution was written, therefore, the Philippines had a Supreme Court, Courts of First Instance with seats generally in the capitals of provinces, and justices of the peace in almost every town. As a result of its history, Philippine jurisprudence has a rich and varied body of law and precedent.

The Supreme Court of the Philippines was initially appointed by the President of the United States with the advice and consent of the United States Senate. Judges of the inferior courts were appointed by the Governor General with the advice and consent of the Philippine Senate. Although American justices were in the majority on the Supreme Court, Filipino jurists sat on the Court almost from the beginning and judges of the inferior courts and justices of the peace were Filipinos. The United States Supreme Court had appellate jurisdiction in certain cases referred to them from the Supreme Court of the Philippines.

[12] Francis Starner, *Magsaysay and the Philippine Peasantry: The Agrarian Impact on Philippine Politics, 1953-1956* (Berkeley and Los Angeles: University of California Press, 1961) p. 37.

The Supreme Court established by the American administration was incorporated into the Constitution, which also provided for such other courts as might be determined by law. The present system includes a Court of Appeals, Courts of First Instance in provincial capitals (at least one in each of sixteen judicial districts), justices of the peace in municipalities, and municipal courts in chartered cities. All justices and judges are appointed by the President with the consent of the Commission on Appointments and hold office during good behavior until they reach the age of seventy or are incapacitated. With the exception of the Supreme Court, their jurisdiction is defined by the legislature.

The Supreme Court's power of judicial review has been recognized since the early days of the American regime, although no express provision was made either in the Organic Law of 1902 or the Jones Law. The right of review in specified cases was written into the constitution and made explicit in the Judiciary Act of 1948.[13] The Supreme Court of the Philippines also has original and concurrent jurisdiction with the Courts of First Instance in actions between the Roman Catholic Church and municipalities and towns, and in actions brought by the government against the Church in disputes over titles to lands used for hospitals, convents, etc.

Undoubtedly the Supreme Court is the most respected body in the Philippines. As in the United States, a justice of the Supreme Court is ranked among the highest in prestige and respect. By and large, the courts have been free of politics, and judges and proceedings remain neutral in the current political context. But they have been a definite conservative force in the society, protecting the rights of private property and to some extent the privileges of the elite. Probably the most important problem of the Philippine judicial process has been the volume of litigation that must be handled. The court system has been unable to cope with it. Court cases often confer status and importance and are thus entered into on the smallest pretext. The large number of lawyers in the society only increase this propensity. Special Courts of Agrarian Reform and Industrial Relations seek to relieve the

[13] Republic Act No. 296 as amended by Republic Act No. 1186.

weight but the process is slow and often years go by before a case is finally settled — often out of court. The courts serve an important conflict adjustment function by means of this delay. Disputants who are unable to agree on a solution to their dispute, will enter into a court case that will drag on and on, postponing any solution but at the same time postponing open conflict. In time, the difficulties and costs of pursuing the case will cause the parties to weaken or even to find an acceptable compromise. The emphasis on self-esteem and family honor often creates situations in which compromise is impossible, and the court system provides a face-saving device.

The Supreme Court is the most important legitimizing institution in the Philippines. Distinguished jurists have given it remarkable popular respect. The Supreme Court is the most important of the formal structures for adjudicating disputes between informal and formal aspects of the political system and between the requirements of problem-solving and the constitution. The impact of the court is seen in the constant references of legislators and executives to the constitutionality of legislation they are attacking or defending. Since practicing lawyers dominate political roles, this relationship takes on even greater import.

The Macapagal administration, which began with a dispute over the midnight appointments of the preceding administration, has had its more controversial and innovational actions judged by the Supreme Court, some of them adversely. Macapagal's attack upon the court and particularly upon one justice aroused much opposition and controversy. But, more important, there was no question that court decisions would be upheld and respected in practice.

Because of the factors discussed above, the judicial system is the formal structure for adjudication. The courts do not "legislate" in the sense that the American Supreme Court does. The higher judicial roles are free of political involvement and are the most clearly defined in the political system.

LOCAL GOVERNMENT

We have already noted the unitary character of Philippine government and the dependence of the local governments on

Manila. As one would expect, the lack of local autonomy has drawn young men in search of political careers to Manila, has given little prestige to local government, and has drawn off the best local leadership. It has also reduced the possibility of direct experience in the problems of self-government for the majority of the population. Younger political leaders have seen this situation as a barrier to political development and as encouraging the apathy and the dependent attitude of the rural Filipino. They feel that the establishment of local governments with real powers and the opportunity for direct popular participation would go a long way toward changing the attitudes that underlie the present pork barrel and patronage system. Many of these younger politicians played important roles in the Magsaysay administration and encouraged him to adopt local autonomy as one of his policy goals. As a result of this agitation and despite the opposition of most congressmen and many senators, the idea was gradually accepted, and in the late 1950's two local autonomy bills were passed. One of these increased the power of the provincial and municipal governments and gave them broader financial authority, and the other provided for limited barrio self-government. These measures were limited in scope and in practice, but they have indicated a new direction for Philippine political development.

The powers of local government are defined by the legislature, not the constitution. Provinces, municipalities, chartered cities, and *barrios* are created by legislation.

> Under the law, Provinces, Towns and Chartered cities occupy a dual status. On the one hand they are agencies of the national government performing purely governmental functions. On the other hand, they are entities resembling private entities organized for the purpose of attending to the corporate needs of people.[14]

Provinces are classified as regular, those populated mainly by Christian Filipinos, or special, those populated mainly by non-Christians. Regular provinces are administered by gov-

14 José M. Aruego, *Philippine Government in Action* (Manila: University Publishing Company, Inc., 1954) pp. 604-605.

ernors and three-member provincial boards, both elected for four-year terms. Electoral success in gubernatorial races is the result of a combination of three factors, one of which may dominate: personal popularity, family prominence, and party support. Party support is manifest as pork barrel or patronage allocated by the national government in support of a particular gubernatorial candidate. Candidates may be genuinely popular personalities, members of prominent local families, or simply party hacks forced on the province by the national party machine.

The governor appoints all subordinate officers and employees whose salaries are paid solely from provincial funds. He has limited appointment power and general supervisory power over municipal governments in his province. Legislation aimed at decentralization and increasing the tax powers of local governments, as well as setting up elected barrio councils, has been passed. But the pull of the center still dominates and the most important provincial officials, such as the provincial engineer, the registrar of deeds, health officers, and superintendents of schools, all are appointed from Manila. These officers work directly under the national administration. As a result, the governor's position depends upon his political leadership and his ability to command local votes that will give him bargaining weight with the national-level politicians and executive agencies. He finds it necessary to gain support in national politics for his provincial position and aligns himself with senators or congressmen, trading his local vote-getting power for a share of their pork barrel and patronage.

Provincial politics is an open and continuous struggle between ambitious local personalities backed by one or another national politician. National political conflicts are fought out on the provincial level with a heavy emphasis on personalities and patronage. Hiring labor for public works projects is a function of the Office of the Provincial Engineer, who works out of and for Manila. He distributes the available jobs according to directions from the center. Short-term unskilled labor jobs are very important in election campaigns and must be allotted by the provincial governor among the municipal mayors in order to gain their support for his election. Under the circumstances, provincial governors find it expedient to switch parties should they find themselves in the opposition. Provincial politicians, like those at the lower level, cannot survive without a patron at the national level; they are judged by their ability to secure for their province the services available at the national level. This situation allows provincial politics to disintegrate into little more than a struggle for power among competing political bosses. Since there is little real governing authority at the provincial level, political officeholders are either men with greater ambitions who are building local machinery to realize those ambitions, or front men for national-level politicians.

The next lower level of government is the municipality, which is equivalent in some respects to the county in the United States. A mayor, vice mayor, and municipal councillors are elected; the municipal treasurer is appointed by the provincial treasurer and the chief of police, the justice of the peace, and the health officer are appointed by the President of the Philippines.

Each municipal councillor has direct supervisory authority over several of the barrios into which the municipality is divided. Before passage of the Barrio Autonomy Act, which became effective on January 1, 1960, the municipal councillor appointed a barrio lieutenant to serve as governmental representative in each barrio.[15] The municipal council sessions were the most direct experience in representative government for most Filipinos before the new law. They were well attended and were often the scene of lively exchanges between councillors and mayors on matters of direct local interest. The acts of the council are recorded in resolutions and ordinances and are financed by such license fees as they are empowered to collect, supplemented by grants from the national government.

The aim of the new Barrio Autonomy Act is to give Filipinos direct experience in governing themselves and to encourage local initiative and reduced dependence upon the national government. Under the new act, the barrios are recog-

[15] Republic Act No. 2370 (H. No. 3156). *An Act Granting Autonomy to Barrios of the Philippines* (June 20, 1959) Section 4 (13).

nized as legal entities with the right to elect their own council and barrio lieutenant, to impose limited taxes, and to enact ordinances. A Barrio Assembly, made up of all persons who are qualified electors and residents of the barrio for at least six months, meets once a year to hear the annual report of the council concerning their activities and finances.

Although the municipal mayor and council exercise power of supervision over these new barrio officials, the people themselves now have a more direct voice in their own affairs. The barrio lieutenant is the law-enforcement officer and is directly responsible to those who elect him. The barrio council has the authority to construct and maintain public works and to cooperate with higher levels of government in other enterprises that will improve economic conditions. It thus encourages local initiative and local participation in government, but such initiative is limited by a lack of funds to carry out projects. The barrios may collect money from voluntary contributions: licenses on stores, signs, billboards; taxes on gamecock and cockfights; and grants from higher levels of government. A percentage of the real estate taxes collected is under special circumstances returned to the barrio. The financial limitations reduce the authority of local government.

The act has been in force too short a time to provide any meaningful results. The barrio people seem enthusiastic about increased autonomy and encouraged to undertake some projects on their own but are not clear about the financial responsibility that devolves on them. Accustomed to pork barrel projects arranged by national politicians and carried out largely by government agencies, they find it difficult to organize and accept their own responsibility for improvement.

THE CIVIL SERVICE

One of the most fundamental requirements of a modern government is a trained, efficient administration capable of putting into operation the policies adopted by the legislature and the executive. Economic development experts have found the lack of such administrators one of the greatest weaknesses in the emerging nations. In the Philippines, the civil service is, like the rest of the society, highly political. We have already

pointed out the patronage service it provides political officeholders and the way in which the legislature and President
both seek to use the civil service for their own ends. As in the
United States at a comparable period, a merit-system civil service has become a major goal of those who would reform politics. But traditional behavior patterns and a high rate of
unemployment combine to make this an extremely difficult
task. Since the beginning of Filipinization of the civil service
during the American period, the attraction of a government
post has conditioned both the attitude toward education and
the content of that education.

During the first decade and a half of American rule, recruitment to the civil service was carefully controlled by more or
less objective standards with well-established regulations and
training periods. The top offices, like the policy-making machinery, were in the hands of Americans who could be independent of non-objective political considerations. But as the
Nacionalista party under Osmeña's leadership established a
pseudo-parliamentary system, they also gradually acquired influence in appointments to the bureaucracy. The use of this
patronage to reward protégés gave the Nacionalista party
directorate inordinate power over the administration and execution of public policy. In later years attempts were made to
restore the rigid independence and efficiency of the civil service, but the increased production of high school and college
graduates and their demands for places in the bureaucracy
increased the difficulty. With so many qualified applicants
for so few positions, choices turned on more subjective considerations. The familiar pakiusap procedure dominated recruitment and the paternalistic authoritarian relationship of superior–inferior showed itself in the wide variety of extra-official
duties undertaken by both boss and subordinate at each level
of the administrative ladder. An imposed system of objective
administration appeared to be hopelessly entangled with traditional roles.

The establishment of the Commonwealth only intensified
already existing habits. Complete Filipinization further encouraged young *provincianos,* and private universities and
colleges sprang up in Manila to provide night schools for

ambitious young men to get that all-important degree and to prepare for the civil service examinations. Filipinos regard the government job as an end in itself, with promotion resulting from political considerations rather than merit.

Selection of men for the highest administrative offices is dependent not only on their appointed and political department secretary but also, often, on the support of one or another congressman, or even the President. Furthermore, the protection of the department's budget and programs necessitates congressional support and such support is won on considerations of political reality. The same situation exists in every bureaucracy. One need only point to the extremely close relations between congressional committee chairmen in the United States Congress and the personnel of the executive department that is the committee's concern.

Low salaries and the high cost of living encouraged this trend. The use of public office for private gain became so widespread that it seemed a way of life. The imposition of controls on the economy to stop the terrifying drain on foreign exchange provided additional incentives for influence-peddling, which could not take place without the cooperation of the administrative service.

A senator or congressman, for example, would come to a government office as a lawyer representing his client in some business matter, and the bureaucrat, recognizing that the congressman also voted on his bureau's budget and even its existence, would provide special consideration. Private citizens bearing letters from political officeholders or accompanied by staff members, friends, or relatives of the President and even those without such connections who were willing to pay, demanded special service from the administrator. The ordinary citizen waited his turn and was caught in the trap. The lower levels of the civil service could not help but be influenced by the activity and engaged in "fixing" cases or "hand-carrying" applications and papers to speed up the process, always for a fee.

A whole class of fixers and speculators was created by the back-pay problem. This situation grew out of the legislation passed by the first postwar session of the Congress, declaring that those who had held government office would be paid for the wartime occupation period. The Congress paid itself for the period from their election in November, 1941 to their resumption of office in 1946. But the government did not have the money to pay and, therefore, issued back-pay certificates to those supposedly qualified under law. Later, as government reserves fell, employees' salaries were often withheld and back-pay certificates were issued. Government marketing agencies that purchased supplies and produce also issued back-pay certificates for their purchases. The administrative work required to keep track of these promises to pay was terrifying to contemplate. Someone had to determine who would be paid and when. Fixers and politicians became involved in securing back pay for clients and constituents and any attempt at a fair system was impossible. Speculators would travel through the islands buying back-pay certificates for 30 per cent or less of face value. After accumulating a large number of these, a deal would be made with the Treasury Department or a politician to cash them with a profit for all concerned except the original holder.

In short, the entire structure of government administration had been so corrupted as to make it seem there was no honest man in office and no way to remedy the situation. A series of circumstances, however, led to determined efforts to purge the civil service and restore it to its prewar standards. Disgust with the 1949 election served as a convenient symbol for sharpening the widespread disillusion and fear.

Part of the reformist movement that coagulated around the person of Ramon Magsaysay and his administration was a demand for reform in the civil service. This demand was expressed by old-time civil servants proud of their achievements and the prestige of the prewar period but disgusted and insulted by postwar events, a group of young American-educated political and social scientists and educators who had come to believe that a merit system civil service was the answer to good government, businessmen who resented the waste of time and capital on politics and politicians required in order to do business; and the middle-class urban citizens who found that the system of graft and corruption froze them out and made their government disgusting in foreign eyes.

The University of the Philippines Institute of Public Administration (IPA), established in 1952, engaged in research into the operations of the government service and conducted programs of in-service training to bring about improvement. The Civil Service Act of 1959 was largely the result of both this upsurge of interest in reform of the civil service and the Institute's activities.[16] Under the act, the IPA is given primary responsibility for the training of executives in the government. Legislators began to utilize the staff and resources of the IPA in drafting legislation. The Civil Service Act of 1959 defined the scope and organization of the central personnel agency, established the qualifications, powers, and duties of the Commissioner and Deputy Commissioner of the civil service, and provided for a "progressive system of personnel administration to insure the maintenance of an honest, efficient, progressive and continuous civil service in the Philippines." The commission of civil service was given the duty to enforce, execute, and carry out the constitutional and statutory provisions of the merit system. It is undoubtedly a fine law and establishes the formal requirements of a merit system — but the behavior encouraged by Philippine society and socialization are bound to interfere in its operation.

[16] Republic Act No. 2260, "An Act to Amend and Revise the Laws Relative to the Philippine Civil Service," (enacted into law June 19, 1959) as published in *The Philippine Journal of Public Administration,* III (July 1959) pp. 387-400.

CHAPTER VI

The Organization of Political Parties

IN OUR DISCUSSION of the constitutional framework of the Philippine political system we referred to the role that political parties play in these formal structures. Now we need to examine in more detail the background and organization of political parties and their particular characteristics. Unlike American political parties, which were post-independence phenomena created specifically to organize disparate elements in the polity with the purpose of controlling and directing policy, the Philippine parties were organized to work out relations with the occupying power to achieve independence. The Nacionalista party's claim to legitimacy as the independence movement combined with social and economic factors to shape the role that parties would play in the bargaining process.

At first glance, the Philippines appears to have a two-party system that is national in character. But a closer look reveals that the two are not parties but coalitions of factions put together largely for electoral purposes and characterized by constantly shifting loyalties to men, not issues. In the past the factions were built up by landed families who controlled significant numbers of local votes on the basis of personal loyalty or economic threat. This base has given way to a different type of faction, formed around a political leader, who uses the support of the traditional elite but more often relies on pork barrel and patronage to build a strong electoral base. The local politician bargains with the national politicians and the administrators for the wherewithal to build his machinery and offers, in return, votes for national candidates. As a result of this factional character, party discipline and loyalty are weak, and highly personal struggles for power are frequent. Since there has been little difference in the base of party organization, party platforms have meant little. Economic interests distribute their financial support with an eye to probability of success, further reducing any distinctions.

There are elements of strength as well as weakness in this party structure. The party's role in the bargaining over policy within the institutions of government has been limited. Instead, the parties preside over the power struggle between members of the elite and are unable or unwilling to incorporate constituent demands into meaningful party programs. On the other hand, the basic similarity of the parties in organization, support, and policy has provided a common interest and a predictability that allows the political elite to bargain with one another. Because of this elite character, they have not found it necessary to exploit the disparate elements and divisions of the society. Potential separatist groups have been smothered and unity has been encouraged. The personal and traditional form of organization and the penetration of these old loyalties by the pork-barrel system has provided a means for incorporating the mass of citizens into the political process. It is the traditional social structure and direct economic interest that are most meaningful to citizens first entering the political process. Economic development plans and legislation mean little to the rural Filipino. The barrio schoolhouse or feeder road are matters of greater import.

The parties, in search of electoral support, have served to mediate between citizen and government and have created a hierarchical distribution system controlled by the center, with terminals at the barrio level. Despite the lack of formally assigned bargaining power, local government is a very real part of the political system. The bargaining weights assigned to national-level politicians and groups have their roots in local politics.

We must look more closely at the party organization and

operation to understand why Philippine parties have been uniquely successful in expanding meaningful political participation but have failed to aggregate interests for policy purposes. The parties too are undergoing transition. Recent developments reveal significant changes in attitudes toward policy disputes, party loyalty, and the party's role in government.

THE HISTORICAL ROOTS

Political organization developed during the Spanish period in the form of secret societies, but the first official political parties organized for operation within an electoral system were established under American auspices.[1] The first organization was the *Partido Federalista,* which came into being in December, 1900 with American encouragement. The party's goal was not independence but statehood within the United States, and it disappeared in the face of outright demands for independence made by later parties.

Meanwhile, a number of groups had formed, some of them based in particular provinces, agitating for immediate independence. After the announcement that general elections for a National Assembly would be held in 1907, these groups combined to form the *Partido Nacionalista* with a platform calling for immediate independence. The party's overwhelming victory established beyond doubt the will of the Filipinos for independence and from that day on the issue was not whether or not but how soon. The party could not hope to become the mechanism for organizing a government, for it was subordinate to a sovereign power that was in no way responsible to voters and parties.

Elections were controlled by the wealthy and educated families, who chose municipal officials from among their own number, who in turn represented them at the provincial level. These early local elections began the domination of the parties by the big provincial families who, in time, controlled

[1] The following history of political party development is based on Hayden, *The Philippines,* Part II; Dapen Liang, *The Development of Philippine Political Parties* (Hong Kong: South China Morning Post, 1939); Maximo M. Kalaw, *The Development of Philippine Politics, 1872-1920* (Manila, 1926).

whole provinces. When it came time to elect a National Assembly, it was these families who coalesced to form the Nacionalistas and delivered the votes of their provinces to the party's candidates. Political campaigns were not mass appeals for votes but negotiations between provincial elites and national political personalities. Party leaders and members constituted a small elite group of wealthy landowners, whose economic status derived from agricultural exports produced on large haciendas by tenant farmers. These were men who understood one another, shared the same values, and lived the same kind of life. Disagreement on issues of policy was unlikely; instead, conflict arose over which personality was to lead. The party became a "national" organization made up of prominent local families who gave their support to one of their own, who served as their representative on the national level and bargained his provincial support to those aspiring to national leadership, in return for policies and patronage for his constituents.

The character of the party ensured that the unrepresented tenant farmers and laborers, as well as the urban middle classes, would have to find other channels for the expression of their demands. The middle classes aligned themselves with sporadic opposition parties in the Manila area while peasant movements, seeking to gain their demands through violence, plagued the Philippines and provided the support for such radical movements as the Sakdalista and the Communists.

The initial slow pace of transfer of government posts to Filipinos picked up rapidly after the passage of the Jones Act of 1916, which organized a two-house legislature with broader functions. In a reorganization of the executive department, all except five of the department heads in the executive branch were chosen by the Governor General with the consent of the Senate, and all other appointments of the Governor General were subject to senatorial confirmation. This move substantially increased the power of the party leadership and gave rise to the first of a series of power struggles between the two foremost Filipino politicians, Sergio Osmeña and Manuel L. Quezon. Osmeña had been Speaker of the House since its inception in 1907 and was recognized as leader of the

Nacionalista party. He was regarded as the top-ranking Filipino in government and had gradually developed for himself
a legislative–executive position similar to that of the prime
minister in a parliamentary system. Quezon had worked
closely with Osmeña but had been slowly building his own
political strength in the party. The establishment of a second legislative body gave Quezon his opportunity, and he ran
for and won the Senate presidency, which gave him the institutional base for challenging Osmeña's leadership.

During December of 1921, Quezon launched his revolt
against Osmeña, accusing him of one-man leadership, which
he labeled "unipersonalism," and demanding collective leadership in both party and government. Both men campaigned
vigorously in what Hayden called "the best political show ever
staged in the Philippines." [2] Quezon's forces, campaigning as
the *Colectivistas,* won thirty-two seats in the House to the Osmeña faction's twenty-one. But an opposition party based in
Manila, the *Partido Democrata,* won twenty-six seats, leaving a
fragmented party situation in both houses, since no party
possessed a majority.

The strong showing of the Democratas indicated widespread discontent with the ruling clique of the Nacionalistas.
Formed as the coalition of two small parties, the Democratas
opposed Nacionalistas of both factions and attacked the open
cynicism of the Osmeña–Quezon power struggle. The party
had its main support from urban middle classes and professional people in the Manila area.

The evidence of opposition among the electorate was a
hopeful sign for the development of an opposition party,
but the fragmented character of the election results and the
homogeneity that existed among the Nacionalistas eliminated
the possibility. Since the Democratas and the Colectivistas had
presented similar programs during the campaign, it was expected that they would combine to form a majority coalition.
Instead, the coalition was built between the two wings of the
Nacionalistas and the established leadership maintained control of Filipino participation in government. The Democratas
denounced this move as a betrayal of the public trust.

2 Hayden, *The Philippines,* p. 332.

The formal reconstitution of the Nacionalistas took place in April, 1924. The new party was named the *Partido Nacionalista Consolidado* with Quezon as President and Osmeña as Vice-President. The Democratas maintained their opposition, attacking the Nacionalistas for mismanagement and corruption in government-owned business and arguing that the government should get out of business entirely. After 1926 the Democratas lost much of their support when they joined the Nacionalista leaders to form a National Supreme Council, uniting all Filipino groups against General Leonard Wood, then Governor General, who was trying to reverse the process of Filipinization of the government. In the 1928 elections they lost control over Manila and in 1933 they were dissolved.

The fight over the independence bill during 1933-34 again split the leadership of the Nacionalistas but it further strengthened Quezon's position as leader of the nationalist movement. The election in 1934 saw Quezon's faction of the party emerge as the overwhelming victor, allowing the Osmeña faction only three out of eleven Senate seats and nineteen out of eighty-nine House seats.

The surprise of the election was the evidence of a new opposition with its base in the high-tenancy rural areas of central Luzon. This was the Sakdalista party, which had been gaining strength in central Luzon for a number of years. Many of the Sakdalistas did not possess the qualifications to vote but "enough of them voted in 1934 to elect three members of the House of Representatives, one provincial governor and numerous municipal presidents, vice-presidents and councilors." [3] Their platform demanded immediate independence, reduction of taxes, and a program of economic reform that would end rural poverty. Their electoral success generated apprehension in Manila, since it was evidence of the existence of a significant group of people who felt their interests were being ignored while a socio-economic oligarchy struggled for personal power and status. The class character of the Sakdalista appeal was repugnant to upper- and middle-class Filipinos.

Nothing really divided the two branches of the Nacion-

[3] Hayden, *The Philippines*, p. 363.

alistas; both had voted for the Tydings-McDuffie Act, the Osmeña group arguing that it was the same as the Hare-Hawes-Cutting Act. By the end of the year, overtures were made and public debates on the prospects of unity took place. Senator Juan Sumulong, the Democrata leader, argued that the whole fight over the independence bill had degenerated into a struggle for personal power that perverted the idea of political parties.[4] The proposed coalition was simply an answer to a threat (by the Sakdalistas) to that oligarchy which had ruled the Philippines for two years. Such an oligarchy corrupted representative government and did not allow for the representation of the poor. But Sumulong was crying in the wilderness. The leadership of the two factions formed a coalition to support Quezon and Osmeña for President and Vice-President of the new Commonwealth. They were elected in September, 1935.

The personalizing of power became an established part of Philippine political life largely as a result of (1) the conditions under which party development took place and (2) the existence of two imposing personalities who led the early struggle for independence. The basis of party organization and this personalizing resulted in a one-party system with factions forming around personalities and loyalty given not to a party but to an individual. The failure of the Democratas to maintain its independence meant the failure of a rational alternative to the personal politics of Osmeña and Quezon. Opposition was provided by factions within the major party; opposition not to policies but to particular leaders. Under the circumstances, party unity and party loyalty were bound to be tenuous.

The establishment of a Philippine government with a strong executive weakened party activity. Under the Commonwealth, however, suffrage was expanded by the removal of the property qualification and by changing the literacy requirement (the voter must be able to read and write, but no restriction to Spanish or English). In addition, a plebiscite was held on female suffrage, and, when the electorate indicated their consent, female citizens over twenty-one years of age be-

[4] Senator Juan Sumulong, "After the Coalition, The Deluge," *Philippines Herald,* April 21, 1935, as cited in Hayden, *The Philippines,* pp. 369-370.

came voters, expanding the electorate greatly. Furthermore, the American concentration on public education was beginning to have an effect. Large numbers of Filipinos of the lower economic classes acquired literacy and entered the voting lists. The immediate effect of the expanded franchise was disappointing partly because of the social and economic system. The Filipino voter turned to his patron for advice and his economic dependence made him susceptible to influence. As a result, political leadership remained in the hands of the same group of men up to the outbreak of World War II.

THE POSTWAR PARTIES: INCORPORATION OF NEW ELEMENTS

In the postwar period, the expanded electorate began to affect party organization. Several factors accounted for the changes: (1) the rural people seemed more interested in politics, (2) it had become usual for citizens to come to Manila with their problems and demand help, and (3) a group of younger men with quite different backgrounds and resources entered political life.

These changes were the result of the wartime dislocation, the temporary removal of many of the old political elite on charges of collaboration, and the feelings of national unity and pride that derived from the bravery and persistence of the Filipino resistance. New men entering politics came from two groups. First, the buy-and-sell operators who had, not always by legitimate means, grown rich during the war and liberation periods. Many of these people turned up as candidates for public office with the cash necessary to finance the party. As congressmen, they continued their operations but now used their political position to get cooperation from government agencies for their business deals.

The other group of newcomers were authentic local heroes, guerilla leaders and people who had shown themselves to be natural leaders in the chaotic and unorganized situation of the wartime Philippines. They won places on the party tickets because of their local popularity and because they would campaign loyally for others, but they were at a disadvantage in the legislature. They did not have either the legal training of the old-time elite or the financial base of the new commercial group. Their lack of the skills required for political success forced them into an alliance with the *status quo* interests and they soon lost their identity as men of the people. One who did not was Ramon Magsaysay, who rose by a combination of circumstances and political instinct to challenge the elite politics of the past.

The increased interest in politics and the attitude that government should help with personal needs changed the character of the party's operation. All political parties run on patronage and public works projects, and the Philippine parties had been no exception. The Nacionalistas had maintained their hold on the electorate largely because they controlled appointments and patronage and used it to their advantage. The postwar period saw the development of a new and more persuasive system of patronage. Guerilla forces and government personnel were entitled to back pay for their services during the war; those who had property destroyed were to receive payment. The United States government provided the funds but someone had to determine who was to be paid, how much, and when. Surplus army equipment cluttered the cities and ports; it was turned over to the Philippine government. To whom was it to be sold and for how much? Large numbers of rural people flocked to the city for jobs, but there were only a few jobs. One did not get something for nothing, one had to have a *quid pro quo*. People carried their personal demands to the political officeholder and offered in return their family's vote. They wanted jobs in government, quick action on their back pay, financial help, advice. Politicians found it expedient to use their influence with government administration to cut channels and meet these demands. The executive's powers of appointment and control over government funds were such as to make his office the central distribution point for such patronage and influence. The party became a distributive mechanism that traded favors and public resources for votes. But, since the incumbent administration held control over these resources, loyalty to the party never developed.

The most important development of the postwar period, however, was the establishment of a two-party system. The loss of the dynamic, almost charismatic Quezon left a vacuum in the leadership, since both of the aspirants could claim legitimate heritage. The intensity of the issues that divided them made a bitter fight inescapable. The struggle for power between the various groups in 1946 established the principle of competitive, two-party elections that has continued to the present. The fact that real issues divided the two parties meant that there was a continuing logic in an opposition group. Both parties are factions joined by highly personal ties of loyalty and little divides them on policy matters. But the two-party system has become the arena for imposing limits and order on the struggle for power and weaving it into the fabric of the daily tasks of the political system. This development has created some interesting new problems for an incumbent administration that can only be understood in the context of three related factors: the absence of party loyalty, the local base of party organization, and the prevalence of third-party reformist movements.

Party Discipline. The domination of the party by a single leader has been basic to Philippine politics since the days of Osmeña's leadership of the Nacionalistas. The overwhelming pull of the presidency has made party identification meaningless.

When the Liberals won the presidency in 1946, numerous local officials, although elected as Nacionalistas, defected to the administration's party. After Magsaysay's victory, large numbers returned to the Nacionalistas. After each change in the presidential administration, local officials, whether elected or appointed, found it expedient to take an oath of loyalty to the President's party. Barely a month after Macapagal's election, his press secretary was able to report that one congressman, six governors, four vice-governors, six provincial board members, more than 100 municipal mayors and as many vice-mayors, and literally thousands of municipal councillors and barrio lieutenants had taken the oath of loyalty to the Liberal Party.[5] An opposition leader found the count even higher a few

[5] Napoleon G. Rama, "Why I Turned LP!" *Philippines Free Press* (December 8, 1962).

days later: at least seven provinces, one senator, thirty-one congressmen, and thousands of municipal and barrio officials had switched. By the end of the first year of the Macapagal administration, the Liberals controlled local government and the House of Representatives, and the President had declared his intention of working for the election of a Senate sympathetic to his program.

Some of the candidates who defected after the 1961 election declared that they had done so because the Nacionalista leadership had treated them unfairly by declaring free zones or allowing more than one official candidate in the elections. They argued that they had won without party support and, therefore, were free from any obligation. Others pointed out that it was a matter of survival that the district or province would get no national help if they remained in opposition. One mayor testified:

> Let's face it. When you are not in the majority party, you don't get anything from Malacanang. You don't get pork barrel releases. No improvement in your town, so, no re-election.[6]

And the governor of a province that had staunchly supported former President Garcia explained:

> Surigao del Norte is an underdeveloped province. It cannot afford the luxury of fighting Malacanang because the province has a mere 320,000 pesos annual income and therefore cannot stand on its own feet.[7]

Politicians themselves see no difference between the parties in their platforms or policies, so there is nothing to be gained from fighting the President.

Switching from party to party is not confined to the local offices — it is an established practice at the national level and accounts for the legislative majority enjoyed by Philippine Presidents. The Liberal party, as we have seen, was formed out of the Nacionalistas. Roxas, Quirino, Magsaysay, and half the senators have switched parties during their careers. Often the defection is due to a dispute with the leadership. Some-

6 *Ibid.*
7 *Ibid.*

times, failing to secure a nomination from one party, they move to another or even form their own party. Magsaysay, denied the Liberal nomination by Quirino's decision to run again, became the Nacionalista party candidate. Cebu's Senator Mariano Cuenco, whose family has carried on a running fight with the Osmeñas for control of Cebu, was a prewar Nacionalista who ran with Roxas in 1946, returned to the Nacionalistas in 1953 and, after falling out with Garcia in 1959, ran as a "guest" on the Liberal ticket. In 1962, he became a Liberal.

The parties are seldom united at election time despite loud protestations of loyalty. During the 1957 elections, factions within the party itself were in outright opposition to the party candidates. In the spring of 1964 the vice-president and Senate president, both elected as Liberals, were campaigning openly against Liberal President Macapagal and by the end of the session both were considered possible Nacionalista candidates for president.

The lack of party discipline does little to encourage party loyalty among voters. To most citizens, the parties are meaningless; it is the individual officeholder who provides service and it is accepted that he will build alliances with offices on the national level in order to get the resources he needs. Citizens who do identify themselves as party members are committed to individuals and will follow them from party to party. Ticket splitting is common and in 1957 resulted in the election of the Liberal vice-presidential candidate, Macapagal, by a greater number of votes than the victorious Nacionalista presidential candidate, Garcia.

The parties remain factions, formed into electoral coalitions of dubious tenure. Opposition to the administration is provided by factions within the administration's own party. Should that opposition go too far, it can be eliminated by the administration, using its authority over the party caucus. Only membership in one of the two major parties can provide the funds, nomination, election inspectors, and organization necessary for election.

The system encourages opportunism and corruption and leads to a heavy measure of cynicism among populace and

politicians. It underlies the sporadic reform movements of the
Philippines, which search for honest men who will take politics out of government.

Party Organization. In an island country with some seven
million voters scattered over more than 1,000 islands, organization is vital. Obviously, party organization is more important
to candidates running at large than to congressmen or local
candidates who can build their own machinery. The parties
are organized as electoral coalitions. Therefore, we must begin
our analysis of the organization by looking at the electoral
system and the role the parties play.

Although government administration and service are organized formally on a functional, objective basis, they operate
in the citizen's perception as extensions of political personalities. The citizen's contact with governmental services will
be conditioned by his relationships with the personalities that
count. As a result, politics, parties, and politicians are ever-
present realities. The citizen must maintain the support of particular personalities by the reciprocal means provided in his
society. The voter is continuously confronted with political
propaganda of the act or the word. In every barrio there is
someone known to be on good terms with municipal officials,
and he serves as the local representative of the municipal officials. Such leaders are the local machinery of the party and
to be effective their operation must be continuous. Every two
years the local leader is judged, there is a rededication of the
machinery and probably a realignment of forces — in short,
an election. Presidential elections that fall in odd-numbered
years generate the most open disputes and activity, for they
call into play the local alliances and coalitions that form
the party's organization. The provincial and regional organizations of senators and congressmen constitute the basic party
coalition that a presidential candidate must integrate and
unify. But each of these organizations is made up of a number
of municipal political machines with direct representation in
the barrios. It is this machinery which the voter recognizes,
bargains with, and eventually supports.

Local leadership has been controlled by the municipal

mayor or persons at the municipal level. These are the people in direct contact with the voter and the services they perform for constituents are direct and personal. Their subordinates in the barrios serve as their direct link to the barrio communication network, reporting a wedding to be attended here, a funeral there, and bringing the barrio people's personal problems to the attention of the municipal government. The barrio workers complain that the people just will not go themselves to the hospital or the treasurer but insist that the worker go with them and talk for them. They believe they will not be served if they go alone and that they will have to wait a long time. Requests for money, transportation, or contributions for celebrating fiesta or some family event are common. There is also competition for a few days' labor on public works projects. Throughout the year, a citizen may have several such requests, and often he will solicit help from both parties. In the weeks preceding elections, requests for help multiply and the politician seeking re-election finds it necessary to make choices as to which request to meet, which to turn away with a promise, and which to laugh off. He relies on his local leaders for this information.

The administration of elections is in the hands of the Commission on Elections, which has direct and immediate supervision over the provincial, municipal, and city officials directly involved in the conduct of elections. The corrupt elections of 1949 stirred great interest in providing for clean and honest elections, and several legislative measures have attempted to clarify election procedure and provide for policing of the polls. As a result, elections in the Philippines embody some interesting innovations. The polls are manned by local school teachers or other nonpartisan people appointed by the Commission on Elections. The two parties that received the largest number of votes in the previous election are allowed to have poll watchers to watch the balloting and the counting of the ballots. These poll watchers can challenge the validity of the ballots and make sure their party is not being cheated out of its votes. Given the nature of the ballot, this service has been extremely important to political success and serves to exclude third parties and to maintain the two-party system. The failure of the reformist Grand Alliance senatorial candidates in 1959 was attributed in part to their lack of poll watchers. Mistakes in spelling or simply illegible writing force the election officials to decide how to count the ballot. It is an obvious advantage to have a party member present with the right to challenge the decision. In the Legaspi city election of 1959, for example, a major problem arose in the gubernatorial race in which the Nacionalista candidate Seva was pitted against the Liberal candidate Ziga. Many ballots could be read as either name.

Since the voter must write out the names of all the candidates he chooses and usually more than twenty names are listed, the parties distribute sample ballots that the voter can take into the booth and copy. A new dimension is thus added to the political campaign, for the major effort of local leaders is concentrated on making sure that the voter has a copy of the party's sample ballot with him as he walks into the voting place. But it also leads to a rash of sample ballots with every possible combination of candidates. Each candidate prints up his own and attempts to make his ticket as attractive as possible. In 1959, sample ballots distributed by Nacionalistas and Liberals often included popular candidates of the Grand Alliance and dropped official candidates of their own parties. Local leaders are swamped with sample ballots and requests to include names of non-party candidates on their lists. The key technique is to keep the ticket before the voter's eyes but have a supply of the official ballot ready and pass them out in front of the polling booth on election day. In such circumstances, the candidates must have dependable local leaders. The local leader has become the key to electoral success.

The system means that the party must have in each election district someone to protect the party's position and someone who can be in constant contact with the voters, processing their demands and keeping in touch with local issues and personalities. These leaders usually owe their jobs in the local government to one or another municipal politician, and are, therefore, committed to his success. Senatorial and presidential candidates who must campaign at large are forced to rely upon the municipal politician and his machine for support.

Congressmen, who are usually far better known in their district and have a smaller area to cover, are closer to the voters themselves and often have their own men in the municipalities and barrios. As a result, the most violent political battles in the Philippines take place at the local level as senators, congressmen, and President battle for the support of municipal and provincial candidates.

In most areas, the rudiments of party organization exist but the possibility of disloyalty and of personal ambition disrupting this organization are very great. The results can be disastrous for the party. The candidates are therefore forced to rely less on the party as an organization and more on established *quid pro quos* with local political leaders. In Philippine elections, to a much greater extent than in the United States, it is every man for himself.

We need to look more closely at the formal organization of the party and here we concentrate on the Nacionalista, which has the most interesting and best articulated organization. The Liberals presently owe their organization to Macapagal, who campaigned for nearly four years building an organization loyal to himself. By mid-1964 the coalition he had put together fell apart.

In the Nacionalista party, members join the organization and must be accepted by majority vote of the party committee at the level joined. Members can be expelled from the party for committing "improper acts or acts inimical to the Party." [8] Such expulsions must be approved by the National Executive Committee.

The party is organized around the Municipal, Provincial, and National Conventions and Committees. The supreme authority, by party declaration, rests with the National Convention, but, in practice, a National Directorate made up of leaders of the party holding national office has been all-powerful. The National Convention is composed of five delegates from each congressional district, elected by the provin-

[8] "Revised Rules of the *Nacionalista* Party" in Pedro L. Baldoria, ed., *Readings; Documents and Literature on Philippine Government and Foreign Relations* (Quezon City: University of the Philippines, 1954) pp. 351-364, Article I, Section 3 (b).

cial conventions, and ex officio delegates composed of present and past elective national and provincial officials. The National Convention nominates candidates for president, vice-president, and senator. The presence of sixty per cent of the members is necessary for a quorum and the vote of sixty per cent of the members present is necessary to nominate a candidate. The National Convention meets once every two years at least ninety days before the general election. The supreme council of the party, the National Directorate, is composed of the members of the party in the legislature, provincial governors affiliated with the party, and a delegate from provinces not represented by an elected official. This body is the real arena of bargaining and discussion. An Executive Committee that includes three each, senators, congressmen, and governors, in addition to its officers, serves as a standing committee of the directorate, meeting once a month. The role of this committee depends to a large extent on the relationship between President and party leaders in the legislature.

If the President of the Philippines belongs to the party, he is titular head and, as such, has extraordinary power to adopt whatever measures he feels necessary. The presidential nominee assumes direction of the party's campaign. An incumbent President controls the party, chooses the senatorial candidates, and has the wherewithal to attract members of the opposition. "The President *is* the Party," one senator said of Garcia. But he does not have unchallenged control. Intra-party battles for control of the local machinery are the spice of Philippine political life.

The local machinery is the key and it constitutes the most important limit on the President's influence. Control rests with local political leaders who can deliver the vote in the barrios. But local politics is a reflection of the national battles, since local officials are dependent on national officeholders for their election necessities, public works projects, and patronage. Municipal mayors and councillors as well as governors find it necessary to spend a good part of their time in Manila negotiating with senators and congressmen for funds and pork-barrel allocations. Most local officials are protégés of one or another national officeholder but their loyalty depends upon the ability of their patron to deliver. Sometimes local politics is a reflection of traditional family rivalries, often dating back to the Spanish era. In such cases, national candidates attempt to exploit this rivalry for their own ends. But the problem of controlling local machinery is, for the party, a reflection of the method of determining local candidates.

At the top of the party hierarchy a majority party caucus dominated by the President chooses candidates for national office. Considerations of regionalism, voting strength, and the other party's likely candidates are taken into account. Presidential and senatorial candidates are distributed according to region in an attempt to attract the largest number of votes. Luzon, being the most populous area, dominates the senatorial slate, but candidates must be distributed among regions and the party leadership will attempt to ensure that they have, either in the Senate or on the ticket, a representative of each major region. In choosing regional representatives, the leadership will try to take into account traditional rivalries in the area.

In the postwar years, the Mindanao vote has become increasingly important and has been used by the Liberals, for example, to offset the Nacionalistas' traditional control of the Visayas. The 1961 Liberal ticket, for example, included former Senator Emmanuel Pelaez as the vice-presidential candidate to offset Macapagal's strength in Luzon. It was expected that the Liberals would pick up the central Luzon and Ilocano vote on the basis of Macapagal's background, and the opposition vote of the Manila area and the Mindanao vote on the basis of Pelaez's strength. This would offset the expected Nacionalista strength in the Visayas.

During the leadership conferences, local organizations and control of votes are weighed and traded for places on the senatorial slate or in the administration. But this caucus system is not effective at the local level. An agreement made with a senator for the support of his machinery in a particular province, for example, will be challenged by a congressional candidate who has his own machinery. Both will attempt to name the local candidates.

As early as the Commonwealth period, the problem of deciding on local candidates was acute. The party adopted the practice of declaring "free zones." When more than one potential candidate appeared to have the capacity to win and a conflict over the choice developed at the national level, the party would declare an open election and name no official candidate. This practice has continued and erodes any semblance of party discipline. Gubernatorial races and mayoralty contests will often attract several candidates, all supported by different national officeholders and claiming to be the official party candidate. In Agusan in 1959, for example, five candidates ran for governor, four claiming to be Nacionalistas. This practice badly splits the electorate and destroys the local party organization. Furthermore, it results in election of candidates with an extremely small number of votes.

It should now be clear that party organization is subordinate to organizations based on loyalty to candidates personally and not to the abstract entity of a national organization.

Reform Movements. Characteristic of Philippine politics is the sporadic reform movement. These have been of two kinds, the radical reformers such as the Sakdalista and Huks, who base their appeal on agrarian unrest, and the liberal reformers such as the Democrata party and the more recent Grand Alliance, who appeal to the urban middle class and to intellectuals. Both types of reform movement have been led by upper-class, well-educated men. The Sakdalista, Communists, and other agrarian movements have had middle-class leadership and seldom developed directly under natural leaders, but were formed around agitators often foreign to the region. Leadership of the liberal reformers has come from within the intellectual groups, themselves beneficiaries of the *status quo* but disgusted with the inequality, graft, and opportunism of politics. They seek honest men who will eliminate politics in favor of statesmanship.

Despite similarities of leadership and goals, reform movements have been unable to weave together intellectual, middle-class, and peasant support for political success. The Democratic Alliance of 1946 came close to succeeding but the Socialists and Huks were too radical for the middle class and for most of the intellectuals and the movement split. Even peasant support, which was widespread in central Luzon while the Huks controlled the region with their military forces, swung easily back to the government when it proved energetic. Neither of these two radical movements was able to attract enough support throughout the islands to give them a political base from which to challenge the elite by legitimate means. As a result, violence proved to be their only hope.

The intellectual reformers, on the other hand, easily capture the imagination of the middle-class and urban voter, but they have shown little willingness or energy to engage in activities that would bring them peasant support. Their greatest success was with Magsaysay, but, like their leader, they proved incapable of establishing a strong base for their reforms and unwilling to make necessary compromises. Once Magsaysay was gone their organization fell apart and most of them left public office rather than engage in the activities necessary to remain there. They looked for leadership, for an honest man and, with appalling self-righteousness, condemned the political process and its actors. By 1961, the remnants of a reformist group that had its roots in the old Democrata joined the Liberals in opposition to Garcia and placed three of their men in the Senate, where, in alliance with remnants of the Magsaysay era, they have been an effective voice for land reform and public morality. If one traces this movement down through history, it is clear that many of the reformist group have slipped quite naturally into the political parties and public office, where they have been notable for their advocacy of constitutionalism and modernization.

The Philippines has not lacked outstanding men, many of whom have come to public office through the sporadic reformist movements.

THE POLITICAL PARTIES AND BARGAINING

As should be obvious from our discussion, Philippine politics cannot rely upon a continuous network of party loyalty for stability. Unlike the United States, where the majority of voters record, at each election, their loyalty to a particular party and only a small number switch from one to the other, the majority of Philippine voters record, each election, their loyalty to a particular personality who has served to mediate for them the government's impact on their lives. As in all aspects of Filipino life, politics is highly personal and involves the individual voter in a reciprocal relationship whose *quid pro quos* are well understood. The Filipino bargains directly with the political process for his own highly personal needs. He does not bargain through a group or for community gains. As a result, attempts to create loyalties to a broader group, nationwide in character, have little chance of success.

The ramifications of Filipino political behavior for the political parties have been pointed out above. The parties, like the individual, build a coalition of personalities on the basis of highly particular and personal considerations. Continuous negotiations between barrio leaders and provincial and municipal officeholders, between local politicians and national officeholders, and among congressional politicians and the President are the life blood of the political system. Based on personalities rather than broad coalitions, the party is in a constant state of flux, so that little in the way of a stable, distinctive program of government policies is possible. Public policy seems to develop with little regard to or effect on party support. As we shall see in our discussion of political functions, this weakness is overcome by the very pressure of the bargaining that the party structure necessitates and encourages.

CHAPTER VII

The Political Culture

THE BARGAINING process that Filipinos have developed as the basis of their political system is rooted in the institutional, emotional, and value orientations that underlie political behavior. Because of this relationship, the system provides rewards according to criteria the Filipino readily understands. It is these personal commitments to specific conceptions of authority and problem-solving that give the political system legitimacy and the ability to perform necessary functions. Modernization in the Philippines has meant transferring traditional behavior to the new patterns made necessary by the imposition of westernized institutions and by the development of conflicts within the body politic that were insoluble by the older methods. The unique success of democracy in the Philippines, as well as the problems of contemporary government, stem from adaptation of the tradition to the new situation. An understanding of the attitudes and commitments that have resulted is essential for the study of the functions performed by the Philippine political system. The concept of political culture provides a framework for examining the character of that adaptation and also for weaving the relevant strands of Philippine life into a political context.

"Every political system is embedded in a particular pattern of orientations to political action," Gabriel Almond writes.[1] The particular set of behavior patterns that arises out of the limits of assigned authority, the bases upon which calculations are made, and the values that can be sought legitimately through the political system, constitute the political culture. The concept of the political culture seeks to relate the emotional, subjective, non-rational components of political action to the structures and roles through which such action is undertaken. It embodies the psychology of a people, in the form of political identities, as well as their institutions. Perhaps its greatest usefulness is to find room in the study of comparative politics for the sentiment expressed by Macauley: "When will people learn that it is the spirit we are of, not the machinery we employ, that binds us to others?" [2]

The question of the type of spirit, personality, or behavior that democracy requires is crucial to students of the emerging nations. For, as Lucian Pye has pointed out, their political elites have been torn from their traditions and set adrift in a world of conflict and passion in which their own identities and personal integrity are in doubt and the risks and costs of action are often too terrible to contemplate.[3] Those who would understand the politics of nation-building must look to the individuals engaged in that process. For "political culture can only be found in men's minds, in the patterns of action, feelings, expectations which they have internalized and made part of their existence." [4]

Having recognized these considerations, we find the Philip-

[1] Gabriel Almond, "Comparative Political Systems," in Heinz Eulau, *et al.* (eds.), *Political Behavior: A Reader in Theory and Research* (Glencoe, Ill.: The Free Press, 1956) p. 36. The author's understanding of this concept is based on the Almond article and Lucian Pye's use of it in his *Politics, Personality and Nation Building: Burma's Search for Identity* (New Haven: Yale University Press, 1962).

[2] Cited by Stephen K. Bailey, "New Research Frontiers of Interest to Legislators and Administrators," in *Research Frontiers in Politics and Government: Brookings Lectures, 1955* (Washington: The Brookings Institute, 1955) p. 19.

[3] See, for example, his "Personal Identity and Political Ideology," in Dwaine Marvick, ed., *Political Decision Makers* (Glencoe, Ill.: The Free Press, 1960) and *Politics, Personality and Nation Building.*

[4] Pye, *Politics, Personality and Nation Building*, p. 124.

pine experience even more remarkable. Our examination of Philippine history, economy, society, and political institutions reveals that Filipinos have suffered some of the same disorientation as other developing countries, have faced many of the same problems, and yet have achieved a substantial measure of stability and political integration. They have created a polity with a definite democratic orientation. We now wish to make clear that they have done so because Philippine society and culture made possible, indeed made necessary, a bargaining spirit. Philippine political culture is a bargaining culture, which is made evident by the Filipino way of perceiving and responding to power, conflict, and human interaction.

Our examination of Philippine society revealed some key elements of Filipino behavior. For example: the highly personal and reciprocal nature of authority; the tendency to see all relationships as a matter of power; the expectation that all action in favor of another created a credit, to be drawn as needed; the use of manipulative language; and the pakiusap practice of using middlemen in sensitive negotiations. These elements appear again in the political culture, providing the requisite capacity to bargain. For they make up a uniquely manipulative attitude toward human interaction and a perception of politics as an extension of the set of human relationships created for dealing with strangers. The Filipino personalizes his ties to the political system, uses his vote as a *quid pro quo,* and fully expects that his demands will be met if he is skillful in exploiting his relationship to those with power. Within this context, there have developed pragmatic, hardheaded politicians who understand the reciprocity that exists between themselves and the voters and know that if they help people they will be helped in return.

It is precisely this emphasis on manipulative skills that has enabled the political system to mobilize sentiments for development and to establish legitimacy for its authoritative decisions. But the highly personal character of political life has made corruption a major problem of Philippine politics. An examination of the key features of this political culture will make clear the weaknesses and strengths of Philippine democracy.

The Scope of Politics. Almond has pointed out that the political culture is related to, but not the same as, the general culture.[5] Since the political system is only one of the social control systems in the society, it partakes of norms and behavior patterns of other systems. In the Philippines, as in other transitional societies, the boundaries between the political system and other subsystems are poorly defined. The political system, as an order-maintaining system, operates on a daily basis, with traditional social controls as its most effective police agent. A broad range of matters is brought to the political process for resolution, in part because of the family basis of Philippine society and the traditional leadership patterns. Authority roles have been, by definition, multi-functional. The datu, for example, made decisions and exercised authority over village, family, religious, and economic matters. The friar was the local government, religious leader, director of the educational system, and an important influence on the local economy. The landlord in his turn came to perform many of the same functions, even to solving family disputes and advising on career plans for the children of his tenants. The transfer of authority to the politician embodied in that role some of these same multi-functional qualities.

The lack of differentiation between political and other spheres is related to the family base. Because family relationships and obligations were the clearest and most meaningful ones the Filipino knew, he sought to transfer the same behavior and obligations required in the family to realms outside the kin group. Philippine barrio society is a reflection of familial behavior, as is the attitude toward and expectations about government officials and politicians. Today Filipinos go to the mayor, congressman, or senator for aid, support, and advice in all life's problems. The citizen seeks the help of politicians for the simplest of his daily needs and perceives the scope of the political process as unlimited. He asks his congressman for jobs, medical help, transportation money, school expenses for his children, protection from government regulations, and for advice on how to deal with his relatives and how

5 Almond, "Comparative Political Systems," p. 36.

to settle arguments with his neighbors. Mayors and senators alike are beset with constituents demanding help in their intensely personal concerns. A mayor reports that a woman came to him for help in getting her wayward husband to give up his mistress; a senator tells of an irate father who asked the senator to find his daughter, who had eloped with a local rascal.[6] These are everyday occurrences, for the Filipino takes his politics personally.

> Today hundreds of thousands, nay, millions all over the islands seem to have no thought for anything else than politics. They talk, dream, eat, etc., politics. One would think politics is the most important thing in the world. That it is the key to peace, plenty and happiness. Work is neglected in its name, in the pursuit of this dubious goddess, the country's real needs are disregarded. Yes, one would think there was no peace and order problem, no food shortage, no inflation, no unemployment — that all is well with the Philippines.[7]

As a result of this politicizing, political roles are diffuse, and clear norms of conduct according to function are absent. Voters judge the men they elect to office on the norms of social life, how well they deal with local problems, how careful they are of others' hiya, how approachable they are. There is little knowledge of or concern for legal authority or the formal structures of government. The legislative performance of political candidates, except for their fiscalizing activities, are seldom, if ever, referred to in political campaigns. Indeed, members of Congress have been strong advocates of land reform even though their legislative record is one of consistent opposition to land distribution proposals.[8] Filipino voters have little knowledge of and less interest in legislation. Politics is the trading of votes for jobs on public works projects or in return for school houses or roads. The result is a highly per-

[6] Author's interviews.

[7] Editorial, *The Philippines Free Press* (October 1949) p. 1.

[8] Starner, *Magsaysay and the Philippine Peasantry*, reports this also. In her interviews with peasants in central Luzon, she found those who supported Magsaysay did so for his personal qualities and knew little of his program. They tended to rely on him as a man whom they could trust. See pp. 78-80.

sonal commitment to political leadership — criteria for judgment are particular and immediate.

For the politician also, politics is broad and varied in scope. Legislators interfere directly in the administrative process, personally distribute relief goods in time of flood and disaster, carry out raids on executive bureaus, serve as employment agencies for their constituents, and engage in a wide variety of activities not directly connected with their policy-making role.

The Sources and Uses of Power. Since the family relationships and obligations provide the basis for judgment of other relationships and the Filipino seeks to bring all those with whom he has dealings into that family pattern, individuals are conceived of according to their power, and no relationship can be effectively neutral. Others are either "in" the family structure and, therefore, understandable and calculable by the modes provided, or "out" and, therefore, dangerous, demanding the use of spokesmen and other ritual means. In any interaction there is a superior and an inferior, and this relationship will determine what takes place. But various forms of power are perceived, some other-worldly and others strongly this-worldly.

Traditional Filipino belief in the spirit world that governs men's lives includes also an understanding that some men are powerful and successful and others are weak and failures. The reason is simply the presence or absence of luck.[9] Man's status is determined by God and nothing can change it. A man who has a spiritual grant of luck has power. This belief underlies all Filipino attitudes toward power. And it connotes a special attitude toward privilege as the right of those who are divinely selected.

Wealth, for example, is also power. But its acquisition is determined by a man's luck, and Filipinos do not envy those

[9] Agaton Pal's studies of levels of living in Negros Oriental have revealed the importance of *swerte* (luck) in Filipino minds. Most recently, he has applied his findings to a study of attitudes toward wealth and savings. See his section "The Philippines" in *The Role of Savings and Wealth in Southern Asia and the West,* edited by Richard D. Lambert and Bert F. Hoselitz for UNESCO (Paris: UNESCO, 1963).

who have managed to acquire wealth. Old families whose holdings in land have been passed on for several generations have great status, whereas the new rich who acquired wealth through commerce activities or foreign exchange manipulation in the postwar period have lower status. But both have recognizable power.

Certain skills are a form of power also. In politics or local affairs, eloquence and good human relations are vital and lead to influence over the lives of other men. To be able to manipulate people and make them do your will without objection and without damage to your self-esteem is power.

The government, since it is the source of jobs, licenses, money, etc., is also a source of power. Even the lowliest clerk in a government bureau is influential. He can hold up your papers or pass them on as the whim strikes him.

Among politicians, power is a combination of popularity with the electorate, influence with the President, and a strong organization. A man is powerful when he can free himself from the dictates of party leaders and President. Magsaysay, for example, was very powerful, too powerful for Filipino politicians. Because he did not need to rely on the local organizations or on pork barrel, he could eliminate other politicians from his calculations. There is a wholehearted common interest among Filipino politicians in preventing the rise of a new Magsaysay who could, like his predecessor, "take all the pork barrel," "never listen to us," and generally operate free of restraint.[10]

Those who have power are expected to use it to promote their own interest and that of their family. There is no moral contempt for those who benefit from their power. It is as it should be, and a man would be a fool to ignore his opportunities.[11] Those who have power lead interesting and eventful lives. And those without seek to establish close contact

[10] Author's interviews. Unless otherwise noted, all quotes are from these interviews.

[11] Like much else in Philippine politics this is reminiscent of George Washington Plunkitt who, it will be remembered, wanted engraved on his tombstone, "He seen his opportunities and he took 'em." See William L. Riordon, *Plunkitt of Tammany Hall* (Dutton paperback).

with those who do. The politician is surrounded by well-wishers who want only to serve him and bask in the power he wields. "My boss is a powerful man," says one senator's assistant, "When we go to Malacanang, he gets his way." Power is predominantly an instrumental value, to be used and not kept for its own sake.

But these attitudes involve cynical calculations and the assignment of self-seeking motives to those who have power. Philippine politicians deny publicly that they are professional politicians and seek to present themselves as public servants, but in their calculations about one another cynicism is the most obvious characteristic. It is assumed that men seek personal gain. If a senator supports a bill, it is because he has some personal stake in the outcome. Thus, one senator privately revealed that he thought a measure unconstitutional and poorly conceived but would vote for it because "they will say I have been bribed." The discrepancy between public statements and private views will be discussed in the context of the measure of trust that exists in political calculations.

The Nature of Conflict. As we saw in our look at the society, Filipinos are aware of the risks involved in human interaction outside the family and seek to overcome potential conflict by ritual means. The fear of conflict is related to the perception of all human relationships as a power struggle and thus dangerous to one's self-esteem. An unwillingness to make open commitments and a tendency to rely upon implicit cues and social obligations is the result. The Filipino feels he can accomplish his goals without ever articulating his own self-interest. But, as the necessity for dealing with strangers is indisputable, more so as urbanization, communications, and transportation expand, some means must be found for dealing with those for whom the social obligations, utang na loob, and family status have no meaning. A recognizable base for negotiations exists in the *quid pro quo* of the vote, which has led to an expansion of the pakiusap practice into the realms of politics and a vast expansion of matters to be dealt with through political frameworks. The Filipino's understanding that politics is simply a new form of the old power struggle, in which his vote is the *quid pro quo,* allows him to interact with strangers in what he perceives to be a structured situation. Conflict is still dangerous and is to be avoided, but a covert bargaining process, masked by forms of the old ritual, is possible.

In modern societies, a well-developed system of functional roles removes much of the inherent conflict from the arena of personality and identity. A man's action as an administrator, for example, is governed by a widely accepted pattern of norms, which include objectivity, equality, and adherence to rules. No role system achieves perfection, yet most Americans applying for a driver's license would recognize that the men who handle the application are operating according to objective norms and their formal role. There is a consensus of expectations about the behavior of persons assigned to various statuses in the society, eliminating conflict and mitigating the effect of personality on the performance of the functions required. It allows for, in fact assumes, a distinction between the individual and the role he plays.

Such an objective system appears heartless and cold to Filipinos accustomed to the warmth, security, and pragmatism of human relations based on highly personal commitments. Filipinos do not distinguish between the man and his job. Any action involves a deep personality commitment and Filipinos expect that personal obligations and desires will dominate the behavior of everyone. The administrator is expected to adapt his treatment of citizens according to their relationship to him. He is expected to help his relatives and those to whom he owes utang na loob. In dealing with government offices or private business, the Filipino attempts to use his network of personal relationships to get someone who has influence to talk for him. The omnipresence of the pakiusap practice is illustrated by the use of *suki* (special customers) in the simplest of buying and selling operations. Good customers establish a special relationship with the seller and are given special prices. Others will seek to exploit this relationship when making purchases.

This type of behavior has ramifications for the performance of political functions. It makes common interest difficult to establish and articulate and thwarts attempts to form groups such as labor unions. Employees place more emphasis on "being in good with the boss" than on cooperation with their fellows. Personal relations, not role organization, dominate Filipinos' perceptions of their world. Highly personal, emotional considerations underlie human interaction at all levels of society and in even the most rudimentary matters. Conflict can only be handled by investing in good human relations and it is the skills this investment requires that the Filipino cultivates.

The Norms of Political Behavior. We have been examining what underlies the Filipino politician's perception of acceptable behavior. Personal loyalties are important and politicians express their distaste for those who "try to buy both sides" or who do not "work through the party but attempt to get the support of both local candidates" by supplying money. "In one way or another, votes are bought," says the politician, "we all engage in it." But politicians who campaign only for themselves and fail to carry the party ticket are not trusted. The mayoralty candidate of a southern Luzon town who managed to unseat the incumbent, although the rest of his party lost, was spoken of with contempt by politicians of both parties. Election campaigns are accompanied by charges that senatorial and congressional candidates have "dropped" others on the ticket or are supporting popular candidates on the other ticket. The difference between what is acceptable and what contemptible seems small to the observer but makes a great difference to the Filipino politician. Those who try to buy both sides and those who actively campaign against the party ticket or members of the party fall in the distasteful category. Those who merely fail to mention certain members of the party are acceptable. It seems to be recognized that no one could possibly accept everyone who turns up as a party nominee, given the overwhelming influence of a few men on their selection. But to keep the party united during elections is of overwhelming importance and those who would weaken unity are unacceptable.

Filipino love for language and eloquence, combined with hypersensitivity to reflections on self-esteem, are the bases for the concept of *delicadeza*. The Liberal Party politician who spoke out at a party caucus during the Quirino administration, accusing the president of being foolish for rooting out grafters in his own administration and shouting "Why be hypocrites? What are we in power for?" was displaying a lack of *delicadeza*.[12] His sentiment would not shock the Filipino voters, who certainly expect this type of behavior. But his open assertion of the venality of political men was in extremely bad taste. The Liberal party leadership, which threw former minority floor leader Senator Ambrose Padilla out of his job during the 1960 session in favor of Senator Ferdinand Marcos, was clearly not acting with delicadeza, but neither was Padilla in opposing them.[13]

When Mayor Arsenio Lacson found it prudent to get rid of his police chief, he asked him to resign rather than be fired.[14] Lacson disagreed with the chief over what he called an unauthorized release of material to newspapers and hinted that much of the chief's life would not bear scrutiny. When the man refused to resign, Lacson listed the possible charges that could be brought against the chief and added:

[12] President Quirino reports being attacked by Senator Avelino for his investigation of graft in the government, which involved loyal party members. Avelino reportedly said: "Why did you have to order an investigation Honorable Mr. President? If you cannot permit abuses you must at least tolerate them. What are we in power for? We are not hypocrites. Why should we pretend to be saints when in reality we are not? We are not angels. And besides when we die, we all go to hell. Anyway it is preferable to go to hell where there are no investigations, no Secretary of Justice, no Secretary of the Interior to go after us." Elpidio Quirino, "Memoirs" in *The Sunday Times Magazine,* January 27, 1957, pp. 25-26. The question "What are we in power for?" is heard all over the islands now, usually in a humorous context but with a measure of acceptance of the idea it contains.

[13] One newsman reported, "If only for *delicadeza* political observers believe Padilla should gradually relinquish his claim . . ." Amante F. Paredes, "How Much Does Ambition Cost?" *The Manila Chronicle,* February 3, 1960.

[14] This account is based on reports in *The Manila Times,* July 7, 1960 and *The Manila Chronicle,* July 8, 1960.

> The decision whether to resign or not rests entirely on Tenorio, and that decision should be dictated not by the question of who appointed the police chief but as a matter of *delicadeza*.[15]

Lacson was urging the chief to resign and save himself the embarrassment of being fired, since that would create an indelicate situation.

Politicians assume that they and their fellows engage in many activities that are extralegal at best, but they find distasteful open assertions of the fact. The norms require that once found out the matter should be handled quietly, and, if necessary, the man involved should resign.

A Sense of Trust. A sense of trust in one another and a knowledge of limits on each other's behavior provides the basis for bargaining among politicians. The basis of that trust is the tradition of leadership by the rich, the well-educated, the westernized. The unity and common social status of the political leadership endowed politicians with an understanding of one another that has tended to limit and make rigid the recruitment process and to ensure the continuation of leadership by men who have much in common.

The growing middle class is imbued with many of the same values that dominated the elite and is undoubtedly a far cry from the middle class that developed in feudal Europe. The demand for economic equality, which Harold Laski found to be the basis of democratization in Europe, is unlikely to develop as a major force in Philippine society.[16] The middle class of the Philippines has found it necessary to seek its goals through the political system and in order to do so has had to meet the recruitment standards of the elite. The dependence of the middle class on the elite seriously mitigates the impact of new ideas and different values, but it provides the continuity and common interest necessary for a sense of trust.

The pattern of social obligations, the norms with respect to hiya, the necessity for solving conflict before it becomes

15 *The Manila Chronicle,* July 8, 1960.
16 See his essay on "Democracy" in the *Encyclopedia of the Social Sciences.*

overt, all hold for the politician as well as for the rest of society. The emphasis on calculating personal commitments rather than formal affiliations, such as membership in political parties, leads to a high degree of pragmatism. As a result, politicians interact with others without the guidelines that an ideology or general policy commitment would provide. Political action requires an assessment of individuals, their skills, and their ambitions, and the limits on their behavior arising from their needs and positions of power.

The trust inherent in this process of calculation is based on distrust, on the expectation that the actions of politicians will be self-seeking and dishonest. Throughout this study, the reader will find statements by politicians and administrators that seem to say: "Why be hypocrites? We all know we are taking advantage of our offices. Let us not accuse each other of what we are all guilty of." Instances abound in the sessions of the House of Representatives. One congressman, angered by newspaper reports about his actions in a committee hearing, demanded time to reply on the House floor. The speaker ruled him out of order:

> Outraged, ———— quickly appealed the chair's decisions to the House. But the House shouted him out of order. Stung by the rebuff, he challenged everyone to fight. "Tyranny!" he cried kicking and pounding on his table. He shook his fist at the speaker. With murder in his eyes, he glared at all his colleagues and ranted: "I know every one of you here is making money left and right!" [17]

Such statements are not confined to the halls of Congress, however. A reporter described an election appeal by a Liberal party candidate during the 1953 political campaign:

> . . . don't vote for the *Nacionalistas* because they are hungry for jobs, hungry for power, hungry for everything! They are like mosquitoes, famished for human blood. Since they have not enjoyed power for almost eight years, they'll swoop down on you, bite you and suck your lifeblood and kill this nation, I tell you.
> On the other hand, we, the Liberals, have been in power since

[17] Napoleon G. Rama, "Inside Congress," *Philippines Free Press*, March 19, 1960.

1946. We have had enough of privileges, everything . . . . We won't suck you any more because we have already sucked you. So, between the *Nacionalistas,* who are out to suck you, and the Liberals, who are now satisfied and contented, whom would you prefer to run our government? Of course, you can't make a mistake! Think it over carefully my friends! [18]

Cabinet officials also are in agreement on the common motives and behavior of politicians. Secretary of Commerce Pedro Hernaez, who also held the post of Nacionalista party treasurer during the 1959 campaign, was accused of telling a visiting delegation from Pakistan that he had raised 4.5 million pesos for his party through Philippine barter arrangements. At the Blue Ribbon Committee hearing on the charges, Hernaez argued that he was not so stupid as to say such a thing.

> I am now old. I can swear to God I did not say I collected that amount by means of barter. . . . Why be hypocrites? We are all politicians. We know it costs money to get elected to public office. But I will not answer your questions, which you yourselves will decline to answer, if they were directed to you.[19]

Since it is assumed that all politicians are engaged in extralegal activities, all are constantly threatened with exposure. But the very universality of corruption provides a sense of trust. If a politician is attacked for such activities, it is axiomatic that he can find similar evidence in the life of his accuser. Both are constrained to limit investigations. Charges of anomalies are perceived as the result of political rivalry or another's anger at their actions. "Do you know why he is gunning for me?" an administrator asks. "It just so happens that he is now facing a robbery charge in the fiscal's office. It was filed by one of my employees." [20]

Little credence is given the argument that a legislator sup-

18 Leon O. Ty, "Hungry for Jobs — Power — Everything," *Philippines Free Press,* January 2, 1954.

19 *The Manila Chronicle,* March 11, 1960.

20 The Chief of the Backpay Division, explaining why the Finance Investigator had brought charges of *anomalous* releases of back-pay claims against him. Reported by Napoleon G. Rama, "The Terrible Backpay Jungle," Part V, *Philippines Free Press,* January 9, 1960.

ported or opposed a bill because of the interests of his constituents, who would then take his support or opposition into account at election time. There is little evidence that constituents know what happens in the legislature, and, since most bills are passed in the rush of the last days and roll calls are rare, the voter has little information about the actions of his congressmen. Electoral success depends on quite different considerations. Constituents are "bought off" by pork barrel, patronage, and cash paid for their votes. If there are issues, they are local in nature — the barrio version of the parish pump — but with the important difference that help must come from the national level, and local do-it-yourself projects are rare. The politician must appeal to an undifferentiated and unorganized public, and he finds it impossible to weave out of that public a policy stand. The politician in his legislative or executive role is free to determine the public interest on any issue. His actions are highly personal and subjective and are open to question by himself as well as by others. The requirements of political success, the demands made on him as an individual and in his law firm or business, all demand compromises raising doubts about the legitimacy of his position on policy issues and his own integrity.

Bargaining as Corruption: The Politician as Ward Heeler. Two related phenomena tend to corrupt the Philippine bargaining process: the lack of clearly defined political roles and the absence of universal interests. A major concern of politics is the development of power relationships among decision makers, but if all relationships are defined in terms of power then the political process must carry an impossible burden. Power must be functionally related to policy decisions. For example, the influence and success of politicians must, to some extent, be a product of their effectiveness in consolidating the interests of their constituencies into a series of national goals that can form the basis of decision making. But when, as in the Philippines, the demands of the constituency are expressed through personal relationships with those who hold public office, then the aggregation and integration of the interests of the total society is inhibited and the formation of national goals suffers accordingly. Political influence and success will be determined by the ability to manipulate public resources to meet fragmented, particular demands, and political roles will be hopelessly entangled with the other roles the individual plays in the society. Philippine culture, colonial experience, and the extreme centralization of government have hampered the development of a limited political arena and clearly defined political roles.

Political brokerage requires that the value orientations and interests of the population be collected, aggregated, and translated into legislation on the basis of the weight and intensity of preference of groups in the body politic. In order to be effective, these groups articulate their interests in the broadest and most inclusive terms. Policies are based on broad general principles and seek universal values. But in the Philippines, interests and values enter the political arena as particular demands and the national interest has not become the standard for assessing legislation. The politician recognizes that he and his fellows are promoting particular interests for electoral purposes.

On one level, the Filipino politician recognizes himself as a "ward heeler," a political necessity. The loss of integrity involved is the fault of the people who demand government resources in return for their votes. On another level, the Filipino politician views himself as a Burkian representative deciding important matters of nation building on the basis of his educated convictions, which are beyond the comprehension of the voter. The people are ignorant of the problems of nation building and the politician must decide for them.

Politicians themselves doubt that the second view is meaningful. They are not confident that they can act as Burkian representatives, and they distrust any of their number who maintain that they are acting in the national interest rather than their own. Private motives rule, but not without acute self-disgust on the part of the politician. Activities required for election and for success in politics engender anxieties about the loss of integrity involved. The politician regards himself as a "practical politician" who understands the reality of power, but that realism borders on cynicism. For the Filipino politician is not sure how much loss of integrity is required by his political role and how much is simply useful for his private ends. Since he calculates political action according to the probable motives of his fellows and their relative power, he cannot escape from a constant sense of his own venality.

The politician is a "ward heeler" but wishes to be a broker. The change from one to the other probably cannot be accomplished until political roles are understood to require specific functions and until this understanding has spread to significant numbers of people at all levels of society.

The Themes of Political Action. We have seen that Philippine political culture is dominated by such highly personal views of political action that institutional roles and formal functions have scarcely mattered. There are recognizable limits to action and the unique place that power holds in the society necessitates constant calculation and negotiation in any social intercourse. As the older set of economic and social relationships succumbed to the impact of new technologies and aspirations, Filipinos found they could transfer the patterns of behavior they had established to the political system. Rapid politicizing and the bringing of large numbers of people into the political bargaining process was the result. But the very success of this transformation has raised other problems for Filipinos. Doubts and fears of their own capacity for democratic government appear in Philippine politics. This cynicism is matched by an equal measure of idealism.

Filipinos often indicate that they hold a highly idealized image of a democratic political system. In this image, politics does not appear, men carry out their duties according to some mystical public will, and the political system operates efficiently with machine-like ritual. The heavy emphasis on personalities rather than issues in their own milieu creates an ever-present reformist theme that seeks honest men who will conduct public affairs in morally acceptable ways. But those who search like Diogenes themselves demand that their social status, family connections, and honest needs be given special considerations in the offices of government as well as other arenas. Filipinos beset with ideas of men as the important commodity are unable to accept the complex assortment of forces that allow the public interest to be articulated. Skepticism about the motives of men and about the basis for their idealism prevents Filipinos from accepting this idea outright. No man in public office can be wholly trusted and none is worthy of blind support.

Doubtful about their own political process, the Filipinos see always the danger that they will go the way of other emergent nations. Fear of becoming a "banana republic" is openly articulated. Filipinos were shocked by the infant uprising in Batangas, engineered by supporters of José Laurel after his electoral defeat in 1949. They were similarly disturbed by the report that Magsaysay supporters were prepared to use the armed forces if he were denied election through fraud in 1953, and by Macapagal's use of the rangers to prevent Garcia-appointed men from taking over the Central Bank in 1961.

Macapagal's actions in office against members of the economic elite have actuated fears that he is becoming a dictator. Even though the absence of graft and corruption in his administration has been noted and the rationalization of economic development plans has been praised, still, three times in the first six months of his administration, his actions were overruled by the Supreme Court.[21] All this adds up to a dilemma for the Philippines. On the one hand, personalities and individual men only can act, produce policy, and bring about

21 A rash of articles in the *Philippines Free Press* during 1962-63 dealt with charges that the President was becoming a dictator. For example: The *Philippines Free Press* began the first year of Macapagal's administration by naming him the "Man of the Year" in a story with a second headline: "Macapagal's love affair with the poor ends in Malacanang" (January 6, 1962). The following year they again named him "Man of the Year" but this time the cover proclaiming him so held a background of question marks (January 5, 1963). In the intervening year, stories headed: "The Abuses of Macapagal" (February 10, 1962), "Divide and Rule" (March 3, 1962), "Macapagal: What Kind of President Is He?" (May 19, 1962), "Four Strikes" (four adverse decisions from the Supreme Court, September 22, 1962). After the beginning of the second year, there appeared: "Democrat or Dictator" (March 9, 1963), "More Against Macapagal" (March 2, 1963), "Unprecedented Act" (May 11, 1963), and "The Plot Against the President: Has the Philippines Finally become a Banana Republic?" (May 11, 1963).

change. On the other, individual men are not incorruptible and power accumulated in one set of hands is dangerous.

This dilemma is reflected in the way in which political functions are performed in the Philippines.

PART III

The Political Functions

The Political Economy

I N THE FIRST parts of this study, we surveyed the historic evolution of the political system and examined the economic and social base that conditioned its development. We described the political institutions and the organization of the political parties, the operating structures of the system. Throughout this discussion we repeatedly made reference to the process and character of modernization in the Philippines. Formally, rapid social change has modified traditional concepts of leadership and social behavior to fit modern institutions. On a deeper level, these modifications themselves are changing basic attitudes toward political action. In order to understand how these two levels of adaptation have combined to create a stable, unified, democratic Philippines, we must turn now to the specific means by which the system mobilizes the population for action, creates a unified nation, and gives a sense of legitimacy to political institutions.

The Philippines, like other developing countries, adopted institutions modeled after those of Western states to perform the tasks of rule making, rule execution, and rule adjudication that are the essence of government. But the formally designated tasks of government must be more than mechanical or bureaucratic formulas, for they involve the polity, which must live by those rules. In a democratic system, the authority of government is based upon widespread acceptance of its right to make legally binding decisions and to enforce them, if necessary, by its exclusive right to use force. The people take their demands to the political system fully expecting that it is the legitimate mechanical means for working out an accommodation of conflicting interests. That is to say, popular attitudes support the function of the political system, and citizens participate in a variety of organizational forms that allow them to influence political action. The formal designation of specific tasks and structures through which they will be performed is insufficient to explain a political system. For the operation of these formal structures is rooted in a pattern of interaction and organization of the society and polity. This pattern may be rudimentary and ritual or it may be highly complex and pragmatic, but some form of relationship between formal governmental structures and the society is present in all systems.

Some means must exist to teach people the rules of political action, to recruit people into political roles, to provide information about political actions, to organize the polity into broad political groupings around interests they have in common, and to find means of aggregating those interests within the formal structures of government. In the Western democracies, these patterns of interaction evolved along with the formal authority structures, providing a popular base for action that correlated well with the form and action of government. In this slow process, the modification of attitudes and social behavior could keep somewhat abreast of the demands made on the political system. In the Philippines, this process has been speeded up and disjointed. The formal structures were established without provision for a popular base relevant to them. The modification of Filipino attitudes toward political action lags behind the development of formal structures. Like other developing countries, the Philippines abounds in imbalances in the modernization process and traditional behavior is only partially adapted to the new structures. Despite these dysfunctional characteristics, the Philippines has evolved a political system unique among developing countries. It is a system highly sensitive to popular demands, and it operates to bring societal and economic conflict into the formal structures of government, which has led to its successful development. Our intention here is to make clear how this system functions.

In order to better organize our discussion of this relationship between people and government, it is helpful to think of the political system as involving the performance of a number of particular functions. The functional approach to politics assumes that the same functions are performed by all political systems, although the structures regulating their performance may vary widely. We differentiate five particular functions: political socialization, political communication, political recruitment, interest articulation, and interest aggregation. The first three (socialization–communication–recruitment) can be broadly described as concerned with the generation of specific expectations about the rewards, risks, and rules of political action. The other two (interest articulation and aggregation) are more concerned with the organization of the demands of the polity into a form negotiable within the formal structure of authority.

It should be noted, however, that the differentiation of these particular functions is a framework for analysis and thus an abstraction from reality. These functions are, in fact, related and, perhaps, inseparable. We use them here to define the pattern of interaction that underlies and gives meaning to the structures of authority in the Philippine political system.

In our analysis, we shall be particularly interested in the relationship between how the functions are performed and political modernization. Lucian Pye has asserted that "the ultimate test of development is the capacity of a people to establish and maintain large, complex but flexible organizational forms." [1] Such a capacity is crucial to modern industrial systems. As we have already suggested, it is related directly to the culture, social structure, and values of a people. The capacity to associate with others for common goals is rooted in man's view of the universe and his place within it. Our purpose here is to investigate and evaluate the capacity of the Philippine system to organize people for action. In judging developments, we must keep in mind the peculiar process of change going on in the Philippines, in which transition is from a special type

[1] Lucian W. Pye, *Politics, Personality and Nation Building*, pp. 38-42.

of traditional system to a modern democracy. The old system of an agrarian hierarchy, which operated the political structures as a private game, while incorporating into their economic roles a paternalistic concern for the masses of the population, is being modified by the operation of a political bargaining process. In this section of our study, we shall point out how that bargaining process is accomplishing the transformation, but we shall see also that certain aspects of the performance of these functions are only partially modernized and that serious conflicts appear in the operations of the system.

CHAPTER VIII

Political Socialization

A S WE HAVE already noted, Filipino political culture is a
mixture of Western ideas and structures and traditional
modes of behavior. Contradictions abound and the integration of political orientations with the structures available for action is only partial and fragmentary, in large
part, because of the contradictory and fragmentary quality
of the socialization process. Socialization is "the whole
process by which an individual born with behavioral po-
tentialities of enormously wide range, is led to develop
actual behavior which is confined within a much narrower
range — the range of what is customary and acceptable for
him according to the standards of his group." [1] Through
this process, the society continues to maintain its identity
by instilling habits of response in its members, which ensures conformity to the rules. A wide variety of social institutions are involved, and the effectiveness of the process
is related to the degree of relevance between the values
and behavior promoted by these institutions. In the Philippines, the effect of rapid and unbalanced social change
has meant that mutually antagonistic values and behaviors are demanded by the different structures that are the

---

[1] I. L. Child, "Socialization" in *Handbook of Social Psychology,*
edited by G. Lindzey (Cambridge: Harvard University Press, 1954)
II, p. 655, as cited by Lewis A. Froman, Jr., "Personality and Political
Socialization," *Journal of Politics,* 23 (May 1961) p. 341.

principal agents of socialization. In addition, urbanization and industrialization have demanded new and more complex skills that cannot be transferred through the traditional structures. As a result, the formal institutions of socialization, for example the schools, have come to play a more important role. Despite the imbalances of this transitional stage, the Philippines has been remarkably successful in orienting its population toward national goals, which, as we have already made clear, is due to the dominance of the political system and its highly pragmatic bargaining spirit. Now we turn to the ways in which the traditional behavior encouraged and demanded by family, religious, and village structures lends itself to this transformation.

A thorough study of the process of socialization would take us far beyond the purpose of this book. Here we concentrate on political socialization and those behaviors and structures which are most relevant to our analysis of the political system. The aim of this process of socialization is to instill a shared view of the general role of the citizen and a consensus on the values, structures, and methods that are the legitimate concern of political life. All political systems perform this function, although the structures through which it is performed may differ greatly. In the Philippines, a variety of formal and informal groups are engaged in the process of transmitting ideas about government and politics, but the most important is the primary human group, the family. The means by which the child is incorporated into the family conditions his behavior in broader sets of relationships throughout his life. The culture transmitted through the family during the earliest years of life indicates the range of identity opportunities open to the individual; the set of responses to environment and to other people that the family demands places the child firmly in the human society. In this sense, the family is the architect of the personality.

The Philippine family system encourages behavior that is manipulative in character and is oriented toward highly personal relationships. This social behavior underlies Philippine political behavior, promoting a bargaining spirit and allowing for the mobilization of all levels of society through highly personal alliance networks. But political socialization does not stop with the family. The community, the schools, churches, economic organizations, and mass media all contribute aspects of the consensus throughout the individual's life. The degree of correlation among the contributions of all these relevant structures will determine the degree of stability in political life and will contribute to the sense of trust required by a democratic system.[2]

In order to understand how political socialization is accomplished in the Philippines, we must look at the contributions of the most important structures: first, the family, and then the most important structure for communicating the modernizing ideas of the elite and building a shared view of what it is to be a Filipino, the schools.

SOCIALIZATION THROUGH THE FAMILY

We have already noted the overwhelming importance of primary groups in conditioning Filipino behavior. It is the expectation of reward or punishment generated by the individual's immediate personal relationships that dominate his expectations, hence his behavior with respect to the broader society.

The Filipino child is born into a well-ordered human group in which his position is clearly defined.[3] He is made to see that he has a special status on a hierarchy of authority and reciprocal obligations that stretches above him and extends outward

[2] Harry Eckstein suggests that governmental stability is in some measure related to the degree of congruence between its authority pattern and the authority patterns of other structures in the society. See his *A Theory of Stable Democracy*, Research Monograph 10 (Princeton: Center for International Studies, 1961) particularly p. 6.

[3] Camilio Osias writes: "The Filipinos look upon society as having, like an individual, a mind (*isip*), a heart (*puso*) and a soul (*kalulua*). These are concepts that are clear and distinct in the Filipino languages. It is usual for them to speak of the spirit of a people or the soul of the people. Their primitive religion of Anitoism contributed to the people's possessing such a concept . . . . Society is not considered a heartless and soulless machine concerned only with material and mechanical efficiency . . . ." *The Filipino Way of Life* (Boston: Ginn and Company, 1940) pp. 117-18.

into the community through a generational respect and authority pattern.

We are here concerned with the process by which the child born into such a family becomes a Filipino identified with a political unit, the Republic of the Philippines, and sharing with his fellows ideas about the ends and means of political action. We have asserted that in order to bargain, a people must be willing to accept conflict and assert self-interest, must have a sense of a common interest in preventing mutually destructive conflict, and, as a result of these, to have a sense of predictability in human interaction and a measure of trust in others. We need now to look at the contributions of the family to these necessary attitudes.

Attitudes toward Conflict and Self-Assertion. The Filipino's sensitivity to his own self-esteem and the respect ritual that makes him fear other-worldly intervention in his life combine to make conflict fearful and its avoidance a major concern. Carried over into the political arena, this attitude toward conflict would seriously impede action. But the problems of living in a world full of such unbearable risks has given rise to mechanisms for masking conflict that enable Filipinos to act without fear of the consequences. Feelings of personal shame are still present, however. Filipinos do not accept political defeat easily and take such matters very personally. The existence of a set of behavioral styles for incorporating strangers into the known and predictable family system, and the use of middlemen in dealing with others has also been transmitted to the political arena. The style of Filipino landlord–tenant relations combined with the recognition that the vote is a more effective *quid pro quo* than those normal for the tenant in such circumstances has brought about a high degree of direct interaction between politician and voter. The manipulative use of language, which is a highly prized skill among Filipinos, is a recognized political skill in democratic systems. Thus, the behavior developed for interaction in a society in which the individual's self-esteem was a dominant concern and in which obligatory and ritualized but at the same time reciprocal and warm personal relationships were the established pattern of organization, is similar to the behavior required for pragmatic politics. It has given rise to a highly personal political relationship between politician and voter, administrator and citizen, and a style of politics that recognizes that the demands of both sides are legitimate and negotiable.

Attitudes toward Organization. The fear of conflict and the omnipresence of power in all relationships underlies the Filipino's attitude toward organization and the common interest. The Filipino attempts to organize his power relationships to make the most of them. He seeks to extend the network of reciprocal relationships through such means as the compadre system and utang na loob, which will bind others firmly to him.[4] Any assistance he provides constitutes a firm claim on the other, just as help received incurs a reciprocal obligation. He seeks to extend his set of claims to those who are influential and to use the influence he secures to further extend his alliance system. Human relationships are the Filipino's social security. John Provinse has pointed out that in the West, social security means economic security and independence but in the Philippines it means well-being and interdependence. "In the West we diversify our stock market holdings in order to protect ourselves; in the Philippines you diversify your human relationships for the same reason." [5]

It is not what the Filipino knows that counts, it is who he knows. To the Filipino, the government is obviously influential and the men who run it should be, whenever possible, incorporated into his network of relationships. By using his votes and those he controls by reason of his claims on others as a *quid pro quo*, he can bargain with persons in the political

[4] The concept of the alliance system is brought out by Frank Lynch, S.J., *Social Class in a Bikol Town*, Research Series 1, Philippine Studies Program. University of Chicago, 1959, pp. 51-2. Somewhat the same idea is inherent in other works, notably Agaton Pal, *A Philippine Barrio: A Study of Social Organization in Relation to Planned Cultural Change* (Ph.D. dissertation, Cornell University, 1956). See particularly pp. 128-131.

[5] John H. Provinse, "Western Research Techniques and Non-Western Values," paper presented to the Council on Economic and Cultural Affairs conference on "The Teaching of Agricultural Economics in Southeast Asia" at the University of Malaya, Kuala Lumpur, May 8-14, 1960, p. 6.

system. Political action is simply an extension of the arena of human relationships, and he is an eager participant in a highly personal form of politics. Through this means, Filipinos have been integrated into the larger society.

But the emphasis on personal and individualistic considerations inhibits the development of community rather than individual goals. The idea of a common interest is poorly developed. Conformity to social norms is high, but it is a negative sort of common interest. In the rural areas, cooperation in work arrangements such as rice harvesting or planting, house moving, fiesta planning, etc. are common because of tradition and the strength of the social pressure. Government community development workers have found a great deal of resistance to their attempts to extend the traditional cooperative work arrangement (*bayanihan*) to new projects such as road building and irrigation construction. The idea of mutual self-help exists but the political process expressed as demands for local public works interferes with the extension of this idea to wider activities of modern life. Rural folks resist the community development workers' attempts to arrange a barrio cooperative self-help project because they feel the project can and should be done by the government. The community development workers, as representatives of that government, should so arrange affairs.

The commitment to personal and individual goals and alliances is obviously in conflict with the functional requirements of a modern industrial society. In a modern society a complex division of labor and function creates demands and conflicts that can best be handled by broad, impersonal groups dedicated to specific universal goals. In the Philippines modernizing forces are attempting to overcome the effect of primary group socialization and to establish new norms and attitudes more consistent with the needs of national decision making. By far the most important institutions for promoting these new criteria are the schools.

THE SCHOOLS AS A SOCIALIZING STRUCTURE

Beyond the family and the cultural values enforced by socialization in the community, the Filipino is subject to other institutions that seek to communicate the broader goals and loyalties of the national identity. One of the basic problems of nation builders is to inspire in citizens a sense of belonging to a larger entity and a feeling of loyalty to the Philippines and its position in the world. This process calls for a breakdown of some of the old patterns, stronger ties to broader organizations, and commitment to a national ideal. In this slow process, public education plays a crucial role.

In the Philippines, the schools are just about the most important elements for promoting the national culture, the national society, and the national identity. They are channels for distributing an understanding of the values of the national elite to the entire country. Since the schools are controlled by the central government, they become channels through which the Westernized elite can promote its goals, setting the stage for a conflict of values. Before we discuss this conflict, we must examine briefly the Philippine educational system and the level of education.

The Educational System. Public education in the Philippines has two principal goals: to instill a common language and heritage and to train people in the skills required by the new economy. Philippine educational institutions from the primary grades through graduate school attempt to inculcate an ideal of citizenship that relates the individual and his career directly to the job of nation building. The ability to accomplish these goals is undermined by two factors: a high rate of dropout after the fourth grade and a traditional emphasis on law as a career of high status.

The level of education in the Philippines is high in relation to those of other developing areas. The 1960 census showed the median grade completed was 5.1, in comparison to 4.2 years in 1948, and 72 per cent of the population reported literacy in at least one language. Most children complete the first four grades and increasingly large numbers complete high school. The Philippines has a larger percentage (14.5 per cent) of its population of college age enrolled in colleges or universities than any country in Europe or the

British Commonwealth.[6] The 1960 census reported that nearly 4 per cent of the population had completed high school. This figure is particularly significant in that as late as 1890 less than 4 per cent of the high school age group in the United States were enrolled in the public schools.

Most barrios have their own primary-grade schools. One study in the early fifties reported that 86 per cent of the 17,-405 barrios had public schools but only 33 per cent of these offered course work beyond the primary grades. By contrast, there were only "344 public high schools nearly all of them located in *poblaciones* and large cities." [7] The heaviest drop-outs occur at the end of the fourth grade when children have to go out of the barrio to attend school. The dropout rate of rural areas is significantly larger than in urban areas (see Table VIII.1). Going on to the higher grades means

TABLE VIII.1   *The Proportion of Urban and Rural Populations Five Years or Over Completing Selected Grades, May, 1956*

Completing at least:	Urban %	Rural %
First grade	77.8	65.0
Fourth grade	58.3	40.1
Sixth grade	39.1	18.5
Fourth year high school	14.4	3.2
Two years college	6.5	1.2
Four years college	3.1	0.4

The Philippine Statistical Survey of Households Bulletin, Series 2, I, p. 5.

added costs for tuition, transportation, textbooks, and, per-haps, even board and room. In the city of Manila, the public schools do not charge tuition, which, combined with the more obvious utility of education, encourages more students to fin-ish high school. In addition to these considerations, the child is less useful to the economy of the urban than to that of the rural household.

The main reason for dropouts has been the inadequacy of

[6] Seymour M. Lipset, "The Value Pattern of Democracy: A Case Study in Comparative Analysis," *American Sociological Review,* 28 (August 1963) p. 524.

[7] Rivera and McMillan, *The Rural Philippines,* p. 147.

family income to meet the additional costs. If intermediate grades were added to the barrio schools, the educational level would rise. But the capital required for such a move is not available to the government. Despite heavy emphasis on education in the national budget, the schools show evidence of falling behind the increase in population: "It is estimated that there were 585 thousand children who were 7 years of age at the start of the school year in 1951, 733 thousand 7 years old this year (1959) and 796 thousand of this age when school opens in 1962." [8] A study of compulsory education in the Philippines carried out by UNESCO reported that the primary problem was how to accommodate those seeking admission and then keep them there. "There is no need to compel them to attend schools. The serious problem is how to keep the children in school long enough to benefit from their schooling." [9]

In order to make the first four years effective, the Bureau of Public Schools has scaled down its goals to concentrate on literacy. Instead of conducting instruction in the national language, which had resulted in the loss of literacy, since the language was not useful in a daily context, the emphasis has turned to teaching the child to read and write in the vernacular and to do simple sums. This practice does not allow the child to learn Filipino (the national language) or English, the second official language. He is, therefore, outside the mainstream of his own "national" culture. The local character of the school makes it a community center, more than a channel to the nation's capital. Many of the schools were built by the residents of the community through private initiative, and public funds to build or repair schools are frequently requested by local political leaders of provincial and national politicians. There is a real interest in the school, at least insofar as it transmits literacy. Beyond this level, aspirations are limited by the costs and risks of further education.

In any case, the majority of the rural people undergo the

[8] Basilio B. Aromin, "Demographic Aspects of Philippine Economic Development," *The Statistical Reporter,* III (October 1959) p. 16.

[9] Antonio Isidro, *et al., Compulsory Education in the Philippines,* Studies on Compulsory Education, 9 (New York: UNESCO, 1952).

socialization offered by the public school system only at the most parochial level. The effect on the individual's perception of roles open to him is to limit opportunities. There is little chance for the schools to provide the young person with a multiplicity of roles to choose among.

Higher Education. As we have already indicated, the number of college-trained individuals in the Philippines is amazingly high even in comparison to developed countries. But the effectiveness of institutions of higher education in performing a political socialization function is limited by traditional attitudes toward elite status and career. The inhibition of this traditional attitude is giving way to the needs of the new society, but meanwhile an inclination toward government work, as the single most important employer, and toward life in Manila has created a large group of unemployed degree-holding young people.

In the prewar Philippines, the civil service and the professions were acceptable career alternatives and young people flocked to the colleges to take degrees in law or medicine in preparation for jobs in the government. This tendency continued in the postwar period, but the opportunities for commercial enterprise drew many young people into business and social science training. By 1957, the profile of distribution showed that 48 per cent of the students enrolled in higher education were working for degrees in the social sciences, 15 per cent toward degrees in education, 15 per cent toward degrees in engineering, and only 5 per cent toward law degrees.[10] Only 4 per cent were enrolled in agricultural courses and 10 per cent in medicine. Another interesting factor was the number of women who, in 1959, constituted 47 per cent of the students enrolled in higher education.

Education is everywhere considered the golden door into the world of the white-collar worker. To the rural people, education means an escape from "life with mud on your pants." High school and college-trained young people do not

10 UNESCO, *Basic Facts and Figures: International statistics relating to education, culture and mass communication* (Paris: UNESCO, 1960), Table 12, pp. 79-80.

go home to their barrios to work and no one seriously expects them to. There is even a strong belief that they would not be successful in the barrio.[11]

The great faith in a degree as the way into government roles has led many young people into the night schools of Manila. Many of these younger people are from lower-class rural and provincial families; they work during the day and attend night classes at one of the Manila universities.

Private education is a big industry in the Philippines. In 1948, there were a total of 3,428 private institutions of learning, including twenty universities with an aggregate enrollment of a million students.[12] The number has risen since 1948. Some of these are legitimate institutions with reasonable academic standards and well-trained staff, but a large number of them are not.

Upper-class children attend private schools from primary grades through the university years. Some of the best schools in the Philippines are private. Most of the lower-grade private schools (kindergarten through high school) are Catholic schools run by nuns and priests; in those there is heavy emphasis on religion and Catholic history. Among the private schools, the Ateneo de Manila, a Jesuit institution, is rated the best. Among the elite, graduates of this institution are regarded as intellectuals of a superior sort. Unfortunately, the kind of intellectual ferment at Ateneo and other top schools is limited to young men of wealthy families, whose role within

[11] Agaton P. Pal, *The Resources, Levels of Living and Aspirations of Rural Households in Negros Oriental* (Quezon City: CDRC, University of the Philippines, 1963) p. 243, has found, in a study of the level of living in Negros Oriental, that the majority of respondents answered "No" to the question: Do you think a college educated young person could be successful farming here? His respondents indicated that education would make it difficult for them to do what they had to do.

[12] Teodoro M. Locsin, "The Diploma Mills: A National Disgrace," *Philippines Free Press* (January 9, 1960) p. 2, citing the *Manila Chronicle*. The *Chronicle* noted that the income of these institutions probably exceeded 150,000,000 pesos. The profits come from student tuition (70-90 pesos in kindergarten and primary grades; 150-200 pesos in elementary and secondary grades; from 250-300 pesos on college level), in addition, students are assessed for all sorts of things during the school year, tickets to raffles, school activities, building funds, examination fees, etc.

the family economic holdings is waiting for them. Enrollment patterns are changing and bright, ambitious boys are now encouraged to enter these schools.

The most hopeful development is the growing number of middle- and lower-class youngsters attending the University of the Philippines. From a student body of 7,500 in prewar years, the University had grown to an enrollment of 30,398 in the school year 1960-61.[13] A full-time teaching staff of 896, many trained in American universities, and a series of special cooperative arrangements with American institutions have given it a research bias and made it the intellectual center of the country. Students from other Southeast Asian states give it a cosmopolitan flavor, and, in many ways, it has the appearance of a large American university. Graduates of the university are highly regarded and the impetus its staff gives to technical training has done much to overcome Filipino reluctance to stray from the professions. A Labor Education Center to train union leaders, an Institute of Public Administration charged with training government civil servants, and a well-developed and research-oriented agricultural college are among its outstanding segments. A Rice Research Institute, with the purpose of discovering better methods of producing rice, and a School of Economics, aimed at training those needed for the economic development of the country both will have Asian, as opposed to Filipino, student bodies. As the university expands, so will its scholarship funds and hopefully the trend now recognizable in the student body will continue.

CONFLICT BETWEEN VALUES
TAUGHT IN HOME AND SCHOOL

Since the family and the school system are of crucial importance in socialization, conflict between the two has serious ramifications for the performance of the socialization function. Such conflict makes socialization undependable, gives rise to cynicism about the content of education, and provides a wide

[13] Arthur L. Carson, *Higher Education in the Philippines,* Bulletin No. 29, United States Department of Health, Education and Welfare, Office of Education (Washington, D.C.: Government Printing Press, 1961) chapter V.

scope of politically legitimate behavior, making political action unpredictable.

In the Philippines the schools attempt to inculcate objective standards, civic spirit, and such virtues as hard work and thrift. But the home life of the students and indeed of the teachers themselves is a daily reminder of a quite different set of standards. Much of the discrepancy between values taught in the home and in the school is due to the heavy influence of American educators on Philippine education. The tradition of American concern for Philippine education began with the soldiers sent to occupy the new territory in 1898 and it continues today with the Peace Corps assisting Filipino teachers in barrio schools. Within three years after American soldiers had shown a propensity to teach Filipino children how to read English, 1,000 American teachers were established in the islands and the idea that education was the golden door to opportunity was firmly established.

It should be remembered that Spanish missions had begun to educate Filipinos in Western values and ideas three centuries before, and Filipinos had long since recognized that education was the means of modernizing their society. Those who led the revolution were themselves beneficiaries of missionary education and, in many cases, had gone on to European universities. Like José Rizal, they found much wrong with the friar's version of education and supported free public schools removed from church influence.[14] The Malolos Constitution and other documents of the period incorporated this idea.[15] Public schools were to be the mechanism for transforming Filipino society.

[14] José Rizal, *El Filibusterismo* (translated as *The Reign of Greed* by Charles E. Derbyshire), (Manila: Philippine Education Company, 1958). Chapter XIII, entitled "The Class in Physics," is among the most scathing and humorous passages in Rizal's work.

[15] Title IV, Article 23 of the Malolos Constitution of June 20, 1899 states that any Filipino "can found and maintain establishments of instruction or education" and "Popular education shall be obligatory and gratuitous in the schools of the nation." Mabini in his *Programa Constitutional de la Republica Filipina* spells out in detail a system of public education in Title X.

The American regime's goal of creating a self-governing democracy fitted Filipino aspirations and won their willing cooperation. The utility of the school house was recognized by both sides. American school teachers adopted Philippine nationhood as their goal and used the same techniques that had proven useful in their own country. Filipino heroes decorated the school rooms, and the national anthem was sung each morning. American educators recognized the undemocratic propensities of the class structure and aimed to use the schools to rid the Philippines of the ubiquitous cacique.[16]

Free public education in the English language aimed at instilling not only ideas of good citizenship and literacy but also new methods of sanitation and hygiene and the skills and motives of the new technology. The effect of the school system, however, was inhibited by three factors: the lack of relevance of American ideas of sanitation and achievement, for example, to Philippine barrio life, the language barrier, and the heavy dropout rate after fourth grade. These problems persist in Philippine education.

American ideas about education have been remarkably successful in other ways. Free public education at the barrio level is an undeniable fact. A larger proportion of Filipinos than any other Asian people outside of Japan enroll in high schools, and a university committed to mass education has become a respected and vital institution. Filipinos ask only "How can we improve our schools?" and "How can we keep more people in school longer?" The commitment to education is apparent in budgetary appropriations for education, which have amounted to nearly one-third of the annual appropriation since 1949.

But the attempt to instill American attitudes set the stage for conflict. The use of American texts complicated matters. As time went on, attempts were made to adapt them to Philippine conditions. Eventually, Filipinos wrote their own texts. But since Filipino teachers are American trained, many of

16 David Barrows made this aim clear in his report contained in *Report of the Philippine Commission,* 1903, III, p. 698. Barrows was General Superintendent of Education. For a description of the operation and accomplishments of the educational system during the Commonwealth period see Ralston Hayden, *The Philippines,* Part III.

the same irrelevancies appear, and the problem of good texts adapted to barrio life is only partially solved. Status is achieved by hard work and discipline, say the texts, but the Filipino does not find it so. Rather, status is assigned automatically by birth and is otherwise achieved only through the right connections. Vocational and technical training is emphasized, but these have no status in the society. Manual labor is held in low esteem, and those who work with their hands are little better than servants.

These conflicts lead to a cynicism on the part of young Filipinos, who have come to see that success lies in having a degree and knowing the right people at the same time that their mentors are attempting to instill in them ideals and aspirations that have little meaning and no hope of success. The conflict between the college text that exalts democracy for its "high regard for the dignity and worth of the individual" and the hiring practices of government offices in which family name and personal favors count more than achievement, is obvious to the student. Democracy, says the text, requires of its citizens "self discipline and self direction, a sense of civic responsibility, economic efficiency and training in self realization." [17] And a high school text asserts that the most important duties of the people are "to be loyal to the government, to render service to the country, to vote intelligently and honestly, to take an active interest in public affairs, to cooperate with the government, to pay taxes promptly, to make efforts toward self-improvement, to show respect for law and authority, to acquire knowledge of the basic laws." [18] But in daily practice, he knows that votes are bought, election scandals are common, politicians and businessmen seldom pay taxes, and finding loopholes in the law is almost a way of life. The textbook view of political life does not match the reality of the Philippines and little has been done to incorporate a new dynamic view of the political system. The image of democratic citizenship encouraged by formal education has

[17] Antonio Isidro, *Philippine Social Life and Youth* (Quezon City, 1950) pp. 283ff.

[18] Arturo M. Tolentino, *The Government of the Philippines* (Manila: R. P. Garcia Company, 1950) p. 68.

no relevance to the bargaining behavior required of the Filipino for the simplest of his daily relationships. These ideals, necessary to the modern state, seem impossible to achieve, given the character and behavior of Filipinos, which makes it difficult for students to develop active interest or loyalty to the aims of nation building. The schools have failed to inculcate in students the sense that their career and future are related to the building of the strong democratic state the government has more or less indicated that it seeks.

In many respects, the schools have contributed to the breakdown of traditional social controls without providing the basis for evolving new ones. During recent years, the Manila press has carried stories of increased lawlessness, hooliganism, and juvenile delinquency on the part of young people, many of whom were college students and large numbers of whom were unemployed. The cause is probably as much the unemployment problem as the inability of young people to find meaningful goals to work for. At the same time, there is a great need for trained young people in agriculture, engineering, and technical fields to work among the rural people and help them improve their standard of living. There are many career opportunities for young people in such fields as forestry, irrigation, animal husbandry, marketing, etc. But these demand a change of goals, and the school system has failed to indicate these goals or the rewards they offer.[19]

Among the upper-class young people from more modernized homes, the correlation between what is learned in school and

[19] The Bureau of the Census, *Annual Report of the Director*, January 1958. Included in this report is the total number engaged in various occupations as of 1957:

Lawyers	21,306
Physicians	13,935
Nurses	12,068
Veterinarians	374
Master plumbers	88
Electrical engineers	210
Chemists	919
Architects	1,045
CPA's	4,994
Mechanical engineers	522

what is learned at home is probably much higher than it is in rural areas, and, consequently, the schools serve the function of reinforcing the values of the family, which are, it must be added, much closer to those of the elite. These young people are, consequently, trained for and recruited into the Manila elite and into the roles that have been opened to them by status and by education in upper-class schools. Socialization cannot be dependable under such circumstances, so that the young person's perception of the wider society, its goals, and the kind of behavior it expects of him are obscure and highly ambivalent.

The differential impact of the agents of political socialization in the Philippines and the lack of congruence apparent in the values and behavior they seek to promote is typical of a transitional system. The adaptation of traditional organization to more complex modern structure involves the development of attitudes and values that allow citizens to associate with one another for common goals. Creating a democratic personality capable of operating in modern organizations is a basic task of the Philippine system. Obviously, the process is hampered if the individual can find no predictability in his surroundings and no pattern of behavior that is acceptable to the society as a whole. It is in this area of personal commitment and attitudes that the conflicts in socialization have their greatest impact and their most serious ramifications.

POLITICAL SOCIALIZATION
AND THE CHANGING POLITICAL SYSTEM

The political system itself has generated conflicts and pressures pushing for changes in political roles. The presidency of Ramon Magsaysay added a new element to Philippine politics. His honesty and integrity in public office were not questioned and his insistence that the government existed to serve the "common man" led the population to expect that their personal demands would be met. But in addition to this aspect of his political career, he rallied about him a large number of Manila intellectuals wedded to the concept of honest, objective government, a civil service based on the merit system, and increased local autonomy. Many of these ideas were incorporated into law, and, although their effect was tempered by a failure to enforce them, they had gained legitimacy as meaningful goals toward which to work.

In addition to the Magsaysay impact, disgust with the graft and corruption that reached its peak after the 1949 election had created a demand for integrity in government and reform which was based in Manila's Westernized intelligentsia but which gradually seeped into the political orientation of the urbanized middle and lower-middle class. By the 1960's, the Filipino voter had come into his own. He found he could "throw the rascals out" and did so with gusto.

The personal relationships and their attendant obligations that dominate Philippine social life have been incorporated into Philippine political roles. Now the increasing complexity of the society is forcing functional requirements to take precedence over the personal obligations. The conflicts engendered by this transition are apparent in the wide variety of highly personal modes of behavior required by the present political roles and by the sense of outrage apparent in Filipinos who come into contact with the new requirements. In this context of rapid social and political change, the behavior of those in public office is unpredictable, and it is never clear whether the public official is performing his special function or doing a favor for a friend.

The problems of conflict can be seen in a comparison of the new, urban–industrial Philippine society with the traditional, rural–agrarian environment. In traditional society, labor was not divided to any great degree and specialized roles were few. A limited number of roles sufficed to handle all areas of life. The designation tenant, landlord, priest, or merchant was sufficient to describe the total life role of the individual. The individual and the role he played were considered one and the same, and there were few opportunities for change or deviance. Social controls were highly effective.

Constant conflict and competition, on the other hand, characterize the urban–industrial society. In the world of business, money wages, division of labor of the new urban Filipino, a man must constantly struggle to overcome his environment. His individual self-interest becomes explicit, and he must use his capacities and skills to acquire the necessities of life. He must bargain with what he has against what there is. Conflict is inevitable and ways must be found to limit and control it. Roles become more specific and involve only part of one's life; they become more impersonal. The articulation and pursuit of explicit self-interest creates more conflict, which must be worked out on an impersonal level.

One of the problems of this transition is simply that the society and its structures of socialization produce individuals with behavioral expectations and responses that do not match the roles they are required to play in the modern system. The sense of predictability, social control, and trust generated by the socialization and the continuity of traditional behavior has enabled the Filipino to find ways of operating the new system of roles in the old manner. But as this behavior proves ineffective, the political system must find ways to handle the variety of conflicts that result.

As we shall see, the Philippine political system emphasizes the electoral process as a means for mobilizing the sentiments of the people. This was a natural outgrowth of the adaptation of traditional behavior to modern structures. And it serves now as a socializing mechanism encouraging the electorate to act in ways that will be effective within the formal structures. This aspect of socialization will be made clear in our discussion of the organization of the system.

The process of socialization also includes the symbols, ideals, and images presented through communication channels. In transitional societies, in which people have little direct contact with the centers of government, what they hear through others is of vital importance in building loyalties and commitments to modernization. We turn now to the communication function in the Philippine political system.

CHAPTER IX

Political Communication

I N THE PHILIPPINES, the development of the political system has been accompanied by increased communication between the levels of society and the adaptation of traditional channels of information to perform functions in the new network. The mass media have penetrated the traditional fragmented communication structures and have been a vital force in the creation of national unity and political commitment. The media have spread the bargaining spirit that provides the dynamism of Philippine politics, for communication is vital to bargaining. Continuous and reliable information is required for the constant assessment of the interest of others, a sense of common goals and limits, and the framework in which interest articulation can take place. The communication process provides a context in which political action has meaning and predictable results. The gap between urban and rural population and the consequences of economic inequality are being overcome by the development of a national network of communication. Modern ideas of political and economic life are transmitted through the media and processed through traditional channels, providing rural people with an awareness of the scope of the political system, the relationship of local to national politics, and the sort of behavior that brings rewards or punishment in the political arena. Political modernization requires that primary communication structures be incorporated into and penetrated by a national communication network that will introduce the concept of a nation and of a political system that has roots in the village.[1] To a very large extent this goal has been achieved in the Philippines.

In order to understand how this function is performed, we must understand the mixed character of the communication structure. Personal and ritual face-to-face communication is the traditional, and still dominant mode of passing information, but key communicators of the traditional society have contact with the mass media and become interpreters of and mediators between the two structures, seriously affecting the impact of the mass media but ensuring that traditional social

TABLE IX.1 *Mass Media Distribution per 1,000 Inhabitants*

Newspapers (daily)......19 copies
Radio receivers ....14 sets
Cinema seats ....12 seats
Television receivers ..... 1 set

UNESCO, *Developing the Mass Media in Asia,* Reports and Papers on Mass Communications, No. 30 (Paris: UNESCO, 1960) Annex II, p. 59.

behavior and structure will influence the messages transmitted (see Table IX.1). The character of the expectations engendered by the media are thus a mixture of both worlds. But, precisely because the traditional modes have been only partially modified, the communication process provides a measure of stability in a period of major and rapid social change. Before turning to the manner in which the function of political communication is performed, we must examine briefly the availability of the mass media in the Philippines.

THE MASS MEDIA

According to the criteria set by the United Nations as a minimal goal, the Philippines is relatively well off in media resources. The United Nations holds that anything less than ten copies of a daily newspaper per thousand and five radio re-

[1] For a discussion of the role of communications in the process of modernization see Lucian W. Pye, ed., *Communications and Political Development,* Studies in Political Development, 1 (Princeton: Princeton University Press, 1963).

ceivers per thousand inhabitants is inadequate. Although the Filipino distribution is significantly greater than those of most other developing countries, it is far from adequate in comparison to the needs of a modern state. Furthermore, the distribution pattern shows a heavy concentration of media resources in Manila and very limited distribution in other areas. Few studies of this problem have been done and available statistics are insufficient. The following discussion can only hope to indicate the nature of the distribution.

TABLE IX.2 *Newspaper Distribution in Manila*

	Manila	Outside Manila
Daily newspapers	18	4
Circulation	300-350,000	150-200,000
Per thousand	310	5

N. W. Ayer and Sons, *Directory, 1953* (Philadelphia: N. W. Ayer and Sons, 1953) and John C. Merrill, *A Handbook of the Foreign Press* (Merrill, 1958).

Newspapers and Periodicals. The overwhelming impact of the mass media is on the Manila area, which is the center of the mass media, as one can see in Table IX.2.[2] Nine of the Manila dailies are published in English, four in Chinese, three in Spanish, and two in Tagalog. The provincial dailies appear in English or in a combination of English and Spanish or the local dialect.

Weekly newspapers and publications have a far wider circulation; forty-one weeklies are published in the provinces. The typical provincial weekly is a four-page tabloid, usually published in English or in English and the local dialect, with a circulation of about 1,000 to 2,000 and sells for 10 centavos or

[2] Circulation statistics vary widely. UNESCO, *World Communications: Press, Radio, Television* (Paris: UNESCO, 1956) p. 169, reports the 1954 circulation as 409,000. N. W. Ayer and Sons, *Directory,* 1953 (Philadelphia: N. W. Ayer and Sons, 1953) reports the 1953 circulation as 415,000. Another source, John C. Merrill, *A Handbook of the Foreign Press* (Merrill, 1958), reports the 1958 total daily circulation at 500,000 copies or more; this includes the *Manila Times,* 100,000; the *Manila Chronicle,* 50,000; the *Philippines Herald,* 40,000; *Bagong Buhay* (Tagalog), 30,000; *Kong Li Po* (Chinese), 15,000; *La Voz de Manila* (Spanish), 10,000. Newsmen have estimated the total daily circulation to be anywhere from 500,000 to 700,000.

the equivalent of 5 cents.[3] An additional fifty-five weeklies are published in Manila. These include the weekly news magazine *Philippines Free Press*, which specializes in political news, tabloids professing to give the "inside story" about political and business personalities and their activities, and the *Liwayway* publications, which are similar to women's magazines of the United States, with fashions, news about movie stars, comic strip serials, and fiction, with love stories as the main interest. The *Free Press* has a wide circulation (60,000–64,000) among provincial elites but does not often reach the rural masses. The most widely circulated in the rural areas are the *Liwayway* publications, which are published in Tagalog, and particularly the Filipino comics.[4] These serve a useful function in promoting the spread of the national language and aiding in the reinforcement of literacy. They also spread the influence of movie stars and comedians and promote a sense of being a Filipino.

Distribution of Radio Sets. There are nine radio transmitters in the country, six of which are commercially operated. These stations broadcast in English, Tagalog, Visayan, Chinese, Spanish, and all other Filipino dialects. Two of the nine transmitters are Voice of America relays, one in Manila and the other in northern Luzon. Most schools and town halls have receiving sets. But the distribution of radio sets reveals the dominance of the Manila area. In the province of Rizal, which surrounds Manila to the east, 50 per cent of the households have radio sets, but in the province of Albay in southern Luzon only 4 per cent of the households have sets.[5]

A study of the Dumaguete City trade area found that only 1.6 per cent, or sixteen out of every thousand householders, had a radio.[6] However, about 100 householders listened at these sixteen households with radios, or six householders per

[3] Merrill, *Handbook*, p. 84.

[4] Two publications, *Liwayway* and *Bulaklak*, have a combined weekly circulation of more than 147,000.

[5] *Census of the Philippines, 1960.*

[6] Robert Polson and Agaton Pal, *The Status of Rural Life in the Dumaguete City Trade Area*, 1952, Data Paper 21, Southeast Asia Program (Ithaca: Department of Far Eastern Studies, Cornell University, 1956) p. 18.

radio. An ICA study of 600 households in 1956 found only twenty or 3.3 per cent had radios and three of the radios did not work, leaving only 2.8 per cent of the total sample with radios in working order.[7] In this study, respondents named news in the dialect and popular music as the most popular; 33.5 per cent of the listeners reported they had heard news in the dialect. The greater part of this news originated from government offices and public relations men.[8]

Much of the difficulty of building a national radio audience has been due to the lack or high cost of electricity in many areas. Now, transistor radios are available, and have become highly prized items. The number of receiving sets grew from 305 in 1957 to 550 in 1959.[9] The government and CARE (Cooperation for American Relief Everywhere) organization in the Philippines have undertaken a project to place a transistor radio in each barrio. The radios were to be located in a central building convenient to all residents, and it was hoped that the people would gather to listen to special information programs presented by the government.[10] As it turned out, the radios were used more for entertainment than for information.

Radio has become a popular medium and the speed with which popular songs spread through the islands is indicative of its effectiveness. Filipino entertainers and particularly comedians have acquired national reputations through Tagalog programs and the movies. Information programs lag far behind entertainment in communicating with the rural people, which is true of all the media. The entertainment aspects of radio, however, are as useful in building national identities

[7] J. C. Tuvera, "Mass Communications and Culture Growth," *Progress 1959* (Manila Times Publishing Company, Inc., 1959) p. 126.

[8] In another recent survey reported by Tuvera, 106 out of 126 government offices surveyed had public-relations people on their staffs. J. C. Tuvera, *op. cit.*, p. 131.

[9] UNESCO, *Basic Facts and Figures*, 1961 (Paris: UNESCO, 1962) Table 30, p. 161.

[10] The effect of this program is the subject of a study by Dr. Richard Coller, Department of Sociology, University of the Philippines, *An Analysis of the Social Effects of Donated Radios on Barrio Life* (Quezon City: Community Development Research Council, 1962).

and goals as the duller and more informative programs of the government. Commercial radio programs utilize traditional Filipino art forms and humor that satirize modern life and social types who have counterparts in the barrio community. Filipinos can thus identify with a larger community that is recognizable and relevant. These programs contribute a sense of the universality of Filipino traits and foibles and a sense of a shared culture. At the same time, they highlight the similarities rather than the differences between urban and rural life and between upper and lower classes and help to overcome fundamental and potentially dangerous splits in the population.

The Movies. There are about 800 movie theaters in the Philippines, with a seating capacity of nearly 700,000. There are 75 movie theaters in Manila alone, with a total seating capacity of 58,370.[11] In addition, 50 mobile units tour the cities and rural areas. Nearly every poblacion and all provincial capitals and chartered cities have one or more movie theaters. Filipino movie companies produce 80 to 100 feature films a year, which are exhibited in Manila and throughout the country. About 50 per cent of the films shown are supplied by United States film companies and about 40 per cent are locally produced. The remainder come from Spain, Mexico, England, etc. Although some movie houses specialize in Filipino films exclusively, most areas have access to both American and Filipino movies relatively often.

Movies are extremely popular in the Philippines. In Manila, the opening of a new film, either Filipino or American, brings out large crowds of people. The theaters of Manila open at 8:00 A.M. and run continuously until the last show at about 10:00 P.M. In the provinces, there is usually a matinee and an evening show, and these are well attended. Most Filipinos have seen at least one movie in their lifetime and

---

[11] United States Department of Commerce, *Motion Pictures Abroad: Philippines* (Washington, D.C.: Government Printing Office, 1958). UNESCO reported in 1956 there were 450 movie theaters (35 mm) and 250 (16 mm) with an estimated 500,000 seats.

poblacion and urban residents attend regularly. Many of the Filipino movies and most of the American movies shown describe a way of life that the majority of the Filipinos do not share. Manila life, the ways of the upper class, and idealized portraits of rural living are the predominant themes of Filipino movies. The most popular are the comedies. During 1959 and 1960, a film entitled "Juan Tamad Goes to Congress," a satire on politics that made little attempt to disguise the personalities it portrayed, drew standing-room-only crowds for weeks. Advertisements carried large pictures of "Juan Tamad" (Lazy John), a Philippine folk hero known for his indolence, with the caption: "The Best Politician Money Can Buy." The film pictured persons readily identified as the President, the senate president, various senators, and executive branch officials engaging in activities such as bargaining for more pork barrel, displaying more than one wife, making campaign promises, and generally hoodwinking the public. The moral of the piece appeared in a recorded speech of the mayor of Manila accusing the voters of advancing corruption by their apathy and personal demands on politicians and calling for an aroused public to serve as a check on the excesses of politicians.

The movies provide a vivid picture of Manila and the outside world and give Filipinos an indirect experience with a way of life alien to their home surroundings. Filipinos sitting in darkened theaters catch glimpses of a world where the individual is not bound to an ascribed status but has unlimited opportunities to build his own life. There are more things in this movie life than he has dreamed of, and the experience both broadens his frame of reference and undermines his traditional commitments.

THE COMMUNICATION PROCESS

A description of Filipinos' actual contact with the mass media is misleading and cannot explain the very vital part the communication process plays in nation building. The content of the media is processed and broadly disseminated through familiar channels. In this way, the modern technologically advanced communication structure penetrates directly the personal face-to-face communication system of the barrio. American researchers' finding that communication involves a "two-step flow," with mass media content given meaning by opinion leaders at various levels of society, is applicable to the Philippines.[12] The provincial and urban middle class serve as contacts with the national media for most Filipinos. It is through these people that the ideas of nationhood, of politics, of modern life are transmitted. They play a key role, as yet uninvestigated, in relating people to the political system and in encouraging the development of specific attitudes and emotions about politics. More important, they link the two communication structures and ensure that each will be sensitive to the other.

Studies of access to the media report very low direct levels of contact, particularly among rural people. One survey of rural households found that 41 per cent of the households read no newspapers or magazines regularly and only 3 per cent had radios, although about one-fourth of the respondents had listened to the radio at least once during the preceding week.[13] Nearly half the respondents in this study had seen motion pictures during the year, with an average attendance of ten times per year. Three out of ten had seen a movie in a mobile unit during the preceding year.[14]

Several studies have attempted to find out how information reaches the rural areas and what kind of information rural people have at their disposal. In general, these show a heavy

[12] Elihu Katz and Paul F. Lazarsfeld, *Personal Influence* (Glencoe: The Free Press, 1955), and Elihu Katz, "The Two-Step Flow of Communications: An Up-to-Date Report on the Hypothesis," *Public Opinion Quarterly,* 21 (Spring 1957) pp. 61-78.

[13] Rivera and McMillan, *The Rural Philippines,* p. 156.

[14] These mobile units are mainly advertising devices of various companies, which usually present a program of commercials and a feature film, either American or Filipino. The government bureaus dealing with aspects of community and rural development have mobile film trucks that are used to show films dealing with special problems. These are popular in both urban and rural areas, but the number (and quality) of training films for this purpose is very limited.

emphasis on face-to-face oral communication with less reliance on the mass media.[15]

In another study of four barrios in Iloilo, the respondents were asked what recent news they had heard about activities of municipal, provincial, or national government personnel.[16] Over half the respondents had heard some news about municipal activities, whereas only a quarter had heard news of provincial or national political activities. Those interviewed listed three common sources of information about municipal politics: "(1) members of the family or relatives, (2) neighbors and (3) *poblacion* residents." [17] Information about activities at the provincial level came from barrio neighbors and poblacion residents and at the national level from publications or public announcements, barrio neighbors and officials and poblacion residents.[18] Available sources of information listed were mainly persons (*i.e.*, barrio lieutenants, municipal officials, teachers, professional people) with newspapers reported as available to only 6 per cent or six people out of one hundred; magazines to seventy-six people; radio to thirty people. Articles most often read in the magazines were short stories in the dialect or in Tagalog.

The extraordinary emphasis on face-to-face communication seems to deny a role to the mass media. Yet these communication channels are, in most cases, simply links between the mass media and the individual. Thus, the barrio lieutenant, the upper-class educated citizens, and the school teacher read the *Philippines Free Press* and often the Manila newspapers, listen to the radio, travel frequently to Manila, and attend movies.

The elites are important channels of political information.

[15] John de Young, *A Pilot Study on Communication Problems in the Barrio* (Manila: Social Science Research Council, University of the Philippines, 1955) p. 83; Polson and Pal, *The Status of Rural Life in the Dumaguete City Trade Area, 1952*, p. 18; Rivera and McMillan, *The Rural Philippines*, p. 156.

[16] Tito Firmalino, *Political Activities of Barrio Citizens in Iloilo as They Affect Community Development*, Study Series No. 4 (Community Development Research Council, University of the Philippines, 1960).

[17] Firmalino, pp. 24-26.

[18] Firmalino, pp. 35-36.

The nurses, doctors, government officials, lawyers, teachers, etc. are in immediate daily contact with the rural voter. Their education, frequent trips to Manila and contact with the mass media make them a "good source" of information for the barrio people. Furthermore, they are usually from older land-holding families and, therefore, have a special status in the local society. They are, in short, acceptable members of the local social structure. The provincial elites have become disseminators of information, serving as mediators between the Western–urban–industrial center and the traditional–rural–agrarian masses. Their interest in local politics is very high and is related to what they consider to be the needs of the province, usually better roads, electricity, and a more adequate water supply. Their choice of candidates reflects the same reasoning as the choice of the barrio folks. Kinship, favors, accessibility, all are important but with a very great emphasis on finding honest men for public office.

The creation of provincial urban centers and poblacion market and recreation centers has led to the development of a working class, whose ties to the surrounding rural area are intimate and direct. These people have become important communicators in the linkage between the mass media and the nation on the one hand and the rural citizenry on the other. They do not share the upper-class status of the professional elite nor do they share their values. These are usually high school graduates whose skills and entrepreneurship have carved them a significant place in the money economy. Their values are, of course, conditioned by this experience, and they place before the rural people a model for change and a realistic alternative to life in the barrio. They collect information from the chains of gossip that are the main structure of communication in Filipino towns, from the mass media, and particularly from radio, movies, and the professional group, and they pass it on to their rural clients. The extent and character of this growing group of small entrepreneurs and service people are vital to the development of more dynamic attitudes toward individual achievement, for it is they who give weight and meaning to modernization and industrialization, which, in the more grandiose communiqués of the governing elite, are meaningless to the barrio citizen. In so doing, they contribute significantly to the interest articulation function, promoting a goal attainable by the masses of people.

Communication between the national government and the population is carried on mainly through personal agents. In a more direct sense, this communication is the function of the political process. The barrio lieutenant has acquired a respectable elective status due to the increased autonomy of the barrio. Contacts between these local leaders and members of Congress constitute a direct flow of information about politics and about national decisions. One of the aims of increased local autonomy is to create a local political process which will relieve some of the burdens on the national political process and will serve to localize government. In some cases, the barrio elections have become simply contests between area congressmen and senators seeking to build their own coalitions, tying local politics directly to national politics but often subsuming local issues and preventing the mobilization of the community in support of particular projects. The creation of a local political process is hampered by these and other more basic inhibitions, but the arena has been defined, and in time local politics will undoubtedly take on a more meaningful role in organizing local life. At present, the intense and spirited campaigning for national office provide the most direct contact between local and national politics. During campaigns, the Philippines is saturated with information about politics, and the Filipino is overloaded with conflicting views of issues, personalities, and parties. At such times, he turns to his local sources of information for help in making determinations. Thus, at all points of contact, it is this acutely sensitive and personal linkage between the oral communications network and the more formal structure that dominates the Filipino's world view.

Socialization Function of the Media. What sort of opportunities are presented through the media? What sort of orientation to government, politics, and society do they provide? These questions cannot be fully answered without analyzing the content of media that find their way to the various levels of society. Studies of this sort have not been done. Some generalizations, however, can be made on the basis of observation.

The daily press and other media have their greatest effect in the Manila area. It is surprising to find that college students, surrounded by rich media sources, seldom take advantage of them. The society pages, movie advertisements, the lovelorn columns are very popular among the young. But the news and front page are largely ignored. The usual reason given is that the papers are full of nothing but graft and corruption, and it is "disgusting." One does not like to read over and over about the shameful activities of one's government. A content analysis of the major news carried in the Manila dailies for any period would undoubtedly show an overwhelming percentage of space devoted to venalities (or, as Filipinos call them, anomalies) in government agencies. During one two-month period, nearly every government bureau was described in the press as being involved in one or another anomaly. The amounts of money "misused" or "lost" through these transactions, as reported, amounted to more than the national budget.[19] The mass media have presented politics as a rather disgusting spectacle in which nice people do not engage.

At the same time, the Filipino sense of humor about politics and the general good sense of the people in refusing to take politicians too seriously is shown very well in the comic strips carried by the daily newspapers. Comic-strip characters, such as "Sakay and Moy," a pair of somewhat less than intelligent types whose fumbling gets them into a great deal of trouble: "Bindoy," a well-meaning innocent in the big city, who obviously is confused by the skulduggery that goes on around him; and the indefatigable "Gorio," the jeepney driver, whose troubles with the cop on the corner are handled with such imagination that he is usually "one up" on the representative of authority; are daily comments on life in Manila and particularly on its political aspects. These strips satirize aspects of life in the city and poke fun at the authorities for their inability to solve the problems. There is a grim humor in "Gorio" being marooned disconsolately with his jeep on

[19] Author's study of the Manila press, March–April 1960.

top of a house during the flood because despite his predicament he is still trying to solicit passengers floating by on odd pieces of debris. Perhaps the biggest drawback is their obvious orientation to life in Manila, which makes them difficult for readers in the rural areas to appreciate. This type of humor allows Manilans to laugh at what otherwise appears as a matter of deep national shame. It also reflects the skepticism about politics that is necessary to the operation of most democratic systems. Such skepticism mitigates the tendency of those newly participating in politics to expect too much from the government and politicians at a time when the government cannot provide as much in the way of service as the population has come to expect or want.

The general "muckraking" quality of the Manila dailies seems to be discouraging young people from entering politics as a career and leads instead to a mass desire for positions in the bureaucracy. Young people indicate support for idealistic reform movements that search for "honest men" to run things or a "strong man" who could control the venalities of lesser men. At the same time, government is the main activity, and venal or not, politicians are the people who can provide careers in government offices. Through the newspapers, gossip, the general commitment to pakiusap as the way of getting things done, and the well-known success of this method, the young person comes to see that his best interest lies in getting a member of the government or a politician to support his bid for employment. The recruitment process is seen as knowing the right man and not as reward for meritorious achievement.

Although the performance of the political communication function in the Philippines is still oriented to the older face-to-face network, these have been effectively linked to a national structure of communication based on the mass media. Through this linkage, the Filipino is introduced to a whole range of new causal relationships, criteria for judging men and events, and ways of organizing life. His perception of these new styles is highly selective and is colored by his own cultural orientation. But the integration of the new channels into his old network of communication has given a traditional sanction to the content of the messages he receives. The impersonal and undifferentiated character of information transmitted through the mass media or through government administration could have little effect on the Filipino. His involvement in intensely human concerns and his sense of a highly personal society could not be penetrated by such a structure. Instead, a mediating structure with roots in the local community translates messages into a form relevant to the Filipino's view of the universe. The development of provincial urban centers, which provide daily examples of the rewards to be won by entrepreneurial skills, gives meaning and effect to the aspirations of the modernizing forces. As a result, the Filipino has developed a more or less continuous identification with a wider community and an awareness of its common characteristics and goals. But because modernizing ideas pass through traditional channels and are incorporated into traditional structure they have not created acceptance for the idea of a common public interest or a civic spirit.

The structure of communication also serves to relate individuals to the public authority and contributes significantly to the development of the polity. The picture of the political system that emerges through this mixed network is drawn in a behavioral perspective that the Filipino readily recognizes as the proper way to do business. The analysis of political events he receives is couched in a form analogous to the kind of manipulation and calculation that are his basic life style. The negotiation of the President with congressional leaders for support of a particular policy, for example, is presented as the same sort of negotiation that a Filipino engages in with municipal officials for a license to operate a fish corral. It does not surprise the Filipino that somewhat the same *quid pro quos* are involved. Because these bargaining situations are similar, the communication process has not managed to illustrate the specific functional requirements of a modern political system and has failed to engender an adequate set of criteria for judging political action. The dominance of the older attitudes toward dependence on others in an alliance system conditioned by kinship and social obligations has prevented complete transition to a more complex set of *quid pro*

quos that would hold politicians responsible for policy decisions more universal in scope. As we shall see in our analysis
of the interest articulation and aggregation functions, the relevance of traditional behavior to political action creates a
standard for judging political behavior on highly personal
criteria and makes it difficult to build organizations committed to broad policies of common interest.

Despite these limitations, the communication process is a
major element in the success of Philippine political development. It has expanded and intensified participation in the
political system and provides a context for the development
of attitudes more conducive to the modernization of other
political functions. The communication of a common Filipino
identity overcomes the division along class or linguistic lines
and ensures that the gap between urban and rural life will be
modified. By presenting the Filipino with a wider range of
opportunities, it breaks the hold of the traditional society and
mobilizes sentiment behind the expansion of political and
economic life. The performance of the communication function has ramifications for all the other functions of the political system. It has a major role to play in socialization and in
interest articulation, and it underlies major changes in political recruitment, broadening the universe from which political actors are chosen, and attracting people with motiva-
tions quite different from those of the old political elite. It
is to this process of recruitment that we must now turn.

CHAPTER X

Political Recruitment

B EYOND THE general process of political socialization, which communicates a sense of a shared political life to all members of the society, a more specific orientation is required for those who are inducted into political roles. This process of selecting, training, and inducting individuals to perform functions in the political system is crucial to development, for it encourages or inhibits the politician's capacity to bargain. The function of political recruitment may be so performed as to produce politicians actively committed to processing the demands of their constituents and working for the modernization of their system, or politicians whose sense of futility and fear of conflict is so great that they cannot act. In the Philippines, political recruitment has produced politicians imbued with a bargaining spirit and capable of accepting and accommodating conflict. This success has resulted from the retention of traditional elements that provide continuity and from the social similarity of the political elite, which eased the development of a common interest and predictability, producing coherence and stability among the politicians during the transitional period. There has been no open revolt against the traditional elite, yet a new, more businesslike, and much more democratic group of young modernizers now dominate the political scene. These are men who have come into politics largely by the old means and under the aegis of the social elite.

217

The Philippine political system has proved remarkably successful at controlling potential rebels and committing new groups and generations to the social control of the older group. The question arises of how society handles individuals and groups that seek to enter the system. If such newcomers demand too much, they will fail, and failing, turn to attempts to destroy the system. In any society, there is a set of relationships, a hierarchy of status and value manipulated by the ruling group to punish and reward its members. If the rewards are clearly available and no possibility of radical change in the *status quo* exists, the individual will seek to advance his interests and gain status within the system. If there is always a possibility of overthrow, then the need to work through the existing system disappears. Any loss of status would be unacceptable and attempts to overthrow the structure would be common. Furthermore, if the rewards are severely restricted and deviance is too strongly punished, dissatisfaction and alienation will soon create unmanageable tensions. The Philippines has not suffered from these problems.

As early as the Commonwealth period, when independence was already won and the need to unite for the sacred cause of nationalism was removed, there seemed no possibility of overthrowing the elite and there appeared none of the strains and divisions common to other newly independent countries. At the same time, the loss of status for deviance from the elite norm was not so great as to cause unbearable loss. Those who joined the Democrata party or other reform movements, for example, were treated gently and were easily reincorporated into the ruling group. It was assumed that upper-class educated men were interested in the same goals and shared the same values. The ruling group could not believe that those who appeared to be supporting radical causes were in earnest and could not be reformed. As a result, no serious split was allowed. Radical movements in the rural areas suffered from a lack of leadership and even more from the commitment of the Filipino tenant to his landlord and to the upper-class paternalistic attitudes. Social controls were acceptable enough throughout the society to provide the stability required.

Philippine politicians assume that men seek power and

status and will not willingly give up either. It is this assumption that underlies the sense of trust apparent in the political elite and also their sense of mistrust. Men are observed to be seeking something knowable, and one can assess with reasonable accuracy how far they will go and how much compromise can be expected. Power and status are acceptable values, and they inspire further agreement on the norms of conduct that govern their distribution.

The Philippine experience has some general implications for the process of political development in other new states. Economists and political scientists have repeatedly commented on the apathy and lack of commitment of politicians in the developing areas and their incapacity to mobilize their people for modernizing goals. The framework of representative government suggests, as in the Philippine case, that those performing political roles struggle constantly to improve their power position vis à vis others within a circumscribed set of limits, a crucial element of which is the requirement of electoral support. The demands made on the politician by his fellow officeholders and by the voters trap him into a clear role, which is passed on to each new generation. The new recruits acquire the same set of convergent expectations and the spirit of the game.[1] The masses of people as a court of final judgment establish limits on the use of power and give the politician a sense of security and the ability to act. The politician in a system of representative government is given a control over his fellows lacking in a country without popular elections or elections that can be manipulated easily. The politician is completely dependent not on the good will of his fellows but on that of his constituents. Any new group is a potential threat or support, and politicians attempt to woo them into their electoral coalition. The real value of the electoral process in the Philippines is that it makes bargaining necessary and ensures that new groups will be heard and their demands in some way accommodated. More than half

[1] Thomas Schelling, *The Strategy of Conflict* (Cambridge: Harvard University Press, 1960) p. 92. Schelling notes that the individual is "trapped in a particular role, or by another's role, because it is the only role that in the circumstances can be identified by the process of tacit consent."

a century of elections has provided the basis for an open and stable system.

The politician must, in achieving a political identity, acquire a sense that society will not abandon him, that he will be able to find an identity within it and live up to its expectations. A society distinctly out of order or in a state of prolonged disorganization cannot create the kind of person who can play the bargaining role. It must be a society clearly organized to give the individual a sense that he can operate within it and find some satisfaction, which becomes a sense of trust that the elite will not abandon him (inner world) to the voter (outer world). It is probably true, as other observers have noted, that politics provides excellent psychotherapy. Like love, it binds the individual into a system of relationships that gives him the freedom to act and to experiment in ways that otherwise would be frowned on. It allows him, in Erikson's words, to "work out his own inner conflicts on a grander scale." [2]

It is suggested that the kind of structure of human relations that exists in society is not so important as a general belief that such a structure does exist. Men can find through experience how it works and can derive from that experience some workable predictions.

The Philippine political elite has had a sense of camaraderie growing out of the close social and kinship ties that wove them together. Party divisions and open political struggles have not obscured compadre ties and have allowed politicians to be friends despite political differences. Now the performance of political recruitment is undergoing change. New elements are being incorporated into the system at a rate that precludes complete integration and new, more formal relationships must develop. The dynamism of the electoral process has undermined the elite's control of the recruitment process, and it remains to be seen whether or not the sense of trust and predictability is sufficient to meet the needs of the rapid modernization. There has been very little research on the so-

[2] Erik H. Erikson, *Childhood and Society* (New York: W. W. Norton and Co., 1950), and a seminar at Massachusetts Institute of Technology, fall, 1958.

cial backgrounds and means of entry of new people into the system. The generalizations we make here are highly subjective and can do little more than suggest the direction of change.

One further caveat is necessary. It is usual to characterize recruitment in transitional societies as based more on ascriptive than on achievement considerations. That is, status is bestowed by the society on the basis of kinship, class, and ethnic group rather than being achieved by the individual on the basis of his own merit. Further research in Western and non-Western societies may reveal that the opposite is true.[3] Almond has pointed out that both criteria are important in all societies but the difference is that the "performance criterion is less explicitly and generally applied in transitional societies."[4] It could be argued in the American case that even when ascriptive criteria largely determine (and limit) the universe from which recruitment to political roles takes place, performance criteria are ultimately applied, whereas in the Philippines, ascriptive considerations tend to dominate despite the individual's performance capacity. This tendency seems to be disappearing as the system develops. We shall here attempt to describe the pattern of subcultures and structures that regulates political recruitment in the Philippines to see what sort of expectations and performance result.

THE UNIVERSE OF POLITICAL RECRUITMENT

An emphasis on the skills of human relations extends to the political process. Such skills form the basis of political success. The politician generally has been an upper-class, well-educated (usually in law) person whose skills at social interaction and commanding the loyalties of men have provided

[3] Anthropologist Ralph Linton writes "all Societies rely mainly on their ascribed status to take care of the ordinary business of living. Most of the statuses which are open to achievement do not touch this business very deeply. The honored ones are extremely satisfying to individuals who achieve them, but many of them are no more vital to the ordinary functioning of the society than are honorary degrees or inclusion in *Who's Who* among ourselves." *The Study of Man* (New York: Appleton Century Crofts, 1936) p. 128.

[4] Almond and Coleman, *Politics of the Developing Areas,* p. 32.

him either with a measure of popular support that the national elite could not overlook in their calculations, or with
shrewdness enough at the skills necessary to bring him into
close relationship with a member of the elite who would back
him for political office. Combinations of both these considerations account for the recruitment to political roles. The most
significant characteristic of political recruitment in the Philippines has been the extent to which the process has been
controlled by a small group of men.

The elite's recognition early in the American occupation
that they were "in" on a good thing gave them an interest in
maintaining the stability of the system. They found that the
policies of the American occupation enabled them to take
over at once the leadership status they had demanded from
Spain. Nothing divided these men except the question of
who was to lead. The common interest was evident in the ease
with which factions coalesced after each such conflict. During the Commonwealth period, the elite under Quezon's leadership sought ways of consolidating their position in the face
of rising demands from peasant and working-class groups.

By the time the Philippines became independent in 1946,
the elite had developed a two-pronged technique for controlling recruitment to political roles. The demand for immediate independence was used successfully by the elite to obscure all other issues, and the Nacionalista program carefully
embodied all important issues, leaving the opposition to ha-
rangue against Quezon's dictatorship or the oligarchy but
unable to offer anything constructive as an alternative. Furthermore, since the Nacionalistas were clearly committed to
the economic *status quo,* they could command financial contributions from the economic interests, since these interests
were unlikely to support reform movements that would weaken
their position. Quezon himself argued that a minority party
was not necessary and Claro M. Recto, delegate to the constitutional convention and at one time Justice of the Philippine Supreme Court, who was to become the outstanding
Philippine nationalist of the postwar period, summed up the
situation in 1938:

The report that I am about to form and head an opposition party is preposterous, not to say ridiculous. To carry out this purpose, one need either be a knight errant of the chivalrous age or one who is embittered not against the government but against his own self having long entertained gloomy thoughts of self-destruction, and I do not choose to be either.[5]

In the pre-World War II period and even afterward, this double technique proved remarkably successful, but as we shall see, the pressures for change and the increased demands of the population on the political process have created a different situation in current Philippine political recruitment. But first it is necessary to keep in mind the requirements of political success.

Education and Profession. Few men have won political office without a college degree and many have held graduate degrees. The educational attainment of members of the Philippine Congress is probably the highest of any legislative body in the world. Nearly all have legal training and many have headed highly successful law firms. Of the twenty-four senators in the 1960 Congress, fourteen had law offices; two were important in the sugar industry; two were businessmen with varied commercial interests; one was a retired military man; one had been a movie idol; two had been recruited from administrative positions in the government; and the other was the late President Ramon Magsaysay's younger brother, who had served previously in the House. Complete information on the House is not available but again legal training and college degrees are usual, though a wider variety of commercial and professional interests exists and land is still the most obvious form of wealth.

The higher ranks of the civil service also require college degrees. An examination system controls entry into the competitive civil service and encourages young people who seek civil service jobs to seek degrees for the same reason. In the prewar period to pass such examinations and achieve first-

[5] As reported in *The Tribune*, May 31, 1938, cited by Ralston Hayden, *The Philippines*, p. 450.

class status in the civil service was respected, but this respect has disintegrated somewhat under the impact of politicizing. Political influence is the key to the operation of the civil service, which somewhat dampens efforts to restore respect for the administrative services of government and for those who hold such jobs. The socio-economic background of civil servants has always been more varied than that of politicians, and it becomes increasingly so. Whereas politicians have tended to come from the law schools of the better universities, particularly private universities; the administrators have come from the less respected schools or the University of the Philippines.

Dominant Subcultures. Beginning with Quezon and Osmeña, Philippine politicians have come from the mestizo families. Spanish-Filipinos, Chinese-Filipinos, and combinations of all three have dominated social, economic, and political life. Part of Ramon Magsaysay's popularity was undoubtedly due to his acceptance as a "Filipino." The mixture of races that have spread through the Philippines makes it highly doubtful that many pure Malayans exist, but a combination of dark skin and facial features has been accepted as "Filipino," as contrasted to the lighter skin and different facial features of the mestizo groups. But the dominance and acceptance of mestizo elite status has a long history. José Rizal, whom Filipinos point to as "the pride of the Malay race," counted among his ancestors Spanish and Chinese. Filipinos prefer light skin, tallness, and tall noses to their own indigenous dark skin, short stature, and flat noses. The inclusion of large numbers of people with the latter characteristics in economic and political roles may change this social preference. It is difficult to determine whether or not such preferences enter into voting behavior. But the hold that the mestizo elite had on power is disintegrating.

Upper-class status has been important to Philippine recruitment also, and has been related to the financial control of landed interests and the dominance of families with the ethnic characteristics noted above. But the criteria that determined class discriminations have changed. Forms of wealth other than land, commerce and industry for example, are growing in importance. Families who do not share the ethnic character of the old elite have risen to prominence and to political roles. Individuals with professional or semiprofessional occupations, who make up the middle class, have entered politics. People with peasant and urban working-class backgrounds have entered political life, often through provincial or city government, and then to the House of Representatives. Poor men still do not seek active political roles at the national level, but other aspects of the recruitment process often provide them with the opportunity to do so. Diosdado Macapagal, for example, is of Pampanga peasant heritage and is a poor boy who made good. He was enabled to do so by a local patron who supported him through school and on to the study of law in Manila. He holds doctorates in law and in economics, and by acquiring the requisite education he was able to enter politics.

Provincial government and the civil service also serve as fields of recruitment. Aspiring young men with higher education often return to their provinces and practice their profession, building a grass-roots organization as a base for achieving political office. Since, as we have seen, local political office depends in large part on the support of the national administration, the patron system is the main means for such men to gain party support and eventually a provincial governorship. Popular provincial governors often move on to congressional seats and in some cases to the Senate. Upper levels of the civil service also provide recruits. The next step for a bureau chief in the competitive civil service is a political appointment; many cabinet posts and other appointive political roles go to former civil servants. This position often leads to elective office.

Labor has been less than successful in providing recruits to political roles. Congressional candidates often seek labor support and some are known as labor candidates, but few have come directly from the labor movement. Secretaries of Labor have been oddly unsuccessful in seeking political office. In the 1963 elections, a trade-union leader ran unsuccessfully for mayor of Manila on the Nacionalista ticket.

The Catholic Church, because it has an important role in the Philippines, has been able to exercise its influence within the political parties and has backed certain candidates for public office. The *Iglesia ni Kristo,* the independent Catholic Church, is reported able to deliver the votes of its members to the candidate of its choice.

The military forces have been remarkably unpolitical, by Filipino standards. Disputes between high-ranking officers and commanders of the various services are commonly referred to the political system and the patrons of the officers concerned. Promotions are politically determined, as are assignments. Except for Senator Eulogio Balao, who was recruited to run for the Senate by Ramon Magsaysay, military men have not run for political office. Secretaries of National Defense have sometimes indicated an aspiration to use that post to repeat Magsaysay's success but have had no luck.

Women have for many years played active political roles in Philippine politics. They have served in both houses and in the cabinet. The job of Secretary of the Social Welfare Agency seems to be safely in female hands and has been used as a stepping stone to the Senate. Two women thus far have held the post and moved to the Senate on the basis of the reputation they gained, particularly from their tours of the countryside in time of natural disaster. A third occupant of the chair, a former congresswoman, was appointed to the post by Macapagal in 1961 after she lost her bid for the Senate. She ran successfully for the Senate in 1963. Women councillors, mayors, provincial board members, vice-governors, and even governors have been accepted with little evidence of social opposition.

Dominant Structures. Perhaps the most characteristic aspect of Philippine political recruitment is the patron–patronee system. Since the parties are loose coalitions put together for electoral purposes, the underlying basis of party organization becomes dominant in the recruitment process. This theme is characteristic of both political and administrative roles. A brief look at the process will illustrate the system.

Recruitment for the House differs in some respects from that for the Senate, and the factor of large numbers makes it more difficult to describe a common pattern. The most common method of recruitment in both cases is the protégé system. A young man bent on a political career will acquire a law degree and return to his home province to practice law, usually emphasizing relations with the rural people and providing them with free legal service. He will join forces with a local politician of some stature or one who has a good chance of success in national politics. He will build his fences among provincial politicians as well as among rural voters of the constituency he has selected. In time, he will run for provincial office, which will give him a political base among the voters (good public relations, as it is usually described) and a reputation for political skill among the local politicians. His road to a national political role will be either through support of a senator from his region or through direct support of the party machinery and the President. In any case, he needs the support of a political party, and to find a place on a party ticket he must have both national-level support and the backing of the provincial politicians. If he can secure such support and a place on the party ticket as a congressional candidate, he then utilizes the popularity he has built up and campaigns for himself and his patron.

Recruitment to the Senate differs largely because electoral success demands a national reputation. For the incumbent party, which has, as we have noted, a big advantage, the President is the single most important factor in the selection of senatorial candidates. For the party out of power much depends upon the leadership but slots on the ticket are somewhat more open. Incumbent senators have some claim on available seats but this claim is by no means always respected. Their claim will depend on their personal popularity with the electorate and on the condition of their local organizations. Candidates are chosen from the House, the cabinet, and other politically appointive posts. Here, as on the presidential ticket, regionalism is an important factor. The party ticket attempts to cover as many regions as possible and will select only one candidate from any one region, taking into account the regional background of incumbent members of the party. For the same reason, it is sometimes considered good politics to include a

woman. A reputation as a "fiscalizer," that is, a critic or investigator of graft in the Congress has proved valuable in acquiring a place on the ticket. Evidence of previous support
for the party has been most valuable with cabinet members.

Presidential and vice-presidential candidates are recruited
on much the same basis. Quezon and Osmeña, for example,
both had served in provincial offices before their election in
1907; from then on their control of party and governmental
influence determined their success. They themselves controlled recruitment throughout the prewar period. Roxas and
Quirino were both protégés of Quezon, moving into political
roles from administrative backgrounds. Garcia, who also enjoyed a reputation as a poet in his own Visayan dialect, had
been successively governor of Bohol, congressman, and senator
before being chosen to offset Magsaysay's Luzon support with
his own Visayan backing. Macapagal enjoyed a wide, though
perhaps not national, reputation as a fiscalizer in the House
and was chosen to run with Yulo in 1957, perhaps as much because of his peasant background (Yulo was a well-known
landlord) as for his support in the Ilocano areas.[6] The extent
of his electoral success in 1957, his personal efforts to gain
control of the Liberal Party and strengthen its organization,
as well as his four-year campaign, assured his candidacy in
1961. The dominance of the patron system at the lower levels
of recruitment extends also to the upper but takes on more
formal patterns. Popularity with the voters, always recognized
in regional and fiscalizing considerations, has come to mean
more in the selection process than it did previously. But entry
into the party list is controlled still by those with political
influence, and the party as a formal structure has less of a role
than one would expect.

Recruitment to the competitive civil service is also political
in nature and is the result of bargaining among politicians,
administrators, and the executive. Although the examination
requirement is upheld in most cases, the appointment and promotion system is often corrupted by redefining positions as

[6] According to one interviewee, Macapagal's position on the Liberal Party
ticket in 1957 resulted from the insistence of the Church hierarchy.

"technical" in nature or "temporary" so that they do not fall within the competitive categories.

> The approval of the annual budget by the Congress usually was the signal for the mad scramble to begin for the newly created positions in the various governmental bureaus and offices in the Philippines. Even before the fiscal year actually started, congressmen and senators began sending out their letters of recommendation, making telephone calls or personally accompanying their numerous recommendees to the different bureaus and offices where the new positions were to be found . . . . The competition for the new vacancies was a stiff one.[7]

The competitive civil service includes all positions that require appropriate examination and civil service eligibility. The noncompetitive positions declared by law to be unclassified are those which are policy-determining, primarily confidential, or highly technical in nature. The exempt service includes elected officials, members of the armed forces, and others. The total number of positions in the competitive civil service has been estimated at 300,000.

> Most administrative positions belong to the competitive service; whereas the majority of political positions belong to the noncompetitive service and are thus exempt from examination requirements.[8]

The above quotation, taken from a publication of the Philippine Institute of Public Administration, makes a distinction between political and administrative positions that is not at all clear in practice. Political considerations are dominant in the everyday operation of the administration and the administrator must engage in a lot of political bargaining in order to survive.

Below the top administrative level, the regional or line departments are competitive civil service positions. This is the

[7] Gregorio A. Francisco, Jr. and Raul P. de Guzman, *The "50-50 Agreement": A Political Administrative Case,* Occasional Papers, No. 3 (Manila: Institute of Public Administration, University of the Philippines, 1960) p. 3.

[8] Francisco and de Guzman, *The "50-50 Agreement,"* p. 3.

general structure of all government departments, the top commissioner and deputy being presidential appointees in the noncompetitive civil service. Top-level administrative jobs, noncompetitive in character, are often filled by persons from the competitive classification who have worked themselves up through the civil service to high rank.

Executive branch appointments are made, as they are in the United States, on the basis of political considerations. But in the Philippines the "political" role of the cabinet is expected to be far more direct. For example, shortly after the 1959 election the Nacionalista leaders demanded the resignation of cabinet members who came from provinces in which the party's official Senate or local candidates lost in the last polls.[9] These direct political demands on officials have the effect of creating ambivalence and confusion as to the functions of administrators and result in what appear to be serious conflicts of interest.

Senators and congressmen with strong regional voting populations behind them also are able to bargain effectively with the executive on the placement of their political protégés. The general manager of the National Marketing Corporation, for example, in 1960 was a protégé of Senator Primicias "who has a lot to say about politics in Pangasinan with its 450,000 voters." [10]

The appointment of cabinet and executive-branch secretaries and department heads is obviously a matter involving a great deal of bargaining. The appointee's position will always be dependent upon the political considerations that accounted for his appointment. He is therefore forced to seek a broader base of political support while in office and must use his influence and the resources of his office to build such support among politicians. In addition, the fact that he may be appointed as a political gambit may weaken the President's support for him and for the proposals and programs he favors in the bargaining between executive agencies. Thus, with the emphasis on power and political success, conflicts of interest are inevitable and administrators' roles are diffuse.

9 *The Manila Chronicle,* November 23, 1959.
10 *The Manila Times,* January 21, 1960.

Role System Performance. Multi-functionality and diffuseness also permeate political and competitive civil service roles. Bureau directors complain that they cannot control their subordinates who are protégés of congressmen.[11]

Filipinos identify not with the role and its requirements but with the structure through which they are recruited. Loyalty flows not to those in the same statuses and roles but to those whose exertions helped place one there. The demands of these loyalties constitute firm claims on the individual, claims that are often in conflict with the requirements of the role. Whatever pressures exist, for example, to imbed in the administrator's behavior a cognitive map, a set of values and expectations consistent with the formal requirements of his role, are displaced by the demands of loyalty which fit with the cognitive map he already possesses from experience with the society and the recruitment process. The claims on the individual's behavior imposed by the society in general are dominant over those of his political role. No distinction, for example, is made between the individual as family member and as politician. There is no difference in the expectations others have about what he will do and how he will do it.

Roles then are poorly defined, functions are diffuse, and there is little separation of function.

Changes in Recruitment Patterns. The disruptions of war and the creation of a whole new class of commercially oriented urban dwellers badly weakened the position of the land-based mestizo elite. Although that elite has maintained its control and has used its two techniques to maintain its leadership, some significant changes have taken place broadening the base of political participation and bringing new elements into political roles. These included the *nouveaux riches* who had built up substantial fortunes by commercial operations during the war and by exploiting the surplus materials and aid programs of the immediate postwar period. This group was unrestrained by the social controls of the prewar upper class and

[11] Egbert S. Wengert, "Some Thoughts on Executive Development in the Philippine Government," *Philippine Journal of Public Administration*, II (October 1958) pp. 348-362.

their economic position depended upon their ability to convert their operations into some more long-lived economic enterprise. The imposition of exchange and import controls
provided the impetus, and competition with the banking institutions for the scarce import allocations triggered an immense
system of graft and corruption that seeped into every corner of
Philippine government. Politicians used their political offices
openly for personal gain. Congressional law firms and executive personnel peddled influence.

This situation gave rise to several changes. The first was a
demand for an end to the graft and corruption centering in
the Manila middle class but rapidly spreading to the provincial middle class and down to the barrio level. Second was a
search for honest men for public office and a tendency to support young men who specialized in pointing out the graft and
corruption of older cohorts. The increase in communications
helped "the fiscalizer" to come into his own. A third aspect of
the situation was the discrediting of the old leadership and
the search for a new type. This search, if it can be called that,
had two elements. One, the rural-based demand for one of
their own that made the "common man" image an important
concomitant of Philippine politics and reached its epitome in
Ramon Magsaysay and in Diosdado Macapagal. The other,
the urban middle-class demand for intellectual leadership,
centered in Manila, with strong support from the provincial
professionals. Both demands merged in the Magsaysay campaign of 1953, but the coalition fell apart after his death and
only the most intense negotiation and highest of political skills
put it together again in 1961.

Recruitment into politics on the local level of young people
cognizant of rural problems has, in the past, been hampered
by the lack of real authority or power at that level. Politics at
the local level appealed to seekers of small rewards who were
content to be little more than hacks. Ambitious and talented
young people went to Manila to seek their political fortunes,
for there rewards are greater and the possibility of effective
action and effective political roles is open. Reformers and reform movements also tend to start at the top, at the national
level, for it is recognized as the center of power and activities

at the local level depend on the actions of the men at the top. But by the same token, starting at the top has required both money and political organization that can only be had within one or the other major party and through a political patron in the elite. By these means, the politically ambitious have been either forced to conform or effectively excluded from political roles. The extension of real authority to local government and attempts to decentralize open political roles to young people willing to work among the barrio people and to learn government and politics by working up the ladder and gaining popular support. These people, because they will have to work more closely with grass-roots opinion, may be expected to arrive on the national political scene with expectations and interests quite different from those of their political predecessors. If the plans for decentralization carry through, the widespread interest in local politics may bring about important changes in the character of political participation and behavior.

CHAPTER XI

Interest Articulation

IN THE PHILIPPINES, unlike other developing countries, the politician has created a predictable political arena in which a measure of trust allows him to act.[1] The Philippines is moving from a traditional system in which the body politic was organized and differentiated largely through such primary groups as the family, and interests were implicit rather than explicit, latent rather than manifest, and parochial rather than universal. The bargaining spirit of Philippine political culture is the motivating force in modernizing the interest articulation function. The function is performed by a mixture of modern associational types of interest groups and traditional social institutions. Demands enter the political arena as personal requests for special consideration on the basis of traditional social obligations, as organized preferences from economic and occupational groups who voluntarily associate themselves to promote and advance their interests, and as implicit or explicit expectations from essentially nonpolitical institutions such as the Church. The transitional character of Philippine politics is nowhere so obvious as in the complex mixture of channels through which the interests of the electorate reach the politician.

In modern democracies, the function of interest articula-

[1] For an example of the enervating quality of political life, when this ability to trust and bargain is missing, see the study of the Burmese politician in Pye, *Politics, Personality and Nation Building.*

tion is handled largely by broad-based interest groups formed for the purpose of advancing particular and explicit policy interests. Such groups are then aggregated into coalitions in support of particular candidates for electoral office. Politicians act as brokers, processing the demands of their constituents as expressed through these groups and attempting to advance and protect those interests in the realm of public policy. In this manner, the population is differentiated, organized, and represented in the policy-making process. But this is a highly complex set of relationships and is based on some fundamental assumptions about political behavior. The ability to handle such an organization requires a bargaining capacity and such a capacity is, in turn, a product of the way in which self-interest is expressed, the sense of common interest inherent in the polity, and the form and effectiveness of social controls. The political culture, the socialization process, and the form of political communication all contribute to or inhibit the sense of trust and predictability that underlies men's capacity to calculate the risks and costs of political action and to pursue their own interests in recognition and appreciation of the interests of others. Individuals must be willing to match their personal demands to those of others and to form groups that can organize and articulate demands on public policy to facilitate aggregation into even broader coalitions. Thus, they will adopt more universal than personal goals, carefully calculated to attract to their cause as broad a spectrum of other groups as possible. Politicians will then assess the relative weight of policy preferences in the body politic and will find means of accommodating conflicts that arise. One of the main tasks of the politician is to ascertain who wants what policy and how much. The politician is directed by the demands of the electorate and considers them legitimate claims to his attention. In short, a modern democratic system involves constant negotiation and calculation of interests on the part of all political actors; the articulation of interests must be performed in a manner conducive to bargaining.

In this chapter, we seek to demonstrate that new more explicit demands from the body politic are forcing a breakdown of the old hierarchical relationships and gross economic inequality. The small elite that controlled social, economic, and political life in the Philippines until relatively recently did not need complex forms of interest articulation. Political decisions were the product of the activities of a very limited number of people whose common status allowed implicit agreement. Interests did not have to be explicitly articulated since the elite's interests were well known and homogeneous. Now independence has brought a commitment to economic independence, impossible under the old economic system. Pressures for modernization and industrialization have developed, with new groups seeking economic policies more in line with the new requirements but in direct competition and conflict with the older interests. The significant fact of Philippine political development has been the capacity and willingness of the politicians to adapt to this new situation without resorting to bureaucratic or authoritarian means. Instead of turning to an economic development plan for direction, the Filipino politician has turned to the people and to the operation of a pragmatic political process. These new demands have been handled, not by bureaucratic planners as in other developing countries, but by politicians with a democratic bargaining spirit.

In India, for example, the administrator and economic planner have been dominant.[2] The government, under the aegis of Nehru's popularity, assumes that it is working for all the people and attempts, through planning and administration, to organize the population for specific goals, allowing for a somewhat neater operation but not preventing political demands from developing. The tensions that result from these demands cannot be accommodated within the planning framework. Politics in India is not a source of strength and national unity is but an obstacle to development. Impressed by the problems and needs of development, the government has refused to accommodate particular interests on grounds that it would in-

[2] Myron Weiner, *The Politics of Scarcity: Public Pressure and Political Response in India* (Chicago: University of Chicago Press, 1962). For a similar view of this phenomenon from a different perspective see Phyllis J. Rolnick, "Charity, Trusteeship and Social Change in India: A Study of Political Ideology," *World Politics*, XIV (April 1962) pp. 439-460.

terfere with development. The distrust of particular interests as impediments to rational planning alienates them from the political system and leaves them little option but to resort to apolitical or even violent means.

In the Philippines, on the other hand, the bargaining spirit of the political culture and the sense of trust and predictability of the politician has allowed the demands of economic and political development to converge. The acceptance of particular interests as legitimate and the willingness to accommodate them within the political arena commits these new groups to national goals. Though somewhat less neat and balanced than a development plan, this process has allowed the mobilization of national energies for development within a democratic context. In order to understand how this process has been achieved, we need to know more about the attitudes of the Philippine politician and how he has reacted to the emergence of interest groups.

THE POLITICIAN'S VIEW OF INTEREST ARTICULATION

In the process of democratic political development, the presence of skilled politicians is crucial. As we have already indicated, the Filipino politician has played a key role in the development of the political system. He accepts the needs of the people as a legitimate concern of politics and recognizes that his electoral success depends on how well he meets those needs.

In the traditional society, the landlord handled the particular demands of his tenants and the politicians, who were either landlords or their representatives, concentrated on articulating and advancing the interests of the landed economic elite. The landlord, who was in direct contact with the population, could, as the franchise expanded, control his tenants' votes by economic and social pressure. His paternalistic approach to the rural people served their needs in some measure, and it was assumed that by this means the people were represented in political life. But the landlord and his family began to desert the rural and provincial scene in favor of life in Manila and were no longer available to their tenants except on short visits during holidays. In many cases, hired managers with none of the paternalistic concern of the landed gentry took over. The wartime disruptions and the rise of an entrepreneurial group weakened the traditional organization of the countryside, and the downward economic mobility of many old provincial families only further intensified the vacuum in the rural areas. At the same time, the population was growing more aware of alternatives to the traditional way of life, and aspirations for change were vigorously pursued. The politician, who could no longer depend upon votes organized and controlled through traditional social and economic obligations, had to build a new electoral base. He stepped into the role of the landlord and the older social relationship was transferred to the political system but with an important change. The reciprocal nature of power relationships, always well recognized, underwent a major revision as the voters recognized the power of the vote. Because the older leadership had controlled the economic well-being of the tenant and also had lent money, they could use this economic pressure to ensure political conformity. But the politician's position depended on the vote, and it had to be won. This factor energized voter demands as they realized they had, in the vote, a form of power over the politician that they had not had over the landlord. The politician realized that he could operate without the landlord's economic power only if he found ways of meeting people's problems. Election campaigns changed from attempts to organize a majority around family, social, and economic ties to attempts to organize on the basis of direct contributions to the individual needs of the people. Politicians established a claim on peoples' votes by service.

In order to meet the requirements of his constituents, the politician needs the resources to provide them with public works projects, jobs, money, and innumerable favors of a personal nature. The search for the wherewithal to meet those requests and the resolution of the conflicts that inevitably arise as politicians compete for government resources occupies the major part of the Filipino politician's time, and it requires of him skill in bargaining, for which he is uniquely prepared by the nature of his society. Although a broader scope of conflict and a more formal political decision-making process is now necessary, some of the political skills and techniques developed in the older system are continued in the new. Politicians recognize that they have a common interest in the necessities of political success and seek ways of working out a system of distributing these resources that will free them of some of their present burdens. But, because they are all dependent upon popular support, which can only be gained by a service to the people, they can assess the motives and needs of other politicians and gauge their behavior accordingly. There is then a degree of predictability in political action that is crucial for bargaining.

Politicians recognize effective limits on their behavior and on that of their fellows. They are tied on the one hand to the executive, whose constitutional authority gives him control of the resources they need for election; on the other hand, they are tied to local political leaders who are in direct daily contact with voters. Political conflict in the Philippines tends to center on the competition for executive support and on control over municipal and provincial politics. The interest articulation function is performed within this open political competition, which gives rise to cynicism about politics and a feeling of loss of integrity on the part of politicians. In part, this attitude is a product of the unique pattern of rewards allowed public officeholders in the Philippines, and is also a product of the manner in which the interest articulation function is performed. The Filipino politician is caught in a dilemma. He realizes that the servicing of people's needs wins elections and is the ethos of a democratic system. On the other hand, he personally benefits from his success at this process in prestige and social position and economically. This dilemma is apparent in his view of the interest articulation function.

To an amazing degree, Filipino politicians believe that their positions on policy issues and legislation have nothing to do with electoral success.[3] They are convinced that people voted for them because of advantages in the form of patronage jobs, money, or other service provided by local leaders under the politician's direction. Their own personality, repu-

[3] This description of the politicians' views is based on the author's interviews with Philippine congressmen and senators during 1959-60.

tation, and good public relations are seen as helpful but seldom sufficient. To the legislators, the President, who controls the allocation of public works money and patronage, and the financial interests, which contribute to campaigns, are the two most important pressures in the legislative process. The interests of the masses are not, however, treated as insignificant or unimportant. Senators, for example, are particularly concerned about the amount of time they spend dealing directly with local politicians, groups, or individual citizens who demand special consideration. They simply do not consider that these dealings constitute a "pressure-group" type of influence on their actions. They seek to rid themselves of the burden of serving as an employment agency and adviser to individual constituents. They introduce and back legislation that would create more jobs, more rural credit, more help for increasing agricultural productivity, more barrio autonomy, in the hope of relieving the burden. Although their own perception of a modern political process does not include this sort of electoral demand as a proper way to do political business, they are in fact engaged in translating these direct, highly personal demands into explicit and universal policy programs. This process places a heavy responsibility on individual politicians, for little electoral support can be gained by legislative policies aimed at the rural masses. The majority of voters are, as yet, undifferentiated, unorganized, and highly personal in their orientation to politics. A handful of jobs on a short-term public works project will gain more votes than a legislative measure designed to provide jobs for a greater number of people. For the public works project can be directly related to a particular politician, but the results of the legislative measure bear a more subtle relationship. And very often, measures designed to meet the latent interests of the constituents are in conflict with the explicit and manifest demands of those who directly support political campaigns.

Another aspect of the politician's view of interest articulation is his ambivalence about pressure groups. Most congressmen deny that pressure groups exist. Some refer to sugar or tobacco blocs, said to be powerful groups with their own representatives in Congress. A few argue that they support the sugar interest because the industry is important to the nation's foreign exchange earnings. Congressmen and senators who are reputed to be members of particular blocs deny the association and assert that there is no organization. Among those groups recognized as politically oriented, business groups like the Chamber of Commerce are considered well organized and financially important and thus able to influence politicians and policy. Veterans' groups are recognized as politically important since they are national organizations with local branches all over the islands. Congressmen indicate that labor is potentially important, but they seem to believe that labor's demands are not reasonable and thus not influential. Church influence appears to be waning in the politician's view although no one can ignore the fact that the Philippines is overwhelmingly Catholic, and the hierarchy can reach the people through parish priests. This ambivalence about particular interests is less evident in practice. But the reality of the influence of these groups is hidden by their method of indicating their special policy preferences. To the politician, the most important means by which interest groups bring pressure on congressmen are extralegal in one sense. Such groups contribute to campaign expenses and hire the services of a legislator's law firm. The line between the requirements of pragmatic politics and outright influence peddling is very thin in the Filipino politician's view, and he considers that it is too often crossed. Many congressmen and senators have their own law firms and handle clients who regularly do business with government offices. During the years of the controlled economy, congressional law firms handled applications for foreign exchange, dollar import quotas, and customs and import questions. In this way, legislators came to understand the businessman's problems. But the appearance of an important senator in a government office as a lawyer representing a client did not obscure his senatorial role. Often the means used to protect clients were possible only because of the political role. Interest group activity was therefore touched with corruption, and congressmen themselves doubt that such activity can ever be free of a tinge of extralegal procedure.

In contrast to this form of personal relationship, there is a public forum type of pressure group operation in the Philippines. A congressman described the practice: "The common practice is that any businessman or group of businessmen sends petitions to the presiding officer or secretary of either house of Congress, and copies are provided each legislator. Or a lunch is organized to which the legislator is invited as guest speaker and in 'open forum' he is made to feel the pressure of opinion for or against a measure." This is a particularly useful technique for business groups. The one group whose existence the Filipino politician finds it difficult to admit is the Chinese. The activities of the Chinese Chamber of Commerce are swathed in mystery so far as the legislator is concerned. Chinese businessmen, individually, contribute heavily to political campaigns and consider that the funds they provide are a kind of bribe to protect them from the traditional anti-Chinese feeling of Filipinos. Organized by the Chinese Chamber of Commerce, they have tried to utilize more formal mechanisms of protection, but individual contacts between Chinese businessmen and Filipino politicians are still widespread. Other alien businessmen have also found this type of contact helpful. Filipino politicians recognize the economic role of Chinese business and financial interests but are unwilling to admit of contact with or influence by such groups.

In the Philippine politician's view, pressure groups are evil and illegitimate, for they represent demands that he use his public authority for private gain. He is on the one hand beset with demands for jobs and other services and must compromise with the executive to get them. On the other hand, financial interests that provide him with campaign funds make explicit demands that he use his influence in their behalf. He is not sure that the compromises he makes are necessary to his role as a politician, but he knows that they are in his personal interest. This dilemma is destructive of the politician's sense of trust in himself and his fellows. It lends a strong element of mistrust to political bargaining and is a major threat to the further development of the Philippine political system. Its solution depends to a large degree on the further development of interest group structures to handle this function. We need to look at the structures that now exist before we see how the present development is likely to continue, and what effect this will have on the politician.

STRUCTURES THROUGH WHICH
INTERESTS ARE ARTICULATED

Interest groups organized for specific purposes abound in the Philippines but most often the bonds that unite members, the attitudes toward leadership and the Filipino emphasis on personal loyalties, weaken the unity, continuity, and purpose of the group. Before we turn to a detailed description of the kinds of structures performing the interest articulation function in the Philippines, we need to understand how the traditional social process influences the organization of the electorate.

Philippine patterns of organization are reflections of the pervasive influence of the family system. Because family ties were the basis of social and economic organization, other community ties remained weak and poorly developed. Instead of moving to organize himself and other citizens with common interests for a specific purpose, the Filipino relies upon highly personal obligations and loyalties built into a system of alliances. The purpose of these alliances and the demands made through them are general, latent, and implicit. This framework of action does not fit well with the concept of voluntary associations of numbers of people organized for specific purposes. The Filipino acts as an individual or through his family ties and does not recognize the existence of common interest or the effectiveness of organization and numbers. Thus this traditional system integrated individuals, not groups, into the political system by means of highly personal demands.

The development of associational groups is further inhibited by the expectations generated by the traditional social process. As one would expect, the Filipino does not accept the need for cooperation among the membership but rather expects that the leader, who gains prestige from his position and whose energy created the group, will bear the brunt of financial and organizational responsibility. The support of the membership is sporadic and halfhearted. As a result, organizations are formed with great energy but disappear rapidly.

These inhibitions to organization are being overcome in the urban areas but are still an obstacle to organization in the rural areas. The activities of community development planners and the interaction of modern ideas with traditional social forms have gone far to revise this system. Again the political system, which has developed an integrated polity largely through these individualistic mechanisms, is providing the impetus to change. Experience with a political bargaining process which provides direct rewards is encouraging new forms of political organization.

In urban areas, organized associational groups are already dominant. Urban people must interact with strangers; they find themselves forced to play economic and other roles that demand behavior quite different from the old life. Even the fiesta committees in urban neighborhoods must rely on formal techniques, as it was not necessary to do in the rural areas where everyone knew everyone else, and families had historical ties and social status of long duration. As a result, organization is more important and reliance on the kin group less effective. Associational interest groups have developed at a rapid rate. Some serve mainly a social function, but others attempt to organize members for direct action on neighborhood needs, occupational advancement, or commercial advantage. Still the heavy responsibility and weight of action falls on the leadership. Filipinos seem loath to support organizations with financial contributions and expect, as in the rural fiesta committee, that the leader will provide the funds. In more formal organizations, such as labor unions and business groups, a professional staff operates under the direction of an elected leader. The membership pays little attention to the details of the operation. Organization is weak and often funds are solicited in a manner not befitting the group's ends.

Interest groups operate directly in the political system, contributing funds to campaigns, backing candidates recruited from their own ranks, and hiring congressional law firms to handle their legal business. Relations between interest groups and administrative bureaus, which are concerned with the group's policy needs, are very close. Interest groups attempt to place members of their own organizations in administrative posts essential to their operation. Much of this development has been nullified by the tendency of individual members to utilize their own personal relations to advance their interests, to the detriment of the group.

But the fact is that these inhibitory behaviors are being transformed by the objective requirements of the developing system. The bargaining spirit has encouraged and has integrated a wide variety of interests to make demands on the political system. Competition among them is acute and cannot be solved by individual negotiations. The operation of the political system reveals that some patterns and styles of interest articulation are more effective than others, and the electorate is learning to match its behavior to the requirements of the system. The effectiveness of group influence on the political system has been well demonstrated, which is further encouraging an already substantial group differentiation.

Interest Articulation in a Mixed System. The Philippine political system is in transition. This condition is evident in the mixed character of means by which interests are articulated. Perhaps a few examples of recent attempts to influence policy will give the reader a sense of the rich variety of institutional, associational, and traditional means by which the interests of the electorate are translated into policy demands.

In a recent session of Congress, the House Appropriations Committee slashed 800 million pesos from the President's 1.9 billion pesos budget. This cut was reported to be a direct attempt to get the executive branch to honor their requests for a share of the 8,000 to 10,000 new jobs created under the budget.[4] In the same session, the Filipino rice and corn millers, traders, and planters circulated a petition in both houses and publicly urged an increase in government assistance to them from 100 to 350 million pesos.[5] A strike among waterfront workers was declared illegal by the Secretary of Finance, who argued that the waterfront and customs was a governmental enterprise and workers could not, therefore, strike. But more

[4] "Inside Congress," *Philippines Free Press*, March 23, 1963.
[5] "On the Economic Side," *Philippines Free Press*, March 23, 1963.

than one million Filipino workers planned to walk out on all but vital jobs in sympathy for the waterfront workers' position. Only the last-minute exertions of the President prevented the nationwide strike.[6] The Philippine Federation of Christian Churches, representing the major Protestant denominations in the country, made public their strong opposition to a bill granting a franchise to gambling casinos in Pasay City and elsewhere.[7] The Philippine Government Employees Association (PGEA) began a telegram campaign to agitate for a Christmas bonus. Government employees throughout the islands wired the President asking him to change his mind and grant the bonus which he had previously decided against.[8] The Catholic Women's League declared all-out war on motels, calling them fronts for prostitution, pressuring Manila and suburban city officials to investigate the motels.[9] The Philippine Chamber of Industries and Philippine Lumber Producers' Association publicly expressed optimism and support for the decontrol program of the Macapagal administration, saying it had opened a new era to business. The Philippine Automotive Association was not so optimistic and refused to predict the long-range effects. The Nacionalista party leadership declared they would attack the Liberal administration for packing government offices with Pampanguenos, provincemates of the President. And a striking union member picketing his place of employment laid his placard down to run across the street to get his "boss" some cigarettes.

This series of incidents is meant to illustrate the penetration of new styles of interest articulation into older modes based on primary group membership. It shows also the multi-functional character of various structures in the society. Legislators become defenders of interests, bureaucrats act like politicians, labor unions perform political recruitment functions, the Church plays an important role in the economy and among the polity, and the Filipino participates in politics through a wide variety of institutions. Associational interest groups are

[6] *Philippines Free Press,* May 18, 1963.
[7] *Ibid.,* May 18, 1963.
[8] *Ibid.,* December 15, 1962.
[9] *Ibid.*

playing an increasingly important role as the political system becomes dominant over the economic system. They serve a socialization purpose, imbuing their members with new values and modes of behavior; they promote new norms and establish criteria of expectation about political roles by granting status and prestige.

In such a milieu, the dominant role of the politician is clear. It is he who must seek to weigh and understand the interests involved in his electoral success. He cannot totally operate as a representative of a selected group of interests, bargaining with his fellows to protect and enhance those interests. In order to understand his role, we must look more closely at the three types of structure through which interests are articulated: traditional, institutional, and associational.

Traditional Structures. Undoubtedly the most important structure for organizing electoral interests is the kinship system and the network of alliances that is built around family and social obligations. But the significant fact for Philippine political development has been the extent to which these structures have been incorporated into and penetrated by the political system. This integration cannot help but change the character of the older structures. The political activities of a family, for example, will be determined by the fact that they have been tenants on the land of another family or have received loans and other aid from that family over the years. If a member of the family to which they are indebted runs for political office, it is obligatory for them to support him, just as kinship ties, however remote, create an obligation of political support. But these patterns are breaking down. Landed families complain that their tenants do not vote as they are told, and relatives often find themselves on opposite sides of local and national political struggles. More direct means of organization, in the form of patronage and pork barrel considerations, now weaken the older pattern. But the effect is the same: a personal reciprocal claim is established that has no direct relationship to specific governmental policies.

Other traditional non-associational structures include social classes. The upper socio-economic group has direct contact with political officeholders. Similar status implies common interest and allows for direct personal claims. Interests channeled through this type of contact are often diffuse and are communicated by the implicit mores of the group. This situation is also changing as the elite's loss of absolute control of the recruitment process has allowed men from different social and economic backgrounds to hold political office. In many cases, these new politicians are not acceptable to the social elite, and the direct contact of the past is being replaced by other mechanisms. Class interests now must be articulated more explicitly on specific policies. As a result, interests that used to be taken for granted must be organized and must seek to influence political officeholders in more impersonal ways. Furthermore, the assumption of control by landed interests has been seriously challenged by new industrial groups whose policy interests are radically different. Many of the older elite have become the new entrepreneurs, and the social prestige of industry is now equivalent to that of landholding. But the competitive quality of this new situation disallows the older personal relationship between social elite and politician as a structure for interest articulation.

Institutional Interest Groups. A striking feature of Philippine political development in comparison with other developing nations is the lack of conflict between institutional groups such as the military or bureaucracy and politicians. These institutions are completely subordinate to the political system.

Institutional interest groups occur within organizations such as armies, bureaucracies, and churches that perform other social or political functions. Either as corporate bodies or through subgroups within the body, they "may articulate their own interests or represent the interests of groups within the society." [10] In other developing systems, officer cliques, religious sects, ideological groups in the bureaucracy, etc. often play a major role. A high incidence of this type of interest articulation obscures the functional differentiation re-

[10] Almond and Coleman, *The Politics of the Developing Areas,* p. 35.

quired and prevents the development of explicit and integrated objective roles.

In the Philippines, the military has operated simply as the extension of the executive. The military forces are completely subordinated to the civilian interests. Promotions are made on the basis of political obligation and loyalties and military men, like bureaucrats, seek political patrons to ensure their career and enhance their status. Officer cliques within the army do form and open disputes often break out between leaders of various branches of the armed services. But the dispute and its outcome are dependent upon the political influence of the participants. This same pattern of penetration and subordination appears in other establishments, among them the two most important, the Roman Catholic Church and the bureaucracy.

The Church. The Catholic Church in the Philippines, since the beginning of the Spanish occupation, has been intimately associated with the governing apparatus. The religious orders were the medium of conquest and organization of the archipelago into a territorial unit, and Catholicism served as the unifying ideology, giving the native Filipinos a common cultural orientation. In a negative sense, the excesses of the religious orders further unified the Filipinos in a demand for reforms and relief from their oppression. American theory on the separation of church and state combined with Filipino fear of resurgence of the friar situation to ensure a constitutional separation. But such distinctions are necessarily limited in a country 82 per cent Catholic, and the role of the Catholic Church in politics has remained of major significance.

The Catholic Church has been successful in protecting its interests with respect to such church policies as divorce and birth control. But it has also found its viewpoint a matter of dispute on issues not distinctly part of Catholic dogma, and, in such cases, it has had to accept less than the ideal.

The Church's continued supremacy is guaranteed not only by its strength in the population but also by its near monopoly of the best private schools (over 600). The *conventos* and

private elementary and high schools in the provincial capitols
are almost exclusively Catholic schools. Even at the state university, the University of the Philippines, the strongest, most
active student organization has generally been the Student
Catholic Action (UPSCA). Other groups such as the Legion
of Mary, the Knights of Columbus, and the Daughters of Isabela serve to articulate and promote policies of the Catholic
Church. But the increasingly associational character of politics
in the Philippines has forced the Catholic Church to rely on
professional and occupational interest groups, for example
the Catholic Lawyers Guild, the Federation of Free Farmers,
the Federation of Free Workers, and the Catholic Women's
League. In addition, the Church has supported candidates for
office, and certain legislators are regarded as their representatives. The Progressive party and Grand Alliance organizations, for example, were strongly influenced by the Jesuit organizations and were led by Ateneo graduates. But the direct
influence of the Church is on the wane and is subject to attack
as simply one more of a number of interests that must be considered.

The late Senator Claro Recto had been an outspoken critic
of the Church's political role and accused the Catholic hierarchy of actively intervening against him in the 1955 campaign. Cardinal Santos publicly denied this charge, indicating
the Church's concern for popular opinion. Other politicians have voiced similar criticisms of Church interference in
elections and the political role of the parish priest. But few
make such charges publicly.[11] Instead, candidates make a point
of attending Mass and showing their devotion, particularly
during campaigns.

In addition to organized interest groups and supporters in
the legislature, the Church takes public positions on various
issues. These positions are made known through the hierarchy,
published in the newspapers, and channeled through parish
priests. In February 1960, for example, the Church declared
its policy on nationalism and "Filipino First." The Nacionalista campaign of 1959 had attempted to organize all nationalist groups in support of its candidates and a somewhat

[11] Author's interviews.

mysterious organization known as the National Progress Movement had established offices in provincial areas and distributed a document known as the "Nationalist Manifesto," which was virulently anti-American and anti-Church. The Church response was a carefully spelled-out version of Filipino nationalism that was anti-Communist and anti-NPM.

The Church maintains its opposition to birth control and argues that population pressures can be accommodated by opening up public lands and increasing productivity. But pressures for some means of limiting the population have grown stronger since the 1960 census figures revealed that the population was growing at a rate of 3.2 per cent annually. In common with the rest of the Catholic world, the Filipinos and their religious leaders are being forced to rethink their position on this matter. The Church has also led the fight against any attempt to pass a divorce law or to nationalize or exercise state control over the private schools. Censorship of movies and publications has been carried out under Church pressure, but here again the Church position is weakening.

In short, the Church has been a major force supporting the *status quo* but now finds it necessary to move with the times. It is essentially a conservative organization whose leaders have been recruited from the landed elite. The Jesuits have led the change, particularly in the field of labor and trade union organization. In the postwar surge of union organization, leftist leadership was obvious and dominant, and the unions were in sympathy with, if they did not actively support, the Huks. It was clear to some enlightened priests in rural parishes or in the intellectual centers of Manila that the Filipino, ordinarily the most peaceful of men, was not satisfied with his lot and that the only available leadership of that discontent were Socialists, Communists, or simply racketeers. The Bell Report of 1950 and the American aid missions gave impetus to the search for some means to bring the working class and peasants into a harmonious relationship with the government, to find expression for their demands in other than violence, and to find leaders who would accept democratic procedures and serve the interests of their membership. The Jesuit role in the labor movement will be discussed in the context of the trade-union groups, but it is important here, for it pressured the Catholic Church into recognizing that the *status quo* was not good enough. And, in company with the growing nationalism and pragmatism of Filipino society, the Jesuit activity forced the Church to find new methods of exercising its influence — methods more in line with the requirements of a bargaining process. It is becoming one of many groups that must compete for influence.

The Bureaucracy. The bureaucracy suffers from much the same problem as labor in the Philippines: too many people seeking too few jobs and an emphasis on the traditional methods of operation rather than the requirements of the role.

Perhaps the most obvious weakness of the Philippine bureaucracy is that of functional considerations. The Filipino's tendency to see the power aspect in all relationships inhibits the development of functional roles. In a government bureau, power, not function, is the determining criterion. And power is determined by connections; that is, by the relationship of the individual to political officeholders. One reads of clerks or collectors or even drivers who never go to an office but collect salaries, who are transferred and yet refuse to leave, who cannot be fired or removed because they are "protected."

As interest articulators, the bureaucrats serve as spokesmen for the special interests of their bureau's programs. Thus, the Secretary of Labor becomes a spokesman for labor's interests within the cabinet and along with bureau chiefs presents his views publicly on legislative and executive matters. The Bureau of Animal Industry takes every opportunity to make clear the role of better animal breeding and production in the national interest. In a more direct political fashion, bureau chiefs "lobby" directly in legislative committee sessions and defend their budgets and programs by trading available job openings for legislative support. Organizations such as the National Association of Government Public Relations Officers serve as professional associations for the bureaucracy. Another source of the blurring of function is the fact that the civil service is a recruiting ground for politicians. Such men as Senator Lorenzo Tañada, who became a senator after distinguishing himself and winning a national reputation as Solicitor General, and Ambrosio Padilla, who held the same post and later ran for the Senate, and others, such as Senators Alejandro Almendras, Gil Puyat, Oscar Ledesma, rose from political appointive posts. For women, the best political position has been the Social Welfare Administration, with whose nationwide disaster and relief activities Geronima Pecson and then Pacita Madrigal Gonzales achieved their Senate seats.

Senators and congressmen with strong regional voting populations behind them are solicited by bureau chiefs as defenders and helpmates. For such men can bargain effectively with the executive for placement of their protégés and can also protect the bureau's budget in the legislature.

A major part of the administrator's time is taken up with dealings with Congress and protecting his department from legislative threats. He must maintain good relations with the President, the cabinet secretary of his department, and others above him in the hierarchy. But to get his programs and budgets through the Congress, he needs the protection and support of key congressmen on the appropriations committee and other committees dealing with the program. The administrator trades jobs and services in the congressman's or senator's district for support for his programs. He thus performs an interest articulation function, soliciting support for his programs and his use of the public resources.

The bureaucracy, like the Church, has relied on traditional Filipino authority and obligation patterns for articulation of their interests. Very conscious of status, they have an interest in restoring the prestige of the civil service and its efficiency. But, at the same time, the intensely personal and particular character of recruitment and promotion have weakened attempts to promote a genuine merit system. But these types of bureaucratic behavior are being transformed by the requirements of the developing system. The private sector does not now provide sufficient opportunities for employment; until it does, the demand for bureaucratic jobs will far exceed the supply of trained and adequate personnel. As the private sector develops, and it is already beginning to do so, it will draw off the best young people and will provide competition to the government as an employer. A more reasonable balance between jobs available and people qualified for them will make possible a more professional and more objective personnel policy. It remains to be seen whether the rewards and prestige of an efficient civil service will be sufficiently appreciated to encourage young people to continue to seek government service once other alternatives exist.

Associational Interest Groups. As we have already pointed out, many associations have been formed in the Philippines for a wide variety of purposes. They represent voluntary and deliberate commitments of people to group activity. Although the Filipino idea of leadership and organization inhibits their development somewhat, the requirements of the political system are encouraging further differentiation and organization. In modern systems, such groups inject specific universal demands for public policy into the political arena, but in the transitional Philippine system, their demands have been neither so specific nor so universal. However, the organization of specific interest groups has gone far to simplify the problem of the politician in selecting the interests he must respond to. In this section, we shall concentrate on the three most important economic interests in the Philippines (business and industry, labor, and the agricultural export industries) and the character of their organizational attempts.

Business and Industrial Groups. Business groups in the Philippines are patterned after those in the United States. The Philippine Chamber of Commerce was organized nearly sixty years ago by Philippine and foreign businessmen in Manila. American businessmen played a major role in the organization in the past, but it is now a Filipino organization of about 600 entrepreneurs engaged in commerce and industry. It cooperates with other business groups in holding annual conventions of Philippine businessmen to discuss policy and issue statements of their policy goals. The National Convention of Manufacturers and Producers of the Philippines is sponsored by the Chamber of Industries of the Philippines (CIP). The CIP was organized in 1950 and has grown to include most major industrial establishments in the Philippines. During 1960, CIP members employed 273,760 persons and produced goods with an aggregate value of 1.8 billion pesos. They contributed 15 per cent of the national income, with wages of 358 million pesos and taxes of 302.9 million pesos. The Chamber's policy interests were revealed by the President of the organization in his inauguration speech in 1961.[12] He said the failure of Congress to pass necessary economic measures to protect Philippine industries was disastrous. Among these measures were the omnibus tariff bill, the repeal of the barter law, a sound foreign investment law, creation of an industrial licensing board, recognition of a selective export tax, and the institution of dynamic credit policies that would help rather than hinder industrialization. The CIP also objected strongly to the marketing policy of the National Marketing Association, which they felt did not support domestic industries. The Chamber wanted the NMA to distribute Philippine-made goods through their local outlets.

These business and industrial groups rely on the financial support they give to party treasuries to gain support for their policy goals. But in direct individual firm to government relationships, businessmen rely on such methods as retaining a congressional law firm and relying on personal and social friendship with legislators. In dealing directly with government agencies, the businessman uses the direct services of a lawyer, who also happens to be a senator or congressman, and additional Christmas presents from time to time. Under the exchange and import controls of the fifties, this type of behavior became more pronounced. But it generated dissatisfaction on the part of those excluded from influence and disgust on the part of those who had to deal with a system that was neither rational nor efficient. The decontrol of the economy engineered by the Macapagal administration created a different atmosphere for businessmen to work in but did not entirely overcome the more traditional and personal types of interest articulation.

At present, and for some time to come, businessmen who

[12] "On the Economic Side," *Philippines Free Press*, November 11, 1961, p. 14.

pay the campaign bills will have an inordinate influence of a particular and personal character simply because of their control of a vital resource of electoral success. Since electorate interests are not made explicit, political leaders are able to, perhaps even forced to argue that business and commercial interests must dominate. It is obvious also that the Philippine manufacturer has been encouraged by controls to produce for the domestic market. His demand for import tariffs to protect him from more prestigeful American goods and cheaper Japanese and Hong Kong goods can only partially relieve his problems. The as yet untapped mass market of the Philippines can only be effective if cash income rises. In the Philippines as elsewhere, it is the trade union movement that is leading the fight to open that market.

Labor. The development of a united labor movement in the Philippines, which could function as an organization and channel for political action, has been hampered by several aspects of the Philippine situation. In the first place, concentration on the production of agricultural crops, with major capital investment in land and employees organized in line with the traditional paternal attitudes of landlord–tenant relationships, has been an impediment. This situation gave traditional employer–employee relationships the character of a social value and a religious order, preventing the development of a legal structure and an objective criterion wherein rights could be protected and enhanced. The postwar political evolution, which put the industrial elite in a stronger position and which has developed a pattern of objective commercial standards, has been slow and is only now beginning to have an effect on the labor union movement.

Second, the Filipino has come to see government as the supreme landlord, who is expected to handle all problems. This tendency to go to the government for help has tied labor directly to government and has given an unconscionable amount of control over trade unions to the Department of Labor. Government intervention to solve conflict and settle strikes has prevented the development of real labor–management negotiations and relations. It has also encouraged the development of union legalism; that is, leadership by lawyers and a concern with legalistic, not organizational activities.

Third, the historical circumstances of labor's development have weakened the movement. The Philippine labor movement found its ideology in the welfare theories of socialism and the intervention of government on the side of the working man. In its early organization, it became part of the Socialist movement and its earliest leaders tended toward left-wing and Communist ideas and ideology. But Philippine labor came late to the field, and by the time organization was advanced enough to be significant, Communism and even Socialism had been repudiated in the West, and Philippine labor leaders suffered under an opprobrium that was heightened by the hostility of the Church in a Catholic country. Filipino experience with a land-based economy and the American ideology gave them a strong grounding in private enterprise and has made them unique among the emerging states of Southeast Asia in their antipathy to Socialism.

The first organized trade union activity began among printers at the time of the revolution and continued under the leadership of Isobelo de los Reyes until in 1902 the American regime crushed a strike and imprisoned the leaders of the movement. Through the first three decades of the twentieth century, the labor movement grew, particularly in Central Luzon, under the impetus of Pedro Abad Santos' Socialist organization and the budding Communist movement. In their first direct political action they formed part of a popular front under Juan Sumulong in the thirties. But organization was hampered by government antipathy, and labor continued to channel its demands through left-wing groups, who operated outside legal channels. The Commonwealth government established a Court of Industrial Relations in 1936 to handle labor disputes. Compulsory arbitration was required when the dispute was certified by the President to be adversely affecting a vital industry. Although this legislation recognized the right of labor to organize and the need for protection of employees' rights, it tied labor organization to the government and destroyed its independence.

In the postwar period, left-wing influence was still dominant, and the creation of the Congress of Labor Organizations (CLO) in 1948 posed the threat of a strong federation of labor that would support the growing Huk movement. In 1951, the government denounced the CLO leadership as Communist and disbanded the organization. The affiliates organized themselves into smaller federations and have since sought to re-unify the whole movement under a broad confederation.

A series of important legislative measures have given impetus to the trade union movement. A Minimum Wage Law and a Workmen's Compensation law, adopted in the early fifties, gave government support to labor's interests. The Industrial Peace Act of 1953 (Magna Charta of Labor) abolished compulsory arbitration and encouraged free collective bargaining.[13] The number of unions grew from 836 with 151,-547 members to an estimated 3,500 unions with a total membership of 476,856 in seven years. Several attempts at unity seemed successful but fell apart at the last moment. In May, 1963, the two biggest confederations, the Philippine Trade Union Council (PTUC) and the *Katipunang Manggagawang Pilipino* (KMP), merged, but whether they will be able to work out their conflicting interpretations and ambitions remains to be seen. The new confederation represents 700,000 members organized in more than 2,500 registered trade unions.

Labor union leadership in the Philippines leaves much to be desired. The compulsory arbitration of the Court of Industrial Relations, in the early fifties, gave rise to a group of labor lawyers who organized unions to advance their own careers, which were spent, for the most part, in the courts.[14]

---

[13] R. A. 875, June 17, 1953. For a history of the union movement see David Wurfel, "Trade Union Development and Labor Relations Policy in the Philippines," *Industrial and Labor Relations Review*, 12 (July 1959) pp. 582-608 and Flerida Ruth Pineda, "Unity is Philippine Labor's Outstanding Problem," *The Manila Times*, April 30, 1960. Miss Pineda kindly allowed the author to read her manuscript on Philippine labor and its unity attempts. For an interesting example of labor attitudes and the reaction of the government elite to the movement see *Evangelista v. Earnshaw*, Supreme Court of the Philippines, No. 36453, September 28, 1932.

[14] One lawyer and trade union president told the author that "lawyers traditionally collected fifty per cent of the settlement over and above the retainer fee which is something else." Another study reported that lawyers

The Magna Charta of Labor did little to redirect labor from legal solutions. As one study points out, "the difficulty is not the employment of lawyers, per se, but it is the attempt to induce legal solutions where others could do much better." [15] Those labor leaders who were not lawyers or politically ambitious were often simply racketeers. The waterfront unions were, according to a Labor Department investigation in 1955, merely façades for labor contractors. The department tried to educate unions, contractors, and companies in the evils of such a situation, but the powers of the contractors were too great.[16] A Labor Education Center has been set up at the University of the Philippines to train leaders and encourage the development of a free trade union movement that would operate through legitimate means. Another major influence has been the Federation of Free Workers, established as a counterattack on the leftist and racketeering unions that were dominant during the postwar period. Under the driving energy of Father Walter Hogan and the Jesuits of Ateneo de Manila, they have sought to replace the company unions and racketeering on the waterfront with responsible organizations that would protect and advance their membership's interests.

Major achievements have been the result, thus far, not of labor pressure but rather a host of other factors such as American pressure, industrial versus landed interests in the political system, and the Jesuits. The political effect of labor has been latent rather than manifest.

Despite the weaknesses pointed out here, organized labor has become a force to be reckoned with in national policy making. The activities of unions serve to articulate the interests of the working class in national policy decisions. Organization of a "labor vote" is still a long way off despite attempts such as those of the Labor Coordinating Committee for Polit-

---

take a cut of 20 per cent of the amount bargained from management. See H. D. Woods, *Report on Philippine Labour Management Relations* (Geneva: ILO, 1958) p. 85.

[15] *Summary of Labor Situation in the Philippines* (ICA: Office of Labour Affairs, 1956).

[16] Wurfel, "Trade Union Development and Labor Relations Policy," p. 599 and author's interviews with labor leaders.

ical Action, organized by the National Labor Union in the 1961 campaign, and the short-lived labor party (*Lapiang Manggagawa*) in 1963. Labor leaders, themselves, feel their main emphasis must be on strong unions and collective bargaining until the Filipino worker realizes the advantages to be gained from collective action. Union leaders rally support for candidates they feel are sympathetic to their cause, but the deep division in the labor movement and the personal ambitions of leaders weaken the effect of their efforts. A few labor leaders have been successful in achieving local and even national office.

The labor movement now includes about 3,000 unions with an estimated membership of one million. But this number must be compared with an expanding labor force, which reached 10.2 million in 1960 and is expected to "increase at the average rate of 360 thousand each year for the next five years." [17] President Macapagal, like his predecessors, had indicated the problem of finding employment for this rapidly expanding group. In his "State of the Nation" address, he proposed a target of a 6 per cent per annum increase in gross national product over the four-year period to create 330,000 to 360,000 jobs.[18] This problem is the major one with which Philippine labor must deal. Union bargaining positions are hurt by the backlog of unemployed and unorganized workers. Although labor representatives sit on government planning commissions and are given opportunities to present their case to congressional committees, Philippine labor has not yet articulated its broader interests in the realm of economic development. Instead, they have concentrated on protecting free labor unions from frequent attempts at nationalization, extending existing labor rights such as collective bargaining and minimum wage laws, protecting employees in government corporations, and strengthening government recognition of

[17] Bernardo Ople, "Is There a Labor Vote?" *Sunday Times Magazine,* November 5, 1961. See also *Labor Yearbook,* 1962 (Geneva: ILO, 1963).

[18] "Address on the State of the Nation to the Fifth Congress of the Republic of the Philippines, January 22, 1962." Excerpts issued by the Division of Cultural Affairs, Embassy of the Philippines, Washington, D.C. (Larawan Series VII, No. 2).

labor's right to organize.[19] Labor does not speak as one voice nor does it maintain a continuous articulation of labor's policy goals. Philippine unions, like their American counterparts, are pragmatic in operation and not ideological in the European sense. It is unlikely that a labor party with a socialist orientation will develop in the Philippines. As with other interest groups, labor will pursue limited policies within the restrictions imposed by the economic and social situation.

Agricultural Groups. The most important economic and political interests in the Philippines have been the traditional agrarian export industries: sugar, cocoanut products, abaca, and tobacco. These industries, and particularly sugar, have maintained their political strength through traditional ties and direct representation in the legislature. In the prewar period, they provided the financial basis of the Nacionalista party. Since independence, they have found themselves competing with a growing commercial and industrial sector for political dominance and, as a result, have found it necessary to give a continuous and institutional character to the representation of their policy interests. Such groups as the Confederation of Sugar Planters and the Tobacco Growers Association have become the agencies for articulating the interests of the sugar bloc and tobacco bloc, respectively.

These interests are characterized by heavy capital investment in land, the use of cheap unskilled labor, high profits, and high-consumption spending, and production for export. They are interested in low-interest government loans during the planting season, low land and income taxes, export and import legislation beneficial to them, and government help in the expansion and protection of their foreign markets. Their main market has been the United States, and as a result they have had representatives in the United States to protect their

[19] The 1962 congressional session did not pass a bill to nationalize labor that was labeled a "must" by the Macapagal administration. It did pass an administration measure creating an Emergency Employment Administration and appropriating 100 million pesos to implement its program of providing public works project jobs similar, in conception at least, to the WPA in the United States.

interests. Philippine sugar growers and refiners have lobbied in Washington for higher quotas, tobacco people seek protection for Manila cigars against Cuban imports, cocoanut producers lobby against the reduction of United States tariffs on cheaper oil sources that would ruin their market, and ask for protection of their industry, which grew up to supply American soap makers, etc. and now is being destroyed by new oil sources, the abaca interests ask protection as the suppliers of rope. They have all been deeply involved in American politics as a result.

Their common interests have not overcome their own interests entirely and sugar men compete actively for shares of the Philippine sugar quota, planters fight refiners for advantage, and tobacco and sugar have more than once found themselves at odds.

The most significant aspect of their attempts to protect themselves has been the election of men to represent them in the Congress. Because they have traditionally articulated their interest through legislative or party cliques and the direct use of their financial power, they find it difficult now to organize as active associations. Pressured by industrial and commercial interests, the labor movement, and the growing rationalization of the political system, they have seemed confused and unable to break the habits generated in long years of representation through elite ties. Since they continue to maintain their position as the country's chief foreign exchange earners, their interests have not been completely ignored.

SUMMARY

The Philippine political system has integrated individuals, not groups, and it has integrated them into the political system by highly personal bargaining mechanisms. The emphasis on personalism and politics subordinated bureaucratic groups, social classes, and associational groups to the play of politics. The Philippines has experienced none of the fragmentation and disequilibrium of other emergent political systems. The structures that perform the interest articulation function have settled into a role supporting the political system. The division between bureaucrat and politician so obvious in Burma is not at all apparent in the Philippines. The periodic military coup common to Latin American republics is wholly absent from Philippine experience. The Roman Catholic Church, which has played such a conservative role in support of the landed elite, has adapted to the changed circumstances without the violent and destructive political battles that Puerto Rico and other Catholic states have experienced. The landlords, though still powerful in Congress, have found it possible to exist and to compete with other groups. All these groups have been forced to turn to forms of organization more suitable to a modern system. An extremely broad variety of interests are being organized for political influence in the Philippines by the operation of a highly competitive bargaining system.

One other factor must be mentioned, for it relates directly to the future development of the Philippine political system. That is the political socializing and integrating function that these new associational groups perform. The attraction of such groups as identity mechanisms for people newly separated from their tradition and forced to interact in roles they only dimly perceive cannot be ignored. Men alienated from their society seek through these groups an organized way of operating in the new world. It is precisely this psychological quality of interest-group membership that is likely to give rise to ideological splits within the Philippine polity. Thus, such groups have important potentials for socializing people both into the system and into belief and value patterns that might be destructive of unity. That in the Philippines these groups are given a legitimate place within the system commits them to seek their interests through politics and to abjure violence, and is a hopeful indication in the prognosis of the future of Philippine society. For as development continues, competition for policy preference will grow more acute and only a very strong commitment to the system will be able to impose order on the struggle.

In modern systems, the commitment of interest groups to the political system is handled by political parties, which seek to aggregate as large a number of interests as possible in support of particular candidates and parties. In the Philippines, it is the electoral system that performs this function. We turn now to the process of interest aggregation in the Philippines to see how these interests are organized and brought to bear through the authoritative structures to produce a public interest.

CHAPTER XII

Interest Aggregation

T HE DIVERSITY of structures through which interests are articulated in the Philippines makes acute the problem of organizing those interests to express the popular will. In the Philippines, particular interests are organized into coalitions by means of elections. Filipino acceptance of the discipline of elections, as the basis of aggregation, is unique among developing nations. No other developing country has relied so heavily or with such zest on an open, competitive electoral system to organize the popular will in support of certain policies or leaders. The polarization of the electorate is pragmatic, uniting the largest possible number of voters and seeking a least common denominator around which disparate groups can rally. "Politics is numbers" according to the grand old man of Philippine politics, Senator Eulogio Rodriguez, and it is just this sort of pragmatism that has encouraged the Filipino voter to express his demands and seek help through the political system. This pragmatism contrasts sharply with the ideological type of polarization found in many other developing countries in which appeals to the electorate are expressed as specific assumptions about the ends and means of political life. Such ideological assumptions have incorporated populations into coalitions in support of precise formulas for development, and these take on the character of belief systems that cannot be compromised. Ideology is particularly important in developing countries, in which rapid social change has alienated many people from their traditions and sent them in search of a way of organizing an unpredictable universe. It is this aspect of the psychological dimension of politics in developing areas which leads to the frustration of leaders with politics and turns them toward bureaucratic or authoritiarian means. Since compromise is impossible, order must be imposed from the top. Bargaining is inhibited, and the close integration of the electorate with the political system so readily apparent in the Philippines is prevented.

The Filipino's approach to politics is personal and direct. His claims on the political system are based on his expectations about the relationship between himself and the political officeholder. Obligations engendered by primary social groups are still the most influential determinants of voting behavior, but those obligations have been tied to the political system. The voter's loyalty is neither automatic nor continuous; it must be rewon for each election. The Filipino's persistent demand for service and the politician's attempt to meet that demand give the electoral system its unique role.

As a mechanism for organizing and securing a majority consent for a set of alternative policies, the Philippine electoral process fails. This failure is the result of the weakness and instability of the party system. What then do elections accomplish? And what functions do parties perform in elections?

In the first place, elections relate the mass of voters directly to the central government. This is certainly not the most obvious aspect of elections from the voter's point of view, but bringing the national politician to the barrio makes manifest the idea of popular consent and helps develop a sense of nationality and unity. The parties, because they have from the first been national organizations concerned with national politics, have helped to overcome the divisive factors in Philippine life. Regional blocs exist within the parties and struggles for power among Bicol, Ilocano, or Negros politicians are common, but regionalism is subsumed under a centralized government and through national parties. In addition, the elections provide an opportunity for the communication of a good deal of information about the political system and its operation. Much of this communication moves through channels opened by the parties. Elections thus perform an educative function, encouraging the developing national community.

Second, elections provide an opportunity for contact between the traditional and modern role systems. The integration of kinship ties and the old landlord–tenant relationship into the operation of representative government synthesizes the old and the new without immediate conflict. The parties, building on traditional relationships and obligations, have helped this process.

Third, though it is true the Filipino makes his choices on a highly personal basis, he has a well-developed sense of reciprocity. He understands that the government, like the landlord, has certain responsibilities toward himself and his neighbors. Political campaigns help the voter to see that he has interests in common with his fellows and, in a broader sense, with groups and persons he has never seen. This developing sense of broad common interest is the basis for more rational group and party organizations.

Fourth, elections in the Philippines express the consent of the electorate for particular personalities who are perceived as personal agents who will serve as lawyer, employment agency, mentor. The Filipino does not recognize any conflict between the demands he makes on his politician and the high standards of objectivity and public service he recognizes as necessary. The Filipino's most intimate and enduring political relationships are those between him and his local community and region. He recognizes, through party activity, that these local relationships link him to the larger national community. His world is structured by kinship ties and debts of gratitude but is extended politically by his regional representatives to the nation in the same way that his family is extended by the compadre system.

THE PARTY AND INTEREST GROUPS

Philippine political parties, being national organizations, must seek to aggregate the varied interests in the society into electoral coalitions. The weakness of the various associational

interest groups, as illustrated in the previous chapter, has ramifications for the parties in both their function and their organization. In a modern industrial democracy, in which the
electorate is associated and organized by interest groups that
regulate the articulation of interests, political parties are instruments for accommodating contradictory and competitive
interests. Since their main goal is to control the government
by electing their candidates to office, the accommodation of
interests is conditioned by the political weight each interest
can provide for the party's candidates.

In the Philippines, however, the mass of voters are not organized in associational groups but rather bring their political
demands individually to the politician. The political weight
of groups, with the possible exception of labor, does not make
itself felt by the number of votes they command but rather
by the private negotiations that arrange the financing of the
campaign. The aggregation of interests with regard to policy
questions and issues is thus very difficult.

The 1961 presidential election seems to have been a water-
shed in Philippine political development largely because it
revealed a more distinct set of issues differentiating the parties
and the candidates. By 1961, the conflict between agrarian
and industrial interests seeking economic advantage had come
to a head. Disgust with the graft and influence peddling
brought about by important foreign exchange controls was
widespread. The influence of the exporting groups, such as
sugar and copra interests, had produced a partial decontrol in
1960. Although this decontrol had brought their profits more
in line with reality, it had not solved the problem. The change
from the two pesos to the dollar to a more reasonable and
flexible rate of exchange pleased some but did not overcome
the distaste for controls and their by-product, corruption.
Macapagal was known as a "free enterprise" advocate and
promised that, if elected, he would remove the controls and
revalue the peso. In addition, he had vigorously opposed the
Garcia administration's "Filipino First" policy, which was intended to strengthen Filipino control over the economy but
was aimed against alien interests. To many Filipinos this pol-

icy seemed to be discouraging foreign investors, and the country badly needed capital. Macapagal was attacked for his anti-nationalist position but his stand appealed to foreign investors, industrial groups, the Chinese, and agricultural export industries. Legitimate businessmen whose profits were much less than those of men engaged in the "controls game," the middle-class people who felt themselves cut off from American goods, intellectuals seeking an end to the corruption and a return to rational development plans, all were attracted to the Macapagal position.

President Garcia also promised decontrol, but members of his administration and his own family were believed to be deeply involved in the influence peddling that surrounded the operation of controls and thus reluctant to adopt full decontrol. The sugar bloc, the traditional financiers of political campaigns, had gradually lost strength as an alternative source of finances, the industrialists, developed. Since the days of Quezon, the sugar interests had been identified with the Nacionalista party, but the poor showing of that party in the sugar areas in the 1959 senatorial elections revealed a weakness in part due to factional disputes, but in part, also, to disaffection with the administration's policies. Partial decontrol in 1960 seemed to satisfy some of their demands, and in 1961 the National Sugar Cane Planters' Federation publicly announced its support for President Garcia and the Nacionalistas. The Negros growers had two representatives in the Senate, both Nacionalistas supporting the administration, but the party lost in "their own province," Negros Occidental.[1] It would be dangerous to consider the sugar bloc as an organized and effective group that acted in unison. Obviously, sugar money backed both parties and probably support for particu-

[1] David Wurfel, "The Philippine Elections: Support for Democracy," *Asian Survey,* II (May 1962) pp. 25-37. Wurfel writes that this was the first sugar bloc defeat since they had switched to Magsaysay at the last minute in 1953. Because they are dependent upon the Philippine National Bank for loans during the planting season, it is difficult for them to oppose an incumbent administration. After the 1961 election, the president of the Planters' Federation, a Negros Nacionalista, was replaced by a planter from Pampanga who supported the Liberals.

lar candidates dominated. But the inability of the sugar planters and growers to deliver the vote is evidence of a major change in Philippine politics.

Just as sugar has usually been found in the Nacionalista camp, tobacco has generally supported the Liberal party. The "solid Ilocano vote" has been an important basic source of Liberal strength. But the key change in the 1961 election was the force of the new business and industrial groups. The industrial groups have produced some of the most dynamic and competent men in the Philippines today. They are committed to modern business methods and to a government that will create the conditions necessary for their operations. They are interested in social reform and increased public welfare measures, but only as part of rapid industrialization. Only a strong industrial base can raise the standard of living of the masses of people, and concentration on raising agricultural productivity and rural development are useless in their opinion. They expect the same scale of preferences to guide the government and resent the use of public resources in the agrarian sector. The Philippine peasant does not starve, but neither does he change. The agricultural sector should be used to provide the capital investment for industry, for only then, when demand for cash incomes and urban employment opportunities have been created for large numbers of the population, can the peasant be changed. Thus, they support tax reform and particularly heavier taxes on land and agricultural exports; low-interest government loans; and an end to heavy government capital flow to the inefficient sugar growers who cannot produce at the world market price and thus keep the economy tied to the American sugar quota.

Despite the fact that the Nacionalistas ran Senator Gil J. Puyat, an industrialist, as their vice-presidential candidate, the Liberals' program apparently attracted this new group. The Liberal party, under Diosdado Macapagal's leadership, successfully aggregated the demand of the rural masses for agrarian reform, which they express as support for the common-man image, the middle-class demand for higher standards of political conduct and an end to corruption, the demands for decontrol and more businesslike economic decisions of the growing industrial sector, the blessings of the Roman Catholic Church and of their traditional allies, the tobacco interests. This experience does not mean an end to the intense personalism, particularism, and familialism of Philippine politics nor does it ignore the local machinery and the flow of patronage, public works funds, and the money needed to build such an effective coalition. The strength of these considerations is shown in the losses sustained by Liberal candidates at the congressman and local-government level. But the issue-oriented base of this aggregation is indicative of the expanded function the political parties will have to perform as economic, social, and political change continues.

The awesome expense of Philippine elections has important ramifications for this aggregation function. In a very broad sense, Filipino politicians have used their political influence in support of economic interests to gain the financial contributions necessary to obtain the votes needed for election. The difficulties of transportation and communication in an island country account for much of the cost of elections. Senatorial elections at large are obviously very expensive. The costs of building local organizations is also very high, and a great deal of money changes hands during campaigns. An experienced observer reported that the 1961 elections were the most expensive in Philippine history, amounting to a sum equal to 8 per cent of the annual national budget.[2] Candidates are prohibited by law from spending more than the total emoluments for one year attached to the office sought. To meet the legal requirement, candidates submit statements that they have not spent more than that sum. Thus, both Macapagal and Garcia filed statements in 1961 that they had not spent more than 30,000 pesos, the annual salary of the presidency, although estimates of the actual cost of a presidential campaign begin at half a million pesos.[3] But the simple conclusion that public office is bought in the Philippines does not explain the fact that on three occasions Filipino voters have thrown in-

[2] Wurfel estimates that candidates for all offices spent an estimated 80 to 150 million pesos. A comparable percentage of the United States budget would be $7 billion.

[3] *The Philippines Free Press*, February 17, 1962.

cumbent administrations out of office despite the great advantage they had in financing campaigns.

In 1961, the Filipino voter was in a better position than ever to exercise his free choice. Not only did strong safeguards exist to protect the secrecy of his ballot, but Operation Quick Count, an agency supported by the *Manila Times* and private citizens, placed its representatives all over the islands and channeled the results of the count in each precinct direct to Manila as fast as the tally was completed. This method prevented changes in the figures or the ballots after the public counting. In addition, it had become apparent to the voter that public works funds and patronage were not the exclusive province of one party but were public resources over which he had some claim no matter who was in office. The Liberal party ticket was very attractive. Macapagal's four-year barrio-hopping campaign and his peasant background had given him a "common man" image with the voters; the vice-presidential candidate, Emanuel Pelaez, who had been close to Magsaysay, had already proven his concern for the rural areas and his outspoken support for modernization; the inclusion of the Grand Alliance reform group on the senatorial ticket rounded out the over-all commitment of the party to change, clean government, and development. The impact of this party image on the channels of communication, the provincial elites, was bound to be very strong.

At the local level and in the congressional races, more intimate considerations prevailed. The congressman is necessarily closer to his constituents than is any other national-level politician. He deals directly and continuously with provincial and municipal officials, supporting their political aspirations and financing their campaigns. The old system works best at this level and provided success for Nacionalista candidates in a context that Garcia and the Senate candidates could not reach.[4]

[4] In 1959 the Nacionalistas held 48 out of the 52 governorships, 19 out of 24 Senate seats, 90 out of 108 congressional seats. In 1961 the Nacionalistas lost the presidency but won more than three-fourths of the contested House seats. The Liberals took six out of the eight Senate seats.

Given the numerous advantages accruing to an incumbent, including the constitutional limit of eight years in office, which gave vice-presidential candidates a particular interest in supporting Garcia, Macapagal's victory was a landslide. He won by a 600,000 vote margin in a total vote of six and a half million.

The major significance of the election, however, was the revelation of clear and specific political interests. In 1961, it was apparent that the parties were performing their aggregating function in a more efficient and more explicit manner than ever before. In the past, parties had been collections of personalities grouped around a hard core of regulars, giving them the character of loose confederations, a stable center surrounded by unstable alliances. At election time, regulars simply attracted as many of these personalities as they could accommodate and sought to guarantee their loyalty to the party organization by supporting them in their local power struggles and political aspirations. Because of the character of such party coalitions, the heavy weight of the incumbent administration's pork barrel and patronage usually turned the tide. To the old-line politico, the Magsaysay phenomena simply increased the weight of such considerations in the rural areas and necessitated more active campaigning. Beyond these admittedly onerous burdens, astute politicians could prevent the rise of a new Magsaysay by controlling the recruitment process. The election could be fought in the old manner with the same coalition. But certain other factors interfered: increased contacts with urban areas; a continuously expanding group of high school graduates; a deep commitment to free and honest elections as a reaction to the 1949 debacle; a resultant large group of young people committed to a modern, objective political decision-making process but effectively frozen out of the influence network; and, perhaps of great importance, the lessons the "young reformers" had learned during twelve years in the political wilderness. In 1961, they came out of their non-party limbo to the detriment of the old professionals. The summation of this experience was delivered by Raul Manglapus, who had been a leading member of the Citizen's party, the

Magsaysay for President movement, the Progressive party, and the Grand Alliance. When the Grand Alliance jointed the Liberal party in 1961, he said:

> Today, twelve years after we issued our challenge against the Liberal Party in 1949, we ourselves have become Liberals. Twelve years we spent challenging the status quo, seeking to substitute venal men with good men, corrupt government with clean government, the old with the new. But aside from the three refreshing years of Magsaysay, it was always an illusive pursuit.
>
> It occurred to us that the reason the pursuit was so elusive is that we had concentrated on substituting men instead of ideas: that we had condemned corruption in the capitol and thought we had solved it by putting up an incorruptible man — until the uncorruptible man died — and corruption came back. We had failed to analyze why corruption thrived in the capitol and why we almost need a saint to resist it. We needed an idea on how to stop it. For incorruptible men will die. But an idea, a good idea on how to stop corruption might live long enough to see it stopped.[5]

The young reformers had learned the realities of political power. The main "idea" was expressed in the Barrio Autonomy Act drafted under the sponsorship of Senator Emanuel Pelaez and pushed through the 1959 legislative session. Corruption thrived because of the centralization of power in Manila, which froze the mass of people out of participation in decision making. The concentration of so much power over national resources and policy led to corruption.

This was not the only attempt at decentralization. Abortive attempts in this direction have been made for some years. The major point on which they collapse is financial — the lack of independent funds to support the local government and its programs. The most significant change in the reformist group was not the "idea," admirable as that may be; rather it was their recognition that the exercise of governmental power and electoral participation demand an organized structure to regulate and mediate popular consent. Political parties aggregate interests and present alternative policies for government to

[5] As cited in Eugenio D. Apostal, "Orator, Diplomat and now Senator," *The Sunday Times Magazine*, XVII (January 21, 1962).

follow; they must present themselves to the electorate periodically for the consent to govern. In effect, the 1961 election strengthened the party structure by making it clear what the function of political parties should be and how it could be performed.

THE ROLE OF THE PRESIDENT

The key role of the Philippine presidency in this system cannot be underestimated. It is the President who determines the general formula for aggregation, and it is he who gives a particular style and direction to the policies of the government. Through his formal authority, the President has more control over his party than does his American counterpart. To a significant extent, this power transfers the function of aggregating interests to the President, as head of his party. The political influence of the presidency weakens party loyalty and has meant, in the past, that only a few militant party leaders remain in opposition, harassing the incumbent administration. Opposition to the administration has most often been performed by factions within the majority party. In fact, the most important political battles in the Philippines have been intraparty disputes, for example: Quezon and Osmeña during 1921 and again in 1934, Quirino and Avelino during 1949–50, Magsaysay and Recto in 1955, Garcia and Rodriguez in 1959–61. The political scene since 1961 has shown some significant changes. The Nacionalistas had maintained control of the Senate and House as well as provincial governments. Local-government personnel defected in groups to the Liberals, but the distaste for party switching was evident at the national level. Some Nacionalista congressmen switched to the Liberal party but others created an independent organization that allowed them to ally themselves with the President's program without really joining the party. Thus the Liberals gained control of the House and put a Liberal into the speakership. But in the Senate, only one defector left the Nacionalistas, and, as a result, the Senate remained divided twelve to twelve. The resulting struggle for leadership in the Senate was not resolved until the 1963 session, when one Nacionalista, dissatisfied with his party's leadership, voted for the Liberal party candidate for Senate president. The Nacionalistas maintained their control of the committees, however. When the 1964 session opened, the struggle for power in the Senate took a new turn as the Liberal party Senate president showed signs of allying himself with the Nacionalistas against Macapagal.

It is not surprising that the Senate should be more inclined to party loyalty than the House. Senatorial candidates must have a national reputation in order to be elected, which means they can rely more on that reputation than on other considerations for electoral success, giving them more freedom from presidential influence. Congressmen, on the other hand, rely on direct service to their constituents, the resources for which are controlled by the executive branch. As a result, the President controls the House and its leadership and has less difficulty getting his program through that body. The crucial debates on public policy are conducted in the Senate.

Policy issues are inevitably founded on the President's program. With the help of his cabinet, he formulates broad policy goals and indicates to Congress the legislation required to meet them. Legislators from his own party, in consultation with executive agencies, then draft and introduce the legislation. The President's political influence is brought to bear in the form of support for candidates, appointments, and public works allocations in negotiations with members of Congress to gain their support. The energy and determination of the President and his sensitivity to legislators' needs are crucial to the effective operation of the political system. It is the President who guides the formation of the public interest. He is the center of an extensive and continuous bargaining process. In the process, he is also building an electoral coalition aggregating particular demands on the public resources into a policy fiamework at one level and trading public resources for political support on another.

Interest aggregation is disjointed and only partially integrates the interests of the electorate into public policy. The lack of refinement and sophistication in this mode of aggregation is, in part, a result of the emphasis on ascriptive structures for interest articulation. When interests are articulated by traditional means, those interests do not lend themselves to sophisticated and complex organization and accommodation. Rather, interests enter the bargaining arena as unprocessed particular demands and become requests for patronage, public works expenditures, or special consideration from a government office. Attempts to impose universal policy alternatives and to force choices on such a basis are doomed to failure. Political parties are of necessity collections of factions based on ascriptive and highly personal loyalties; the relationship of the voter to his candidate is personal and does not lend itself to aggregation on the basis of policy choices. The President must translate this wide variety of unprocessed claims into a program for using the public resources in such a way as to maintain the support of sufficient votes and financial contributions for his electoral coalition. As this process of change we have noted continues, the parties will have to take on more of this function, collecting and weaving together the claims of individuals and groups. At present, the parties are more important for their role in political socialization and communication, but they serve as regulators for the entrance of demands into the political process, and, as those demands become more differentiated, they will lend themselves more readily to a continuous claim on the support of a particular party. At present, the function of aggregation of interests into public policy is performed by the President of the Phillippines in his role as political leader.

* * *

Contrary to the opinion of those who decry the politics that creep into economic development programs in the new states, the Philippine case illustrates that it is a pragmatic political process that can create the conditions and energy required for development. The capacity to handle organization so necessary to political and economic development is, in effect, the capacity to handle an open bargaining process. Rather than ignore conflict, the Filipinos have encouraged it and have allowed open competition to work itself out in free elections. Interest aggregation through an electoral system that distributes public resources is building a nation that will rest upon the vigorous pursuit of popular needs and not upon abstract formulations such as the Burmese way to Socialism. This type of development is not without its dangers. The open pursuit of self-interest leads to corruption of public office and cynicism about the meaning of the public interest, which may again threaten the legitimacy of the political system, as happened in the early fifties. Periodic purges through the electoral system have gone far to impose a limit on this single-minded pursuit and encourage political officeholders to adhere to standards of conduct and morality more in line with their function. The increased sophistication of the electorate made possible by their experience is already imposing this limit. The integration and operation of the system itself is working to eliminate the corruption and misuse of resources that it has created. For only a society that does not seek everything good in life through the political system can solve the problem of corruption. And such a society is built by the development of its economic and social life. The Philippine political system is directing that development. The rich and the poor, the Westernized and the traditional, the rural peasant and the urban entrepreneur meet today in the offices of the politicians.

CHAPTER XIII

Conclusions

A LMOST TWO DECADES of independence have wrought acceptance of political action as a means of change and have
subordinated all groups — military, administrative, intellectual, and economic — to the political system. Competitive, hard-fought elections have attracted widespread participation, which is changing the pattern of relationships
and behavior and thus the very nature of the society. A
sporadic reformist trend is characteristic of the developing
style, as is the common-man image and its attendant dema-
goguery. The defeat of the Huk rebellion, the beginnings
of economic development, and three changes of government by elections have given Filipinos confidence in their
own ability to operate democratic institutions and modernize their country. This confidence has also encouraged
them to play a larger role in international, particularly
Asian, affairs. After more than three and a half centuries
of experience with Western institutions and values, the
Filipinos have accepted this inheritance and have made it
part of their culture. Now Filipinos look to Asia and
seek to play a leading role in that area and to find the
clues to their own "Asian" identity.

But the very success of Philippine political development
has raised other problems that will put the political system on trial and test its efficiency, flexibility, and responsiveness. Perhaps the most serious danger the Philippines

faces is the rapid growth of population and the widening gap between rural and urban society. We have shown that channels of communication exist and that the development of the rural areas, increased agricultural productivity, and land reform have gained important allies among the new industrial groups. But it remains to be seen whether or not the energetic leadership required for exploiting these advantages will emerge. The agrarian demand for a better life has been established as a legitimate claim on national resources even before the rural people have organized themselves for effective political action. Some means must be found to translate the latent interests of the rural population into manifest support for legislation that will meet their needs. Making rural interests manifest and direct is particularly important because the rapid increase in population will be felt first in the rural areas, where the already existing tensions will be further intensified.

Many of the other problems of the Philippines, for example the need to reconcile economic nationalism with the requirements of economic development, can only be solved by the strengthening of the organizational means by which the nation is held together. Too often the fear of Chinese control of the economy has triggered attempts to eliminate the Chinese entirely, attempts that fail to provide a substitute for the skills and capital of the Chinese. Creation of effective economic and political controls to curb the excesses of the Chinese will demand broader policy-making scope than has heretofore been possible.

The means for channeling these pressures into energy for development lie in bringing the institutions of the political system more in line with the demands made on them by the society. The older, personal forms must give way to new structures through which specific, particular interests may be deliberated upon and incorporated into the public interest. Two interdependent and related structures are available to handle this task, but both presently suffer from weaknesses that inhibit the ability of the system to cope with the problems it faces. The weakness of the parties' organization and discipline means that citizens are not affiliated on a continuous basis with a broad, responsive organization that can give meaning to political participation in governmental decisions and policies. As we have seen, electoral coalitions are transitory and are unrelated to legislative or executive action on policy decisions. Though parties are growing stronger it is by no means clear that they will develop in time to build workable bridges across social classes, geographic regions, and urban and rural society in time to channel the tensions produced into peaceful paths.

The other related structure, the legislature, warped from its assigned function by executive dominance of the means of electoral success, has been unable to serve as the arena for compromising the particular demands of the electorate into policies that would ensure that all interests were in some measure accommodated. As a result the legislature has not forced the parties to serve as governing coalitions. Instead the legislature has acted in a highly fragmented fashion, concentrating on pursuing narrow interests that can be handled through traditional social channels. Until the legislators can be aggregated into parties on a more or less continuous basis, there is unlikely to develop any systematic and regular process of deliberation on broader public issues. Both parties and legislature are changing, but the question posed by the rapidly increasing population and the pressures generated by economic development may not wait for that change to be completed.

As with most Philippine problems, the potential exists for solution, but it will require some hard choices and some political risks for those who would promote and commit themselves to the broad, inclusive policies necessary for development, at the same time that responsiveness to individual, narrow, and short-run demands is the basis of political success. The political system must become the innovative mechanism for encouraging efficient investment, increased productivity, more jobs, and some relief for the countryside. No other alternative seems feasible considering the demands of Philippine economic and political development. The conflicts inherent in this development are already clear. Innovation, a willingness to take risks, an open admission of failure, have marked the Macapagal administration and have led to alienation of the political elite from the presidency and acute legislative–

executive conflict. The Senate, for those reasons we have pointed out, is the battleground for this confrontation between political leadership of an energetic, experimental type and legislative independence of both the young-reformer and the old-conservative types. Such a confrontation is not destructive of democracy in the Philippines but can have the effect of clarifying and focusing bargaining power and weights and posing real alternatives to the electorate. The frustration, and thus the danger, lies in the inability of the government to carry out policy decisions because no strong, continuous, and articulate support for implementation comes from the people who would benefit by them. Nowhere is this danger more evident than in the Land Reform Act. Unless there is enthusiastic and aggressive popular demand for its implementation it is doubtful that the energy and determination of the leaders at the center will be sufficient to stimulate the administrative and local government channels to action.

One other danger needs to be mentioned, the elemental, spiritual crisis that faces Filipino politics as a result of the heavy weight of personalization. Despite the confidence engendered by success, widespread corruption and opportunism have harassed and wearied the population and show no sign of abating. Personalism alienates young people from politics, leads to disillusion and despair and to wildly unrealistic attempts to substitute honest men for effective limits. This fundamental and intense cynicism of the Philippine polity lends itself readily to reform movements but might lend itself just as readily to radical or demagogic movements aimed at destroying the entire system to eliminate its evils. Only continued success in development, which will reorient Filipino behavior to the requirements of complex forms of organization and away from the traditional personal ties, will provide the basis for change as the optimism and confidence now spreading through the elite seeps into the awareness of a broad sector of the population.

In short, the Filipino has learned to operate a bargaining process, has created forms of organization and the basis for a common effort that accepts the unity of the islands and the central direction of the government. Now the problems that arise and the way in which they are handled will shape the development of a formal structure to carry the burdens that highly personal considerations have carried in the past. This change will impose great strains on the developing political system and will demand still more changes in social structure and behavior. Politics has been opportunity in the Philippines and has triggered the successful development of the nation, but now Filipinos must draw boundaries to their political system and create other associations through which to seek the good life.

Index

DATE DUE

GAYLORD   PRINTED IN U.S.A.